C000295159

John A. Keel: The Man, The Myths, and The Ongoing Mysteries

By Brent Raynes

John A. Keel: The Man, The Myths, and the Ongoing
Mysteries

Acknowledgements

I became involved in this field in 1967 at age 14. Going on now to 52 years plus, I have heartfelt and grateful acknowledgements to be made to so many helpful and influential people. Naturally, such an acknowledgement should begin with my mom and dad (Edna and Nathan Raynes), who certainly represent the earliest nurturing and guiding influences in my life. My mom, from time to time, had been the most vocal about my crazy UFO interests and that instead I should devote my time and studies to more normal and productive pursuits, such as higher education that would provide a better livelihood for me and, of course, a future family (who soon enough did come along). My dad, the bread winner, a skilled carpenter, accordion player, and organic gardener, was a man of many skills and accomplishments to be admired, and he understood and appreciated (although he did, on occasion, express concerns) my evolving passion to become what I later learned somebody had termed a "ufologist."

My dad mapped out a family trip to include Toronto, Canada, so I could meet a contactee named Joan Howard, whom I had read about in a Brad Steiger book. One time he drove me and mom all the way to Sistersville, West Virginia (we lived in Maine, by the way) just because I had read in one of John Keel's magazine articles that UFOs had been extremely active there in the 1960s and people were seeing UFOs like fireflies – which is all I ended up seeing. During my high school years I became increasingly active and noticed at the local level due to my interests. The Augusta *Daily Kennebec Journal* wrote two articles about my "hobby" and I spoke on a popular radio station in Augusta about UFOs. My older brother Brian was getting gas in Augusta and the guy who pumped his gas had just been listening to me on the radio. When he found out that my brother had the same last name, he wondered if my brother was that UFO guy he had just heard. I recall my brother saying something to my dad about how I seemed to make a real impression on this man and it was too bad that I couldn't somehow make a living with my "hobby."

Coming from my brother, at that time, it felt pretty good. I often felt like the oddball geek in my family and town. Several years later, I knocked on the door of an elderly Tennessee woman who had claimed (along with others in that neighborhood) to have seen "Bigfoot," while Mom and Dad waited in the car. As I was invited inside, my dad repeated to my mom what my brother had earlier stated, that it was too bad I couldn't make a living at pursuing this particular passion that I had. He commented that I seemed to know a lot about the subject and that I could often approach strangers and instantly win their confidence. They were, incidentally, in Tennessee with me at that time, as I was getting married and was going to put down roots there. A couple years earlier, in 1975, I had spent a summer on the road traveling from Maine to Florida meeting with and interviewing researchers and witnesses, pursuing my passion. In the process I visited a lovely, grand gal in Tennessee who I had been corresponding with (it started out on the subject of UFOs) and she would end up stealing my heart.

It was easier, and I felt the right thing to do, to relocate to Tennessee than to uproot my future wife Joan from the only place she had known, and leave behind her mom, who lived by herself.

As things evolved, I seemed again and again to be in the right places meeting the right people in order to pursue my "crazy" hobby, as my mom had called it. But this so-called hobby brought me into contact with so many, many wonderful people out there that I can't imagine it could have turned out any better. Hmmm. Well, much better, anyway.

Dr. Greg Little, also a Tennessee resident (who too was a Yankee transplant) became a great friend and colleague who helped me tremendously with the magazine I edit, *Alternate Perceptions*. Greg also published my first book *Visitors From Hidden Realms* (2004), encouraging me every step of the way to do it, and so very much more. Then too there are people I've been investigating with over the years, like Sandy Nichols and Bret Oldham. Special thanks to Nomar Slevik for helping me to research some of the barium cloud data described in chapter 4. In the mid-1970s,

Charles and Geri Wilhelm of the Ohio UFO Investigators League kindly allowed this former "ufologist" from Maine to use their Ohio home as a base of operations for weeks at a time.

Sadly so many are no longer with us (to be expected after a half century), like Brad Steiger, Geri Wilhelm, Shirley Fickett, James Carey, Patsy Wingate, Dr. Berthold Eric Schwarz, Betty Hill, Tom Adams, Lucius Farish, Bob Pratt, Ramona Hibner, Stanley Ingram, Madeline Teagle, Earl Neff, Larry Moyers, and, of course, John Keel.

I still know a lot of the old-timers in the UFO field who are still at it, like Timothy Green Beckley (who published my second book, *On The Edge of Reality*), Allen Greenfield, Rick Hilberg, Stan Gordon, Rich Hoffman, Bob Goerman, Patrick Huyghe, and Joe Nyman. It's impossible to mention every single person out there who has touched my life through the years. If you're one of those, even though you may not be mentioned here, know that your friendship, kindness, and help are and have been sincerely appreciated.

One person I certainly don't need to leave out is my daughter Chandra who has done many interviews with me for *Alternate Perceptions* and who has been involved in her share of paranormal investigations too. My wife Joan has long been on this journey with me (not always her favorite thing to do) but she has certainly made a good number of supportive contributions. She especially made me aware of the Native American aspects and helped me a lot on ARE (Association for Research and Enlightenment) sponsored Indian Mound Tours that we both participated in with Doctors Greg and Lora Little.

Joan and I shared dozens of sweat lodge adventures (special thanks to Wanda "Dove" Theiss who led some truly powerful ones!) and we met with Daniel Statnekov at the Pinson Mounds in Tennessee and learned about the mysterious and shamanic Peruvian Whistling Vessels, and Joan played some in the clay and made several whistles herself. We've had some pretty awesome adventures!

A special word of thanks and appreciation to Rosemary Ellen Guiley for expressing an interest in this work, for looking it over and making suggestions, and for the many other great people who shared their stories, ideas, encouragement and a little bit of themselves. Thanks to Hakan Blomqvist for photographs, letters, articles, and assorted vital materials from the Archives for UFO Research in Sweden. Thanks again also to Rosemary Ellen Guiley, and Doug Skinner, Michael Grosso, Sandra Martin, and Dan Drasin who had known Keel quite well and were willing to share memories, impressions, and their own personal takes on things Keelian. Much appreciation also to Timothy and John Frick, and Steve Ward for sharing Keelian data as well. Thanks to Robert Davis and Barbara Mango for their encouraging and supportive words, ideas and information as I shared details with them about the contents of this book.

A very special word of thanks also to Lynn Miller and her daughter DeAnna for working on the cover of this book. It's what the reader sees first!

And last but certainly not least, a very special word of dedication and tribute to two trailblazing pioneers in ufology who showed us (or at least tried ever so valiantly to do so) that the UFO enigma was potentially far more complex and perplexing than mainstream "nuts and bolts" ufology generally portrayed it to be. Those two legendary giants are, of course, none other than Dr. Jacques Vallee and his "ghost writer" John Keel. Well, okay, I couldn't resist interjecting a little Keelian tongue-in-cheek humor here as 'ol big John enjoyed joking and poking some fun at Vallee. He felt that though the French-born scientist had originally resisted his ideas, he later came to very similar conclusions and concepts.

Brent Raynes

Waynesboro, Tennessee

Table of Contents

Acknowledgements..iii

Foreword by Rosemary Ellen Guiley...xi

Chapter One: Like the Moth drawn to the flame.....................1

Chapter Two: "We have just opened Pandora's box".............20

Chapter Three: Will the real John Keel please stand up?........36

Chapter Four: Keel's Ups and Downs...57

Chapter Five: Jadoo, Voices, and UFOs....................................,87

Chapter Six: Is Djinn the Oz Behind the Curtain?...................103

Chapter Seven: John Keel and Swedish Ufology...................111

Chapter Eight: Paul Eno on Ghosts, UFOs, and the Multiverse...........124

Chapter Nine: Winged "Monsters"...131

Chapter Ten: Timothy Frick, a Monster Sleuth...................................152

Chapter Eleven: Odd Lightning, Geomagnetism, and Shamans........165

Chapter Twelve: Elementals Are Everywhere..................................198

Chapter Thirteen: The Enigmatic MIB..204

Chapter Fourteen: Religious Events, Shapeshifters, and Phantom
Landscapes...249

Chapter Fifteen: Paranormal Bigfoots?..278

Chapter Sixteen: Alien Eyes..286

Chapter Seventeen: Hypnotized Minds...293

Chapter Eighteen: What Next?...300

Bibliography..312

About the Author...315

John A. Keel: The Man, The Myths, and the Ongoing Mysteries

Foreword
Rosemary Ellen Guiley

John A. Keel was a man way ahead of his time. In fact, he probably was born that way. His career in journalism was excellent training for the true destiny of his life: to plumb the mysteries of the unknown and blaze a trail for other researchers to follow.

Keel recognized that certain individuals were "wired" differently from others and thus were more likely to encounter the strange beings and entities that exist in a netherworld on this planet. Keel never said that about himself, but I always thought that he too was one of those wired persons, for he had a great many paranormal experiences – and highly unusual ones, such as those that happened to him while he was investigating the Mothman wave. From the get go, Keel had an antenna tuned to the frequencies of parallel worlds, alternate realities and interdimensional realms. And that attunement is what led him – perhaps even drove him – into the investigation and study of all things paranormal. Who else but a wired person would travel around the world in his twenties looking into things spooky and write a book like *Jadoo*?

Keel also was ahead of his time in that from the outset of his research, he saw the big picture – the interconnectedness of all paranormal phenomena, the intelligent trickster elements that permeate the entire spectrum, the shape-shifting of the same phenomena throughout history, and, even more significant, the role of human consciousness is co-creating the phenomena.

Some of these views also were held by other researchers who were contemporary with Keel; for example, Gordon Creighton, publisher of *Flying Saucer Review;* UFO researcher Jacques Vallee; and UFO researcher Ann Druffel, to mention a few, and who are referenced and cited here in Brent Raynes's book.

Rather than being hailed as revolutionary and cutting edge, however, these viewpoints have been trashed by narrow-minded researchers in all paranormal fields, whether ghosts and spirits, UFOs and aliens, or cryptids.

Throughout his life Keel had a mounting disdain for the tunnel vision crowd, especially the "nuts and bolts" ufologists out running around looking for crashed craft and alien bodies, and those wedded blindly to the Extraterrestrial Hypothesis (ETH), that ETs are visiting us and so we must explain the technology that enables them to traverse the huge distances of outer space.

He did not necessarily think that "extraterrestrials" were really beings from outer space. He preferred the term coined by Ivan T. Sanderson – "ultraterrestrials" – which explains all weird visitors to our realm as coming from a parallel world through a "window" (or portal) into ours. Keel also posited, as Brent discusses, that UFOs could be intelligent forms, not mechanical craft, and that human consciousness projects energy that comes back to us in "entity" form.

John was among my good friends in the paranormal world, and I describe later in this book, in an interview with Brent, some of my interactions with him. I resonated with his viewpoints, because I had come independently to the same conclusions myself very early in my own research. I appreciated John's intelligence and knowledge, and especially his acid wit.

He was an indefatigable researcher, always preferring to track down original sources whenever possible, and spending countless hours, days and weeks out in the field. He was in constant contact with other researchers. His files burgeoned with thousands of documents, articles, letters and photographs. His New York City apartment was spartan in furniture but spilled over with papers and books.

I always suspected that John experienced, knew and understood far more than he ever let on about "the big picture." I believe that early on, he realized that the tunnel vision crowd would never come around, and so he kept some secrets to himself. He downplayed his own expertise, claiming not to be an authority on anything, when in fact he probably knew more than most researchers put together.

He was of the opinion that an unknown cosmic trickster was behind everything and was capable – and determined – to keep us constantly confused and chasing dead ends, so that we would never discover the real truth behind any of the phenomena. I think he is right.

The release in 2002 of the film *The Mothman Prophecies*, supposedly based on Keel's best-known book about one of the strangest episodes of paranormal weirdness in modern history, brought his work to renewed attention and a new audience. The film was an unfortunate piece of work, however – if you knew nothing about Mothman prior to seeing it, you still knew nothing about Mothman when you finished. Nonetheless, the film inspired people to get the book. Many of those new readers went on to probe John's work more deeply.

Keel wrote only nine books, but each one of them is a classic filled with amazing insights. (There are more Keel titles, which are revisions of earlier works and collections of selected writings.) His work has galvanized generations of enthusiasts and researchers to shine their flashlights into the darkness too and keep exploring and pushing the boundaries of what we know. His work should be required reading for anyone on a personal exploration mission, and certainly for those entering the field as researchers.

I have my favorites of his titles, besides *The Mothman Prophecies: UFOs: Operation Trojan Horse* and *The Eighth Tower*.

UFOs: Operation Trojan Horse was published in 1970 and was Keel's first book on UFOs. Right out of the starting gate, he blew apart the prevailing "nuts and bolts" ideas about physical craft and aliens coming across vast distances of space to Earth. By that time, ufologists had had 20 some years to investigate the phenomenon (dating the modern UFO age to the 1947 sighting of flying discs by pilot Kenneth Arnold in Washington State). They were still coming up empty-handed with evidence and explanations. Rather than welcome a fresh perspective, the mainline ufology community branded Keel a crackpot and accused him of fabrication.

Over the years, John became increasingly frustrated with ufology's myopic vision and glacial speed to consider new evidence and concepts. The field has improved somewhat today, though the conferences are still like stuck records, replaying the same material over and over again.

The Eighth Tower, published in 1975, delves deeper into the consciousness factor, connecting dots between the paranormal, occult, UFOs, mysterious phenomena and even religion. I believe that human consciousness is the most important, yet most overlooked factor in all our extraordinary experiences. It's a wild card dependent upon the subjective outlook of the percipient; yet there are collective patterns throughout history that reveal glimpses of what we are truly encountering and why.

I have a number of favorite memories about John, too. One was a trip to England in the 1990s, in which we both participated as presenters in a sacred sites tour that took in Stonehenge. I still have a photo of John, standing in front of the megaliths (back then you could walk right up to them and wander among them), sunglasses on and a crafty smile on his face, looking like a man of mystery among the mysteries. That was John.

The last time I saw John was about a year before he died. We met in Manhattan on the Upper West Side for lunch. I wheeled in a small piece of luggage filled with my *Atlas of the Mysterious in North America,* for which he had written the foreword, and asked him to sign them. He obliged, although he protested that no one would want his autograph. He had been having some health issues but overall looked good, albeit a little low on energy. After lunch, we wandered to a nearby favorite bookstore of his and spent some time browsing the shelves.

With Brent Raynes's book, I am glad to see a new spotlight on John. Brent interviewed many researchers who knew and worked with Keel, and he also draws upon his own interactions with John. Many topics – all of which were fascinating to John – are explored in-depth.

John A. Keel is one of the giants, and the rest of us stand on his shoulders. Wherever you are now, John, I hope you have figured out at least some of the answers to the big picture. Let us know, will you?

ONE
LIKE THE MOTH DRAWN TO THE FLAME...

My grandson Conner and I flanked by two die-hard ghostbusters, Kevin
Pauley (right) and Todd Wines (left), with the Stay Puff Marshmallow
Man menacingly towering over us.

It was Saturday and Sunday, September 19 and 20, 2015. My wife Joan, our daughter Chandra, her husband Scott, their eight-year-old son Conner and I made our way to the 14th annual Mothman Festival in Point Pleasant, West Virginia, a small town of less than 5,000 located along the Ohio River. Since 2001, thousands converge annually at this otherwise sleepy little river town made famous by the late New York journalist John A. Keel's book *The Mothman Prophecies* (1975), which in 2002 became a movie by the same name, starring Richard Gere and Laura Linney. Be forewarned, if you don't already know, that many details of the movie were changed and fictionalized from the book's original narrative.

On the night of November 15, 1966, two young couples, Linda and Roger Scarberry, and Mary and Steve Mallette, claimed that they had seen a human-like figure estimated between six-and-a-half to seven feet tall, with wings and red eyes. They said it went airborne and chased them out of what is known locally as the TNT area, a World War II manufacturing and ammunition storage facility several miles north of Point Pleasant. The driver, Roger Scarberry, allegedly floored it, accelerating his 1957 Chevy up to 100 miles an hour down Route 62 as the thing pursued them to the city limits. They soon burst into the sheriff's office at the Mason County courthouse, where they described their terrifying encounter to one Deputy Millard Halstead.

As the Scarberry's and Mallett's fled the TNT area in their car after seeing Mothman, the creature pursued them all the way to the Point Pleasant city limits. Along the way, they saw a dead dog on the side of the road. When they returned shortly, the dog was gone. Later the charred remains of a dog in the TNT area were found by the police.

Keel wondered if the charred dog had been the sacrificial offering of some local warlock and if Mothman itself might have been brought into being by a Satanic ritual. In Gallipolis, Ohio, across the Ohio River from Point Pleasant, a man reported finding his missing German Shepherd lying dead in a field inside a perfect 20-

foot-wide circle of flattened grass. Every bone in its body had been crushed and there was no sign of blood.

Keel made his first visit to Point Pleasant on December 7, 1966, to investigate the Scarberry/Mallette encounter, and realized that this was but the tip of an iceberg. In five lengthy visits to the area, he interviewed over a hundred "monster" witnesses. "Mothman" wasn't the only monster in the region; there was also a Bigfoot-type "monster" and a giant hairy headless-looking critter with broad shoulders. He wrote in *Strange Creatures from Time and Space* (1970) that he found that thousands up and down the Ohio Valley were seeing UFOs but were often reluctant to report their sightings. He discovered too that about half of the "Mothman" witnesses he interviewed had active or latent psychic abilities.

I tracked down a documentary filmmaker, Dan Drasin, now living in California, who had accompanied Keel to Point Pleasant in 1967, hoping to do a documentary for PBS on the matter. For some reason PBS eventually decided against it. Drasin shared with me some of his own interesting sightings that he had while there; some with Keel. (This will be covered later in another chapter.)

I originally visited Point Pleasant in May 1976, nearly 10 years after it all began, with some "monster hunters" from the Cincinnati area, including Ron Schaffner, who once edited a newsletter called *Creature Chronicles*. He had also been a big Keel fan. I talked with a number of witnesses, including Linda Scarberry, who described the initial 1966 sighting that made worldwide news. Authorities quickly tried to dismiss it as an owl or sandhill crane, but the witnesses angrily insisted no way. At the time, *Batman* was a popular TV series and a news person dubbed the creature "Mothman." The name stuck. Locals had simply been calling it "the Bird."

Ron and I had found that Point Pleasant's Mothman story was even a deeper and more complex mystery, incredibly enough, than we had read in Keel's *Mothman Prophecies*. "As you discovered, my book only covered a small part of the overall situation," Keel wrote me in 1993. "It would have taken six books to discuss all of it. What happened there also happened (and is still happening) in many other parts of the country. I was flabbergasted by the scope and complexity of the phenomena in the 1960s. I found the same identical situations everywhere, from Long Island to Hartshorne, Oklahoma. I spent some time in Fyffe, Alabama then, and, as you know, they are still having UFO stuff along with many animal mutilations, poltergeist activity, etc."

"Unfortunately, there was little interest on Madison Avenue in the '60s and there was no place to publish any of my findings. In addition, the hardcore UFO buffs, NICAP, APRO, et al, fought bitterly against things like mutes, abductions, lost time cases, etc. They chose, instead, to attack me and accuse me of making it all up."

When I casually asked Linda Scarberry how many times she had seen the creature, I was startled when she informed me and fellow researcher Ron Schaffner that she had seen it "hundreds" of times! One time she looked out an apartment window where she was living and a mere yard or so away the creature stood looking back at her with it's luminous, protruding red eyes! "It seems like it doesn't want to hurt you," she said. "But you're too afraid when you see it to do anything."

I asked Linda how the Mothman usually departed. "It just stands there, takes its wings out just a tiny bit and goes straight up in the air," she said. I had read about this kind of Mothman takeoff into the air, which hardly seems to make sense for something that size.

Everyone I spoke to who had known John Keel spoke very highly of him. This wasn't long after his book, *The Mothman Prophecies,* had been published. "People actually called up some of those named in the book and demanded to know if it was true, if I had paid them to say such things," Keel told me. "Others rushed to Point Pleasant, as you did, to pester the witnesses and sit up all night in the TNT area. The town finally adopted a policy of running all UFO buffs out whenever they appeared. In 1991, a team from a Baltimore radio station visited Point Pleasant. On their first day they interviewed a number of local people. On the second day they found that no one...absolutely no one...would even speak to them. The buffs blame me for this, of course. I haven't been in West Virginia for over twenty years."

Hopefully, no one felt that I had pestered them back in 1976. However, no doubt the attention and intrusions from outsiders aren't always welcomed. Today, like Roswell, New Mexico, Point Pleasant has turned things around and capitalized on this outside interest with an annual festival, which benefits the community commercially. For a lot of participants, the Mothman Festival is a fun event for young and old alike.

Entranced Mothman witnesses?

While in the area in 1976, I contacted and spoke on the phone with Virginia Thomas, who described her "Mothman" experience on November 2, 1967. Her husband Ralph had worked as a caretaker at the wildlife station, where they lived. On that day Mrs. Thomas stepped outside to cover over some motorcycles as dark clouds were forming overhead. She heard a sound "like a broken fan belt on a car" that drew her attention to a field across the road where she saw a grayish form "shaped like a man" but "running like lightning." It ran so fast she later concluded that it must have been some kind of robot.

Keel noted there were a couple of witnesses who had described hearing an odd mechanical humming noise as their Mothman-type creature was flying overhead. Definitely an odd "bird"!

"It took over my thinking," Mrs. Thomas added. Crackling and popping noises filled her ears. Her eyes were fixed on the creature – she was unable to look away – and although she was able to open her mouth, she was unable to utter a sound.

It sounded like this witness was entranced in some way during her experience, and I later learned that Keel had run into this kind of situation before. He recounted one instance where a banker was at home and heard a noise outside, went out his front door to investigate, and then saw a strange creature outside his home. He stood there for approximately 20 minutes watching it, as though in a trance state. His wife was inside watching television, completely oblivious as to what was transpiring, until he re-entered the house, pale and shaking. "He claimed that during those twenty minutes when he was outside this creature was standing on his lawn, staring at him," Keel explained. "And he couldn't move."

Mrs. Thomas told me she was a devout Pentecostal and that she had had prophetic dreams. One of these Keel had written about, which seemed to foreshadow the tragic collapse of the Silver Bridge on December 15, 1967, which took the lives of 46 people. She said that she had once also foreseen an explosion at a jail in Point Pleasant where several people died.

In *The Mothman Prophecies*, Keel wrote: "Roger and Linda Scarberry were living in a house trailer at the time of their Mothman sighting. In the week that followed they were suddenly plagued by strange sounds around the trailer late at night. Beeps and loud garbled noises like a speeded-up phonograph record. They could not locate the source of the sounds outside or inside the trailer. Worried and frightened, they finally moved out of the trailer and settled in the basement apartment in the home of Linda's parents, Parke and Mabel McDaniel."

Everything went berserk

"We had never heard of a UFO or anything like that before in our lives," Linda's mother, Mabel McDaniel, told us. "Now that's the truth. We had never heard of it before until that happened to the kids and then after that happened everything went berserk." On January 11, 1967, Mrs. McDaniel thought she might have seen Mothman herself while returning home from work. It was about 5:10-5:15 p.m., and it flew low directly over her car near Tiny's restaurant (now the Village Pizza Inn). It had wing-like appendages, though they weren't flapping, and human-looking legs dangling down. She turned into 30th Street, where she lived, rushed inside and got her husband, but by the time they both emerged from the house the thing was out of sight.

Things indeed got "berserk." All sorts of strange happenings plagued them: UFOs, doors opening and closing as though by invisible hands, mysterious footsteps, unexplained odors, and ghostly apparitions. Linda once awakened to see the dark outline of a man standing at the foot of her bed. She wanted to yell at an aunt sleeping in a nearby bed in the same room or grab a flashlight. She felt if she could just shine it over a crucifix on the wall everything might be okay, but she found she "couldn't even move." Several minutes seemed to elapse and then, she stated, "He lit a cigarette and when he lit the cigarette it lit up this crucifix on the wall and he disappeared." When Linda's aunt awakened right after that she said that she had just dreamed that there was a man in the room.

"I don't understand it really, but John Keel seems to know what he's talking about," Mrs. McDaniel told us. She recalled how Keel was spending the night one time and in the morning she had gone to the bank before he had gotten up. While she was driving to the bank a suspicious "black shiny Cadillac" was following behind her, later disappearing down an alley. She returned home immediately afterwards. "He was still here and he hadn't gotten up yet," she said. "John later explained 'he wants you to know that he knows I'm here.'" Keel obviously believed that the driver was one of the notorious MIB (Men in Black) who from time to time reportedly keep a watchful eye on UFO researchers and witnesses. The MIB often wear black business suits, fedora hats and dark sunglasses, and their preferred mode of transportation is usually a black Cadillac.

Keel had a number of UFO sightings while in West Virginia. His most dramatic one occurred on top of a high hill in Gallipolis Ferry during the wee hours of the morning of April 3, 1967. He was sitting in his automobile, relaxed and chewing on a candy bar while he listened to the Long John Nebel radio show being broadcast from New York. At about 1:35 a.m. he observed a clearly defined saucer-shaped object, an estimated 20-30 feet across, that was "glowing red with greenish upper surface" and had "red lights or 'portholes' around (the) perimeter." It appeared to land behind some trees a short distance away from his automobile. Although Keel had been used to prowling graveyards and the spooky TNT area alone late at night, he suddenly found himself very afraid. He locked his doors and remained inside the car for the remainder of his solitary skywatch.

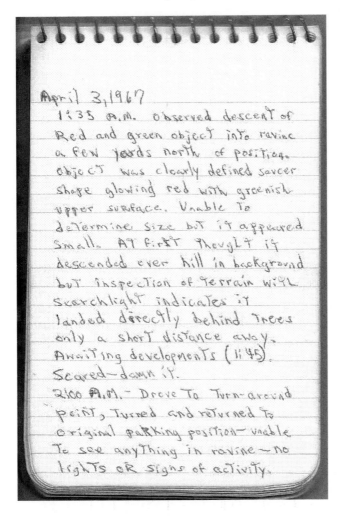

April 3, 1967
1:35 A.M. observed descent of Red and green object into ravine a few yards north of position. object was clearly defined saucer shape glowing red with greenish upper surface. Unable to determine size but it appeared small. At first thought it descended over hill in background but inspection of terrain with searchlight indicates it landed directly behind trees only a short distance away. Awaiting developments (1:45). Scared—damn it.
2:00 A.M. — Drove to turn-around point, turned and returned to original parking position— unable to see anything in ravine — no lights or signs of activity.

Source: johnkeel.com

Keel also described how from a high hilltop that gave him a great view of the Ohio Valley and the Ohio River, he observed "very bright lights" that came down out of the sky and circled the river boats. "The men on the boats would turn on the searchlights and aim them at these lights and the lights would jump out of the way of the searchlights," he explained. "And I thought that was pretty interesting. It went on night after night, and I talked to some of the boat men and they said, 'Oh, they've been playing those games for years with those lights in the Ohio Valley.'"

Keel also reported how strange lights would react to his flashlight. On the night of March 31, 1967, he and a police officer named Harold Harmon had traveled over around Gallipolis Ferry when they noticed two teenaged boys sitting on a hilltop next to a roaring bonfire. Keel learned that they were hoping to attract UFOs with the fire, but he asked them to extinguish it instead, knowing that the fire would likely repel rather than attract any UFOs. Keel then hiked into the nearby hills, under the cover of total darkness, accompanied by the two boys. As his vision began to adjust to the darkness, he noticed what he described as vague purple shapes hovering over nearby woods. Initially, he thought they might simply be stars low on the horizon, viewed through a natural haze. "But when I flashed my six-celled light at one of these purple blobs it suddenly and jerkily moved to one side, as if it were jumping out of my light beam," Keel wrote. "Fascinated, I repeated the experiment several times. Then I tried flashing the light at obvious stars to see if this wasn't just some trick of my eyesight. The stars didn't move, naturally."

On the night of April 2, newspaper reporter Mary Hyre was sitting on a hilltop with Keel when she too observed how strange lights jumped out of the way of his flashlight beam. In addition, Keel flashed the Morse Code for "descend" at one large object in the sky, and she gasped as it began to lose altitude. "It looks like it's going down a flight of stairs," she exclaimed. Keel noted that this was the classic "falling leaf" motion described by many other UFO witnesses over the years.

Swedish researcher Ake Franzen in 1977
Source: Hakan Blomqvist

Back on May 19, 1973, Swedish ufologists Hakan Blomqvist and
Anders Liljegren tape recorded an interview with their friend and
colleague Ake Franzen about what he had encountered during the
several weeks he spent in West Virginia, back in 1969 and 1970.
This interview added a significant variety of intriguing details to
this story from the perspective of another investigator. Here is a
partial transcript that appeared later in the Swedish magazine
Ufologen, No. 12, November-December 1973, two years before
The Mothman Prophecies came out. It touches upon some very
revealing and critical anomalous details that some of the witnesses
had described to Mr. Franzen during his own personal
investigations. The Marcella Bennett story that he related occurred
on November 16, 1966 and is described in Keel's *The Mothman
Prophecies*.

Here are excerpts from Franzen's interview:

Ake Franzen: "Linda Scarberry had to seek medical help because
of the psychological trauma caused by the encounter. None of

those traumatized by close encounters with this creature have recovered completely. Previously they were calm and harmonious which has changed to nervousness. Linda Scarberry woke up at the hospital one morning with her arms and legs badly scratched. She had large scars after this. The witnesses nervousness was above all evident in how much they smoked. My God, how they smoked. Even I who was a non-smoker when I arrived started. One witness, Marcella Bennett, could not be still. Most of the people who had seen 'the bird' had these kinds of symptoms. One witness started crying when she told me of her observation."

"It was like they watched a movie when they told of their observations, talked like they experienced it again. I told them 'you don't need to recount what happened if you don't want to' but they insisted on relating the event anyway. Maybe they noticed I believed them and felt confidence in me. I think it is important to the witnesses to behave in such a manner. It was fascinating but made me ill at ease listening to their encounters. When I talked to relatives they always said 'it is not the same old...' and then the name of the witness."

"Marcella Bennett didn't want to relate her experience to anyone else but John Keel and me. She said she had confidence in me. The night after Linda Scarberry's encounter Marcella and some of her acquaintances were planning to visit friends living near the TNT-area. Because of what had happened the night before they decided to spook their friends by knocking on the window. They parked their cars on a slope and walked towards the house. Mrs. Bennett was just about to take her two-year-old daughter out of the car when she heard a sound like a wet sack had fallen behind the car. She turned around and noticed something gray rise up behind the car. What she especially saw was the shining red 'circles.' She felt like paralyzed by them."

Håkan Blomqvist: "Was this some kind of eyes?"

Åke Franzén: "Yes, that's the theory, but they are placed very low, shining with a hypnotic glow. The witnesses often talked more about these 'circles' than the creature. Mrs. Bennett was unable to move when she saw the 'bird' coming between the cars. Her arms were sort of straightened out and she dropped the little girl on the ground. Not until the child began crying did Marcella 'wake up'. She picked up the girl and together with the others started running towards the house. They were hysterical when they knocked on the door and rushed in. Only three of the children were at home. Their parents had gone to Point Pleasant on an errand. They locked the door. Mrs. Bennett was speechless from fear and the others hysterical. Suddenly they heard something moving on the porch and how the 'bird's' wings hit against the logs holding the porch. Someone picked up the phone and called the police but when they arrived there were no traces, nothing. Only some hysterical witnesses. They were five grown up people so it could hardly be a misinterpretation."

"I also talked to a woman from New Haven. She and her husband were part of the group that investigated the ruin [TNT power plant] looking for traces. They walked around checking the various rooms. When she was about to leave a small room 'it' appeared, crouching in a corner. She screamed and the others – Keel was there – hurried to the place, but saw nothing. The husband made fun of her in front of the others, which of course made her upset."

"On the way home – now Keel was not there – they crossed a field and the woman noticed the creature standing in the field. Now her husband also observed 'the bird' and became very pale. 'The Birdman' disappeared straight up with a terrific speed, like a robot. It simply spread out the wings, but did not flutter with them, like an ordinary bird. Another woman I talked to was one of the few witnesses who had seen the face of the creature. She had observed an incredibly ugly, scaly head leaning towards one side."

Håkan Blomqvist: "Did you estimate how many within the TNT area who had witnessed 'the bird'?"

Åke Franzén: "It is hard to say as I didn't have time to visit all the witnesses. I talked to around thirty witnesses. I found it peculiar that they lived so far away from each other. It was pretty large distances. Inspite of this they told the same story, with insignificant variations. Another common factor was the poltergeist phenomena. Something strange always happened in the house right after someone had seen the 'bird'. It was somehow connected. Certain witnesses received strange phone calls, any time day or night. When they picked up the phone all that was heard sounded like metallic clicking. Four of the witnesses I talked to – among them Marcella Bennett and Linda Scarberry – had experienced this."

"One of the weirdest experiences was related by the Lilly family. One evening they were together conversing in one of the rooms. Mrs. Lilly happened to look in the direction of a bookshelf with a large vase. Suddenly the vase began moving, leaning outwards. Slowly, slowly, like in slow motion it fell over the edge of the shelf towards the floor where it shattered in two parts. Not in small parts, but straight edges! It was only the wife who observed the vase falling through the air and she felt paralyzed. She told me it wasn't like the vase fell through the air, but rather 'sailed.'"

"No one could explain this incident but it was associated with the strange noises heard in the house. Several times it sounded like a woman or child crying in the house in the middle of the night. There were no children in this house and they found it impossible to locate from where the sound was coming. The sound was 'everywhere'. It was heard but they were unable to find out from which direction it came. The area seemed 'infected' in some way. After a couple of weeks so much had happened that the family was forced to move. Nothing happened at the new address."

End of interview.

Linda Scarberry and her parents have all now passed away.

During my attendance at the 2015 Mothman Festival I found Faye Dewitt sitting at a booth, willing to share her own experience, also from back in November 1966, when she was only 14. My son-in-law Scott Harrison and I ducked into the nearby famous Harris Steak House, owned by Carolyn Harris and the official gathering spot for Mothman attendees, to hear her story firsthand. Her account was absolutely riveting!

Faye's brother, Carlisle, 16 at the time, had just gotten his driver's permit. They went to the TNT area because he wanted to prove there was nothing to the sightings. They had not yet been reported in the local newspaper, but word had gotten out at school about them. He was convinced that it was just someone in a Halloween costume. However, he and Faye found out otherwise, as the creature chased alongside their car at impossible speeds for a human on foot. It had reflective red eyes, but otherwise had human like facial features, with a nose and mouth, and appeared to be covered in feathers! Her sighting is described by her in great detail in an interview in Jeff Wamsley's book, *Mothman...behind the red eyes* (2005). Jeff is the owner of the local Mothman store/museum at 400 Main Street in Point Pleasant, and the principle organizer of the annual Mothman Festival. (His website: www.mothmanmuseum.com).

Like Mrs. Thomas mentioned a few paragraphs earlier, Faye Dewitt also had had precognitive visions of future events that would involve family or others to whom she was close. "I didn't have control the three times that my husbands were going to die," she told author Andy Colvin [*The Mothman Photogapher II*, 2007]. "It didn't tell me it was them. It showed me that was going to happen. ...Each time, within 15, 20 minutes after I saw that, I got the call that they were dead."

Fast forward to the 2017 Mothman Festival. While I didn't attend it, I learned from fellow Keelian researcher Tim Frick that he had met a woman named Linda Sigman there who said that she was 16 when she had a UFO close encounter on the evening of April 18, 1967 near Mason, West Virginia. At one point, a dark circular looking craft, approximately 25-30 feet in diameter, with several red and yellow lights on the underside, came very close to the car she was in. It made a faint "vacuum cleaner" type noise. Linda observed a tall dark humanoid figure about 10 feet tall go flying out from it!

She had a precognitive dream, as had others, that was related to the tragic Silver Bride collapse on December 15, 1967. "The night before the Silver Bridge collapsed, I dreamed that there were Christmas packages floating in the river and people screaming, and I can remember hearing this woman going 'God help me! Help me!' and there were pieces of metal and they were all tangled, and I woke up crying and screaming," Linda recalled.

Sigman grew up only about 20 minutes from Point Pleasant, in Pomeroy, Ohio. "I crossed the Silver Bridge many, many times," she said. "My sister taught me to drive when I was barely 15, so we went down there often, sometimes to shop, sometimes to meet with friends. I crossed the Silver Bridge for the last time just two weeks before it fell."

"The Silver Bridge swung like a baby's cradle," Linda added. "Sometimes we would just sit on it in the middle, if there wasn't a long line of traffic, and scare the crap out of the occupants in our car. It was fun, as we were young and crazy."

Was this an early warning sign that these teenagers and other locals ignored indicating that the bridge was becoming unsafe? Constructed in 1928, engineers later determined that the bridge collapse had been the result of a failed eye-bar joint and metal fatigue.

Mary Hyre had had similar dreams of Christmas packages floating in the river. On the morning after the disaster, Keel finally was able to reach Hyre on the phone around 2 a.m. (phone service had been disrupted). "It's the most terrible thing I've ever seen," she told Keel. "But I was kind of prepared for it. You know those dreams I had...well, it was exactly like that. The packages floating in the water. The people crying for help. Those dreams came true."

A core group of researchers who visit Point Pleasant frequently believe that Mothman (and other anomalies) come and go through interdimensional portals. Rosemary Ellen Guiley, a prolific writer on the paranormal and a popular speaker, is one of them. She had attended 14 festivals since 2004. "This is one of the most energetic, vibrant events that I go to," she told me. "I love the energies that the attendees bring, and the top-notch researchers in the paranormal and cryptozoology. You're always getting the latest perspective on trends and cases, and the festival is a lot of fun on top of that."

When I asked Rosemary about her own personal experiences there, she said, "How many days do you have?" Then she laughed and offered a few details. "Out in the TNT area, I've seen shadow people quite frequently in the igloos area," she stated. "They walk along the trails there and sometimes they actually lurk around the igloos themselves." (The igloos are old dome-shaped concrete storage buildings that had once housed explosives). "Shadow people look humanoid but they're not. They're entities that take on like a very dark silhouette of a person. They're drawn to areas of intense energies; especially if there's been a lot of negative energy. The TNT area, very contaminated because of the explosives and the things that have leached into the ground. And then that often creates or enhances the natural portal area that opens the window for a lot of strange things."

"This part of the Ohio River Valley has always been heavily haunted," she added. "Generation after generation have had encounters with ghosts and mysterious creatures. This is in my opinion a portal area."

I asked Rosemary how much John Keel's work had influenced her own. "John influenced just about everybody in this field, regardless of what area of the paranormal they're interested in," she stated. "He was way ahead of his time with his ideas and theories, which are enjoying renewed appreciation among researchers."

"John was a friend of mine. I got to know him back in the 1980s. I attended many meetings of his New York Fortean group. We met in New York City on occasion for dinner and saw each other at events. I admired his work tremendously. John left a great legacy for all of us."

I met and interviewed many other awesome and fascinating folks, like Texan writer/researcher Ken Gerhard, the author of the thought-provoking book *Encounters with Flying Humanoids* (2013). He called Keel "a huge influence" in this field. "It's an iconic story," he said. "Mothman is probably one of the most well-known beings/apparitions in the annals of the unexplained. The community embraces the whole mystery, which is really awesome."

17

"I'm always a bit skeptical," he said of cryptid reports in general, but added: "I've interviewed hundreds of eyewitnesses, many of them very credible and sincere people who claimed remarkable experiences."

Ken's interest in cryptozoology began when he was a young boy and he watched a television program about Bigfoot. After that, he began going to the library and searching for more information. His mother was a travel agent and an adventurous person, and she took him on vacations throughout the world, including the Amazon jungle, Australia, and Africa. Wherever he went, he inquired of the locals about unusual legends about mysterious creatures. At age 15, he visited Scotland's Loch Ness. "I attempted my first field research with a little movie camera and interviewed people," Ken said. "So it's been a life-long passion."

Was Mothman also in Pennsylvania in 1966 too?

I ran into another well-known researcher/author, Stan Gordon, from Greensburg, Pennsylvania, who has been chasing "monsters" and UFOs since 1965. I visited him at his home in August 1975, and here we were 40 years later reunited at the Mothman Festival! We used to both have solid black hair on our heads! (See what UFO and "monster" hunting can do to ya?)

Stan gave me a copy of his new book, *Astonishing Encounters: Pennsylvania's Unknown Creatures,* and told me to check out the many creature stories, including one with a "Mothman-type event that happened in the Pittsburgh area at the same time it was happening down here in West Virginia, but nobody knew about it."

According to Stan, the Mothman-like experiences began in the summer of 1966, in a wooded section of southern Allegheny

County near Pittsburgh. One young man reported that a strange creature leaped onto the back of his black convertible. Frightened, he hit the gas pedal and the thing fell off, leaving behind streaks of a white juicy substance on the back of his vehicle. Soon other teenagers began reporting frightening encounters with a monster in the woods. From the descriptions, it indeed resembled Mothman. Witnesses said it stood about eight feet tall with shoulders about five to six feet in width. It was muscle toned and appeared to be covered with feathers. When one group of teens barged into the local police station, the police didn't seem surprised, saying that they had been hearing similar stories for weeks. UFOs were seen around this time as well.

In West Virginia, Faye Dewitt recalled that soon after the Mothman reports circulated in the media a government agency fenced off the TNT area for about two weeks. She thought that it might have been the FBI.

TWO
"WE HAVE JUST OPENED PANDORA'S BOX"

Despite his fame in the field of ufology for his unusual stories and controversial ideas, John Keel liked his privacy and often preferred to stay out of the spotlight. He shied away from interviews, and often in correspondence asked that his comments remain confidential because he didn't want to generate any further "hysteria and paranoia" in the field.

Nonetheless, Keel had a peculiar knack for drawing attention and high-strangeness into his life. In 2015, I learned of a bizarre incident that he kept out of *The Mothman Prophecies.* During 1967, while Keel was trying to wrap his brain around many mysterious happenings, he received a visit from an old friend, Joe Woodvine. He hadn't seen Joe, a security officer for the Transit Authority, for a few years. This was a man to whom he had once been quite close to for nearly 20 years – someone he had been best man for at his wedding in 1950.

On December 15, 1967 – the day the Silver Bridge collapsed, killing 46 people -- Joe unexpectedly showed up at Keel's door, and they spent hours together, from early afternoon until nearly midnight. My informant of this event, who wished to remain anonymous, also visited Keel's apartment that day and remembered Joe well. "Big guy with a powerful handshake," he recalled.

Nothing seemed amiss about him.

About three years later, Keel sent my informant a letter in which he said he was in a store and found Joe's wife working there. He asked her how Joe was doing, and she told Keel that he had died of a heart attack *in July 1965,* more than two years before Joe had visited his apartment. "I argued that I had seen him in December 1967 and that she must be mistaken," Keel wrote in the letter. "She was most indignant. How could she be mistaken about a thing like that? She was with him when he died. She went through the funeral and all. She insisted it happened in July 1965."

"It looked like Joe, had Joe's memories, was flesh and blood," Keel continued. "But it couldn't possibly have been Joe. Strange, too, that he turned up on what proved to be one of the most important days in my life. You met him. All the people at Moseley's meeting saw him." [Keel and Joe attended a Jim Moseley UFO meeting at a midtown New York City hotel.] I had to leave this out of *The Mothman Prophecies* for obvious technical reasons. It would have been anticlimactic. But this has kept me awake many, many nights."

Keel struggled with this encounter with "Joe," who appeared physical and ordinary, indistinguishable from his real friend. It had his memories too. Was this early experience a taste of the deception that Keel soon believed permeated the paranormal and ufological fields?

I inquired of long-time researchers Allen Greenfield, Rick Hilberg and Tim Beckley, if they had photos from that 1967 Moseley meeting, but no one was able to help.

Researchers Tim and John Frick spent about eight hours with Keel at the 2003 Mothman Festival. Keel told them the same story about Joe. When John Frick asked Keel what he thought about meeting someone under such odd circumstances, he replied, "I don't like thinking about it, because it makes my head hurt."

When something makes John Keel's "head hurt," you know you're dealing with high-strangeness that has been kicked up several notches! But in the paranormal world, such stories are not unheard of.

Keel's world appears to have become one filled with reality twisted personal encounters with high-strangeness. In *Operation Trojan Horse*, he confessed how at times he questioned his own sanity. "I kept profusive notes – a daily journal which now reads like something from the pen of Edgar Allen Poe or H. P. Lovecraft," he wrote.

Keel shared a paraphysical Men in Black experience with acclaimed author and researcher Brad Steiger. Brad told me:

"In January of 1967, I was brought to New York City by Macfadden-Bartell publishers to complete my Valentino, the biography of the great silent film screen lover of the 1920s. I had corresponded with Ivan T. Sanderson for a few years and he had become my mentor. At the time, Ivan was an editor-at-large for a publisher and he had me working on a book on the poltergeist phenomena. When I told him I would be in New York City for a couple of weeks, he suggested that I take time off from work on the book for Macfadden-Bartell to visit him at his farm in New Jersey and sift through whatever info on poltergeists that he might have in his files. While I was there, the Jersey Devil was sighted, and Ivan spent hours on the phone answering queries and doing radio programs. Before I returned to the City, he said that I absolutely must take some time to get together with John A. Keel. Keel and I had corresponded briefly, and I agreed to ring him up some night when I felt I could take another break from my deadline. An editor was stopping by daily to pick up the pages I had completed, so I didn't have a lot of free time."

"When I was able to call Keel, he asked if I liked Chinese food. I confessed that I had never been to a Chinese restaurant. He was pleased to introduce me to some excellent dishes from what we then called 'the Orient,' and I have loved Chinese cuisine ever since."

"Our dinner conversation was laced with talk of UFOs, monsters, and, of course, the nefarious Three Men in Black. The MIB were very much a part of the general paranoia of the field in the late 1960s. It seemed that everyone who considered himself or herself a 'UFO researcher' claimed some personal harassment that just had to be the result of those three mysterious figures of menace. Some researchers believe that they had proof that the trio was comprised of U.S. Air Force officers. Others were convinced that the entities were members of a sinister group of ETs who were intent on silencing any Earthling who might have information that would expose their machinations to the portions of the government and military not already under their domination."

"Keel wanted to discuss the MIB at greater length, and he suggested that we adjourn to his apartment. Once we had arrived, he got right to the point. He believed that the entities who were harassing him were more than human and that it was unlikely that they were extraterrestrials because of the peculiar abilities which they had demonstrated."

"According to Keel, after he had suffered mysterious telephone calls and was made aware that a seemingly all-knowing 'someone' had him always under surveillance, 'they' arrived one night in his apartment. They didn't bother with the door. Suddenly three men simply manifested before him. Keel recalled that their behavior alternated between acting buffoonish to that of assuming 'tough guy' personas as they threatened him to cease all of his research into the UFO phenomena."

"After around a half an hour of cacophony of threats and behavior suggestive of the Three Stooges, one of them asked Keel if he wanted a demonstration of their alien abilities. When Keel shrugged, 'why not,' one of them went to his kitchen sink, pulled out a bottle of bleach from its cabinet, and took several swallows of the liquid, then handed the bottle to one of his companions, who, in turn, passed it to the third member of the strange trio.

"Keel said that they took their turn with the bottle of deadly liquid

23

until the bottle was empty. In his opinion, the beings were most likely paraphysical, for he could not imagine any physical beings who could drink bleach. Unless, of course, they were physical beings of an entirely different composition than we humans."

"While I found Keel's account difficult to comprehend, he seemed completely honest and forthright with his account of the extraordinary encounters with the strange beings. As we discussed his bizarre visitors at greater length, I could tell that Keel was beginning to lean more toward the belief that rather than extraterrestrials threatening those who chose to delve into the UFO enigma, it was humankind's ancient supernatural enemies harassing us in more modern guises of beings from other planets. He had, it appeared to me, begun to think in terms of demonic interference for what endgame goal remained unclear."

"But as I said, UFO research grew extremely bizarre in the late 1960s. Not long after I completed the book on Valentino and returned home to the Midwest, I received a letter from a prominent researcher who swore to me that Keel had been replaced by an alien look-alike. When I asked Keel the next time we spoke on the telephone if I were speaking to the real or the robotic Keel, he only laughed and knew exactly who was spreading those rumors about him."

"After my visit with Keel, I began to examine my disillusionment with what we then called 'flying saucer research.' The more that I got into the field, the more that I traveled across the US and Canada, the more that I interviewed contactees and abductees, the more that I began to pay attention to the nagging voice within me that kept telling me that the initial excitement that aliens, benevolent or malevolent, were visiting Earth was seeming more familiar and more like the world of psychic phenomena that I had been investigating for years. It seemed that we were now abandoning the spirit guides and mediums for the contactees with their Space Brothers and Sisters. And as I continued research for the poltergeist book (which became Strange Guests, Ace, 1966), I felt more and more that the phenomena of harassment by strange sounds and bumps in the night reported by those who had UFO encounters were seeming increasingly similar to the phenomena reported by those troubled by the bothersome rampages of the poltergeist."

Keel got a lot of us back in those days to re-examine our previous notions of strictly "nuts and bolts" ET visitors and look at the larger and more complex picture of these anomalous phenomena.

How was he able to so quickly grasp the bigger picture?

Keel's earliest experiences

In an interview with John Keel in 1984 in *UFO Review* #18, author and publisher Tim Beckley observed that prominent UFO researchers Dr. Jacques Vallee and Dr. J. Allen Hynek eventually validated Keel's UFO/paranormal correlations. "When I first expressed my views in books like *Operation Trojan Horse* and *Our Haunted Planet*, I was met with quite a bit of opposition," Keel responded. "For years people like Hynek and Vallee fought my concepts."

I believe the seeds of Keel's unique psychological evolution were planted in his childhood and teenage years, when Keel had poltergeist and UFO experiences. He began hearing knocks on his bedroom wall. He worked out a primitive code of tapping and asked the unknown communicator questions such as, 'Who will win the war?'"

Around 1940, when Keel was about 10, people on a back road near his family farm outside of Buffalo, New York, began seeing a tall hair-covered creature. They believed that it was a gorilla. "It scared several people badly and the farmers all went out with shotguns to track it down," Keel told Beckley.

One night in 1937, when Keel was seven years old, he saw his first UFO. He was in a car with his parents outside the small town of Canaseraga, New York, when they all saw "a huge, brilliantly illuminated sphere" on top of a nearby hill. Keel's stepfather stopped the car to observe more closely. Initially they thought it might be a barn or other structure on fire, but then it slowly rose straight into the air a short distance and then shot off out of sight. The memory of that experience was burned into Keel's mind and he never forgot it. He added this odd postscript: "But many years later I asked my parents about it and they had absolutely no memory of the episode whatsoever."

In 1974, Keel revealed to author Colin Wilson that for years he had been quietly conducting interviews with warlocks. He intended to write a book that would delve into the experiences of "natural witches and warlocks" – individuals, Keel explained, who were born with the ability to perceive "elementals" and control them to some extent. He believed that he had this ability when he was an adolescent, but managed to distance himself from it by redirecting his attention to the study of physics and chemistry. By age 18, he felt he had lost this ability. However, it was at age 18, while staying in a residence near Times Square, that he had an experience of spiritual illumination. "For a few brief moments, I suddenly understood everything," Keel told Wilson. "I was really one with the cosmos. The next morning, I could remember very little of it, but I'm sure it was all entered into my subconscious."

These are not the typical experiences we hear concerning the average "nuts and bolts" ufologist, but they were a part of John Keel's early life and varied background. These anomalous and dramatic events, along with his sighting of a UFO while exploring Egypt's Upper Nile in adulthood, no doubt had a considerable impact on his psyche. The sighting in Egypt occurred in 1954 when he witnessed a metallic looking, disc-shaped object with a dome on top hovering above the Aswan Dam. Later his extensive treks through Asia to study claims of the unexplained and the occult – he even tracked in Tibet the legendary Abominable Snowman for several weeks - all contributed in various ways to psychologically prepare him for the full-time UFO investigations that he would embark upon beginning in 1966. In his twenties, he was a globetrotting journalist who later served as Science Editor for *Funk & Wagnalls Encyclopedia.* His credentials had become quite impressive, even though he had never finished high school. He rose from humble beginnings in a farmhouse that had no electricity, no insulation, an unheated outhouse, and a sulfuric-tasting well. The only means of heat on cold nights was kerosene lamps. Nonetheless, many people later assumed that he had some sort of doctorate because of the knowledge he displayed on many topics. The editor of a local newspaper, The Perry Herald, was impressed with Keel and offered him the job of doing a weekly column, called "Scraping the Keel," beginning when he was only 14. The editor paid him two dollars a week, which was a big deal back then. He did that for several years, and then at age 17, with a mere 75 cents in his pockets, he hitchhiked his way to New York City, looking to make his mark in the world.

Which he did. Later in life, Keel received two honorary doctorate degrees in herpetology and archaeology, and for a time served as a special government consultant for the Department of Health, Education, and Welfare, the Bureau of Radiology, and the Air Force Office of Technical Research. When it came to his writing career, he was prolific, producing a steady stream of articles. He also created material for television and radio, with an emphasis on humor, and for a time was a head writer for Merv Griffin, Gene Rayburn, Robert G. Lewis, and others. In 1966, he wrote a humorous novel entitled *The Fickle Finger of Fate* that sold over 800,000 copies. He appeared on shows with Johnny Carson, Jack Paar, David Letterman, and many other big names in the TV industry.

UFOs and Ghosts

Getting back to the strange world of UFOs and the paranormal, Keel came to the conclusion that UFOs and the entities/intelligences associated with them were what occultists had long referred to as "elementals," beings existing in a hidden realm who occasionally intrude or manifest into our world. He explored an alternative physics that could explain how we are dealing with energy forms of intelligence that manipulate and traverse the electromagnetic spectrum, often in ways invisible to our abilities to detect and perceive. With his book *The Eighth Tower,* Keel attempted to simplify quantum physics and demonstrate how our perceptions of reality are being manipulated by various natural energies. "Are ghosts really UFOs and UFO entities, or are UFOs really ghosts?" Keel wrote in *Strange Creatures from Time and Space* (1970). "Take your choice." Some researchers, such as Andrew Collins and Dr. Greg Little, have speculated that UFOs are plasma energy forms with intelligence (*Lightquest*, 2012). British science writer Antony Milne, in his book *Fireballs, Skyquakes and Hums* (2011) agreed that we might be dealing with "plasmoid" beings. Trevor James Constable was an early American UFO researcher who concluded that there existed "amoebalike life-forms" in the upper atmosphere that were composed of plasma. He claimed that they existed primarily in the infrared range of the electromagnetic spectrum. Beginning in 1957, Constable and his colleague Dr. James O. Woods took hundreds of still and motion picture film of these UFOs with the aid of infrared film and filters. Some paranormal researchers also believe that some "ghosts" may be composed of plasma energy as well.

Some UFOs are certainly ghost-like. Ufologist Bob Teets described to me an experience he had as a young boy on a farm in Terra Alta, West Virginia, one early morning in the summer of 1958. They were a farm family and early risers, but on this particular morning a loud noise woke young Bob (about age eight) before the others. Looking out his bedroom window, he clearly saw a silver-colored, disc-shaped object, about 30-35 feet across, with "two glowing orange-red orifices" that seemed to be propelling it. "Even with my hands over my ears it still penetrated my head," he said. "It was just unbelievable. It was as if you were standing right beside a freight train that was going full throttle."

Then the most amazing thing happened. The object headed straight for a nearby hill, and Bob feared his sighting was going to end in an explosive crash. Instead, the object "went into the hill."

Yes, like a ghost.

"I had a very clear view," Bob said. "I could see everything."

In 2005, I met an American researcher, Cynthia Newby Luce, who had master's degrees in experimental psychology and anthropology. She had lived for many years in the mountain village of Sao Jose do Vale do Rio Preto, northwest of Rio de Janeiro, Brazil. One day she witnessed something peculiar near her village. "I was driving along the road that has the river on one side of me (the left) and on my right is a steep embankment as the river is in a narrow valley and the road is cut from the hill that comes right down to the river," Luce said. "It was in the middle of the day and the sun was bright and clear. I was going along at about 25 miles an hour. The road winds and suddenly I saw this metallic object with windows half-way into the hillside. It was around eight feet up from the road, and about 10 feet of the object was protruding, and it just slid into the hillside of bare red earth. It went in fast and it really startled me, and I did not have time to stop."

Sometime later she found a drawing depicting exactly what she had seen. It was based on eyewitness testimony of a "comet" observed in Arabia... in 1479 AD! She found the illustration, published in 1557, in William Bramley's book *The Gods of Eden* (1989, 1990).

Luce recalled another strange incident. "I was coming down my stairs into the living room. It was in the summer and the light was bright as my house is on top of a mountain and is designed to maximize the view and the light. I was two thirds (of the way) from the bottom of the stairs when coming towards me was this very strange, nasty looking animal. It was about the size of a large tom cat with a bushy tail and stripes about three-and-a-half inches wide of the oddest colors...a greenish yellow alternating with a brownish purple.

"You might construe the animal as some kind of cat except for the head and teeth. It had rounded small ears set too close together and the head was narrow with a rounded snout and many, many needle teeth. The mouth was open and not at all friendly looking. It came at me as if it did not see me and went between my legs and up the stairs. I turned to stare at it and it reached the top of the stairs and vanished! Just POP! It was gone."

"It was not completely solid," she added. "That's what tipped me off into thinking about dimensions." Luce noted how she had "without any effort, by accident, encountered four other people (at different times and places) who saw the same peculiarly colored, wide-striped, needle-toothed creature." She felt as though she and others were at times "walking around in a dimensional soup."

"For years, on an informal level, ufologists, or people talking about sightings, have noted that it is very common that once a person has seen a UFO, or even experienced any one of a wide range of phenomena, their chances of further experiences outside 'consensus reality' shoot up," Luce observed.

In *Confrontations* (1990), Jacques Vallee described a UFO witness who said she had seen an oval-shaped object rise off the ground a few feet, pause briefly and then shoot up a canyon at high speed, passing through several trees as if they were not there.

Sometimes it is the human experiencers who take on ghost-like qualities. A UFO contact experiencer who lived in the Chicago area shared some puzzling experiences with me. A small "golden ball of light" appeared a mere three feet in front of her face one night. "As I swept my hand across the light, the ball was not blocked by my hand," she said. "Instead, my hand disappeared as it moved across the light." On another night, a thing she described as a pinkish cloud floated into her window and appeared over her head. She decided again to see what would happen if she reached her hand up into the odd cloud. "I did so and my hand and part of my arm disappeared from view in the cloud," she said. "The cloud really didn't feel like anything except some very subtle vibrations."

Such oddball light anomalies are not unheard of. In Clug, Romania, in the summer of 1953, a 17-year-old biology student saw a glowing ball of light drop from the sky into a bush. Taking a stick, he poked it into the bush in search of the light orb and was startled when he could no longer see the stick as well as part of his hand. In addition, he was aware of a tingling sensation throughout his hand and a great heat in the soles of his feet, soon followed by a cold sensation that pressed down over his entire body. Fleeing from the site, he later suffered from vomiting and "mental disturbances."

In a case in Sao Paulo, Brazil, on May 22, 1973, at about 3 a.m., a 40-year-old salesman said a UFO projected a light beam down upon his car, at which point his auto became transparent. He stated that his skin felt as though it were on fire. He ran from his car some distance and then fainted.

Otherworldly reflections

UFO contactee Brian Scott told me he had multiple encounters with small balls of light. One night one of these luminous orbs entered his home. As it passed in front of a dresser mirror, he noticed he couldn't see its reflection.

A man in Ohio told me he was parked along a street in the city one night waiting for a friend when he saw two four-legged animals (he couldn't decide if they were wolves or dogs) running down the street in his direction. Oddly, he noticed that they were about a foot off the ground and appeared to run in "slow motion" even though they moved past him fairly quickly. However, what really surprised and disturbed him occurred after they passed. He looked at them in a side mirror and his rearview mirror. Instead of the "wolves," he saw in the mirrors a young man and woman running. They appeared to be between the ages of 18 and 20 and were nude!

Folklore around the world and dating to ancient times holds that reflective surfaces, including mirrors, have the ability to become doorways to the spirit world and allow the dead and other spirits to appear and communicate. In the 1990s, Dr. Raymond Moody, a pioneer of the study of near-death experiences, revived the use of mirrors for contacting the dead, which he discussed in his book *Reunions [1993]*. created his own mirror arrangement called a "psychomanteum," a term he coined from the Latinized words for "place of spirit." Moody's psychomanteum recreated conditions in which the ancient Greeks used isolation in dark places and shiny reflective surfaces to contact the spirit world. Moody's psychomanteum consisted of a black mirror in a dimly lit room or space. By gazing into it, a person might see or hear the dead. Some have had more remarkable and vivid experiences in which the departed manifest in the environment and make physical contact, such as touching shoulders, giving hugs and wiping away tears.

One of the first subjects to use Moody's psychomanteum was Hollywood celebrity Joan Rivers, who said she was able to connect with her late husband Edgar, who had committed suicide.

My friend and colleague, Dr. Greg Little, a Memphis, Tennessee psychologist, constructed his own psychomanteum after attending one of Dr. Moody's workshops. One day my wife, Joan, and I took our friend Wanda "Dove" Theiss, a Native American medicine woman, to experience Greg's psychomanteum. She sat in front of the mirror and afterwards described her experience. "I did see a young girl about seven to eight years old sprawled across a recliner," she stated. "She had a pink and white striped blouse on. A very clear vision. I also saw ancient ruins, (like an) Olmec temple pyramid."

Dr. Little wrote about Dr. Moody and the psychomanteum in his book *Grand Illusions* (1994). He stated that aliens could be contacted with the mirror as well as the dead. One of his readers wrote him that he had done his own experiment by concentrating on Aleister Crowley's famous drawing of the entity Lam, which closely resembles a modern alien "grey." The man stared into a candle-lit dark mirror for about 20 minutes. "Three of them [aliens] visually appeared for a few minutes staring at me, then faded," he wrote. This was followed by an uneasy feeling that someone was behind him. He forced himself to reach over and switch on a nearby lamp. "The presence and feeling immediately went away, In all honesty, I was actually quite shocked by the success of this experiment."

Other UFO contact experiencers have seen and/or interacted with aliens in mirrors too.

Dr. Little has examined this matter from both Jungian and physics perspectives. He notes, "Certain types of physical matter with particular electromagnetic properties are used by the archetypal energies to assist in the physical manifestation – a mirror is an example. So too are crystals, certain rocks, water, and particular spots on the face of the earth where geomagnetic anomalies exist. Jung just said that an archetype is a psychoid factor – something normally invisible (and very powerful) taking on a physically real shape and form."

The Jungian psychoid is an archetypal expression that manifests somewhere between the human psyche and physical matter - occurrences that may even have a partial and a temporary manifestation in our physical reality. In ufology, as in parapsychology, dreams may occasionally reflect that a transcendent part of life is but a dream. This rightfully belongs on the project display boards of theoretical quantum physicists.

When UFO dreams foreshadowed encounters

Farah Yurdozu, a noted ufologist from Turkey, is a multi-generational "alien contact percipient," beginning with her great-grandfather, a teacher at Istanbul University. In the late 1890s he was visited by two humanoid beings with reptilian features (most disturbing were the vertical pupils) who communicated with him telepathically.

"When I was a high school student I had a dream about a UFO landing on the shore where our apartment was located in Istanbul," Yurdozu shared with me. "It was a very vivid dream. In fact, I would call it an 'astral dream' with amazing details. Ten days later, in the same spot, I had a UFO sighting just like it happened in my dream."

A Native American medicine man shared with me something similar. "During the late part of winter 1974, I began to have a series of unusual dreams about silver-colored eagles," Medicine Grizzlybear Lake recalled. On three occasions he dreamed how the four eagles appeared from the four cardinal directions and flew around in a circular pattern for a time, and then flew out of sight. But then there was a fourth dream, again with the eagles coming in from the four directions. However, there was a new twist. "They all flew in a circle but began to change form," he said. "In place of the eagles appeared four silver-colored discs. The four silver discs then merged into one very large silver-colored flying saucer. All of the dreams were accompanied by a tremendous humming sound, and although I was asleep in each situation, I would feel my entire body vibrate to the point that it became unbearable. I would awake from the dreams shaking, exhausted, bewildered, and dizzy."

In February 1975, Lake consulted a Seneca medicine man, Beeman Logan, who doctored him and explained that the dream was some kind of shamanic vision and contact with the spiritual realm. He added that it might be a premonition that he would be taken up in a flying saucer by the "ancient ones." "As a college professor, and as a half-breed, assimilated Indian, I could not help but laugh in his face," Lake stated. "'You've got to be joking,' I reacted. 'Flying saucers, beings from outer space, and UFOs spiritual?'"

Shortly after his birthday on March 6, the dreams returned. One night, he had the dream again, but this time there was a voice. "Get ready my son, it is time to go."

"Suddenly, I found myself standing next to my bed and I felt compelled to walk into the front room," he explained. "Outside the large window hovered a huge, silver disc-shaped vehicle approximately 45 feet in diameter. Soft blue lights pulsated on it in a hypnotic fashion. I felt as though I was in a trance. This thing was pulling me closer and closer, and I couldn't seem to get away." Next he was hit by a beam of white light and then found himself onboard a craft with flashing lights of various colors, computer looking instruments and four beings, the "ancient ones" -- Native Americans were piloting the saucer!

In his interview with John Keel, mentioned earlier in this chapter, Timothy Green Beckley noted Keel had been a pioneer in tying UFOs to psychic phenomena. Keel remarked that in the beginning, he had met a great deal of resistance to this idea, but eventually fellow investigators around the world discovered for themselves that he was correct.

"So you've triumphed in the end," Beckley replied to Keel. "How does it feel?"

"It's a hollow victory," Keel came back. "We have just opened Pandora's box. Instead of solving the mystery, we've created many new ones."

Psychiatrist Dr. Berthold Eric Schwarz's intense interest in the paranormal developed in 1945 when he and his mother had precognitive impressions of the death of his younger brother, Eric, who was in the army and was killed in action in Germany. More than two decades later, with much parapsychological research and investigation under his belt, Schwarz came into contact with Keel, who pointed out to him the link between psychic phenomena and UFOs. Schwarz took this revelation quite seriously and hit the road to interview many UFO experiencers first-hand himself in several states to confirm Keel's conclusions. Later he penned a two-volume book, *UFO Dynamics: Psychiatric & Psychic Aspects of the UFO Syndrome* (1983) that contained many cases he had personally investigated, including one from Maine that I investigated as well.

There remains still so very much yet for us to learn and better understand.

THREE
WILL THE REAL JOHN KEEL PLEASE STAND UP?

After *The Mothman Prophecies* was published in 1975, Keel appeared on the popular television show *To Tell The Truth*. In the format for the show, a real person and two imposters were questioned by a panel of celebrities, who had to determine which of the three was the featured guest. "John and the two pseudo-Keels were quizzed by Kitty Carlisle, Bill Cullen, Peggy Cass, and Nipsey Russell on Mothman, the Yeti and Bigfoot, and ultraterrestrials," Keel's long-time friend Doug Skinner recalled. "It was certainly odd to hear Nipsey Russell interrogating John about Mothman, and to hear Kitty Carlisle try to figure out what an ultraterrestrial was."

Keel felt early on that he had become misunderstood in the ufological community and was the victim of false rumors and gossip. "Since my very first article in *TRUE* I have followed the same 'line,', but the assorted interpretations have been fantastic," Keel wrote me on November 23, 1970. "Anyone who has read my pieces objectively can see the route I have chosen. Yet people are always concluding that I have suddenly switched somewhere along the line...and this has led to the absurd speculations that I have been brainwashed, kidnapped by UFOs, bought off by the CIA, etc."

Admittedly, Keel's ideas certainly stood out in sharp contrast to the mainstream perspective of ufology, in ways that often raised eyebrows, concerns, and, in many cases, anger and disbelief. Keel was seldom interested in, or concerned with, sugar coating the controversial nature of his ideas and concepts. He was not happy with mainstream ufology and much of the mainstream had an intense dislike for him. They did not like him describing their ideas and writings as "cult literature," and saying that trying to talk to ufologists was like trying to talk to "a group of religious fanatics." Nor did they like his assertion that they primarily wanted "confirmation of their beliefs" more than a critical and objective review of the evidence. Plus, on top of all of that, Keel frequently drew attention to religious and paranormal elements that he perceived as significantly interrelated to the mainstream's beloved "nuts and bolts" UFO phenomenon.

Keel would advise researchers, as he did with me, to carefully "study comparative religion and demonology," as he perceived distinct parallels with UFO events, as examples, to the classic Marian apparitional events and the "alien abduction" cases. "What used to be called demonic possession is now called ufology by the victims," he told me as he told numerous others in the field. He expressed how he saw himself at times more as a demonologist than a ufologist, which certainly drew considerable criticism in his direction. When he got really worked up with the "UFO buffs," as he called them, he'd continue attacking the character of many "self-styled ufologists," complaining how "fragile socially and emotionally" many were. "Since they are unread and seeking something to give them a personal identity to downplay the obvious, they resort to the UFO fantasy. It is a big can of worms."

Keel complained how discord among ufologists had existed since the early days, recalling how back in 1948 he had attended a meeting on UFOs on 14 Street in New York City, held in a small room crowded with about 40 people who yelled and argued with one another about government suppression and such. Little has changed, obviously.

"UFO audiences are often very hostile – that's their nature – but Forteans are much more congenial," Keel noted. He preferred talking before Fortean gatherings more than UFO functions. "They're always terribly disappointed with my talks because I'm not confirming any of the crap that they've been fed through the different cult magazines and things," Keel told me. "You know, they want to hear conspiracies and stuff like that at these talks."

Credit: johnkeel.com
John Keel (left) and Doug Skinner (right)

Doug Skinner is a Fortean and could talk with Keel on matters they shared in common. Skinner is a performer, an accomplished ventriloquist. He maintains the John Keel website, www.johnkeel.com. He agreed to talk with me about the real John Keel who he had come to know quite well.

Brent Raynes: Shortly after John's passing in 2009, in your very nice tribute to him in the *Fortean Times,* you talked about meeting him in 1990 and that soon afterwards you became a regular attendee at John's New York Fortean Society gatherings. You helped him set up some fun and entertaining events at conferences such as the FortFest in Virginia. It sounded like the two of you had a good deal of fun.
I remember reading of one skit that you and John had cooked up where you performed a ventriloquism act in which you had a dummy that naturally had "psychic powers" and was able to locate

a dollar bill taped under one of the chairs. Also, at another time, how you guys placed rubber snails to many of the chairs. You even wrote "the squeals as forteans discovered gelatinous were quite satisfying."

Doug Skinner: We did have fun! He invited me to some of the FortFests held by the International Fortean Organization down in the D.C. area. I contributed some comedy bits to the program, and then started giving talks as well. John was always a magic buff and enjoyed working a card trick into one of the skits we came up with. Those old FortFests were a blast. Where else could you party with forteans, skeptics, Christians, pagans, cryptozoologists, and occultists? I also had a good time drawing a cartoon for the cover of his booklet "The Flying Saucer Subculture," an official publication of the New York Fortean Society. John insisted there had to be a straitjacket and a propeller beanie.

Brent Raynes: Within a short time the two of you became good friends. Could you share with us some about the friendship that evolved between the two of you, what he was like and what his friendship meant to you?

Doug Skinner: I got along well with John, for some reason. I say "for some reason," because he could be rude and difficult. We often had long phone calls and met for lunch. Meeting for lunch always required a long phone call as well. It might have helped that I was open-minded about ufology, but not active in the field myself (and therefore not engaged in the usual polemics), and that I worked in show business, where John spent much of his life. He taught me a lot about Forteana, and I kept him up to date on the miseries of auditioning.

Brent Raynes: I came across a couple articles that you had written for *Fate* magazine and I watched a YouTube lecture you gave at FortFest once where you were filling in for John while he was in New York recuperating from illness. What sort of impact did John's Fortean interests have on your life?

Doug Skinner: I had read Fort before I met John, and even accompanied a dance performance in San Francisco, back in the 1980s (for a dance by Virginia Matthews), by reading some excerpts from Fort. John did introduce me to other Forteans and Fortean groups. I ended up writing for "Fate," "The Fortean Times," and "The Anomalist," on the Count of Saint-Germain, Richard Shaver (especially his paintings), Charles Fort himself, and other topics. I was happiest with an article I did on Tiffany Thayer for "Fortean Times," since nobody had really researched him, and he was an interesting character. I also drew some Fortean comics for "Zuzu" and "Nickelodeon," which puzzled my colleagues who were not Forteans.

Brent Raynes: Have you ever had a puzzling experience in your own life that you couldn't explain and that you always wondered about?

Doug Skinner: Just the usual bewilderment at life on earth and human consciousness.

Brent Raynes: Some people who met John complained that he was difficult, depressed, and negative to be around at times. While I never met him in person, we exchanged letters and spoke on the phone several times, and he consistently had a great wit and sense of humor. You wrote that John insulted people, including you, and would be a bit of a trickster, that if you were going somewhere together and you were the navigator with the roadmap, you'd say something like turn left and he'd turn right. Were those the days and years before John became ill, which certainly affected his social abilities? Toward the end he was battling diabetes, anemia and heart trouble.

Doug Skinner: John was sometimes funny and charming and sometimes rude and negative. He suffered from money and health problems and was often depressed and in pain. He was terrified that his diabetes might lead to kidney failure or amputation, as it often does. The Mothman movie brought him some money (it didn't pay him much, but the book was republished in several countries), which relieved some of the financial worries. In his later years, he was starting to suffer from cognitive difficulties, like problems with word retrieval and memory loss. That was hard for him to deal with too. As he used to say, "Old age is not for sissies."

Brent Raynes: You and other close friends who had been helping to care for an aging and ailing John Keel, were with him to the end. I recall how as John laid there before you in a hospital in an unconscious state, you spoke to him of how he'd be missed and promised that we'd keep reading his "crazy books."

Doug Skinner: At the end, Larry Sloman and I were his medical proxies. We saw him a couple of days before he died, and he was in bad shape. I got a call from the hospital telling me that he had died and been resuscitated, and that Larry and I needed to decide if he should be kept alive with a respirator.
So, he had already taken his last breath the last time I saw him. We gave the final directive. Larry was out of town, so I was left to say the last goodbye, although I'm sure John didn't know. I had to do it anyway.

Brent Raynes: John Keel had been a Fortean and a ufological legend. Whether you agreed with him or not, he had made his mark in those fields. A big, very big mark. He is known by researchers and readers all over the world. He was a unique individual with many thought-provoking and original, pioneering insights, ideas and information that just might one day help us eventually solve some of this world's greatest mysteries. Maybe his books weren't all that "crazy."

Doug Skinner: Crazy is good! I meant it, of course, in the sense of "wild," not "insane." John's books were surprising and iconoclastic, crazy in the best sense of the word.

Brent Raynes: Thank you Doug for being there for John, and for the website you maintain with monthly postings of letters that he had written and received, along with reports, photos, clippings, and articles, all posted at: http://www.johnkeel.com

Doug Skinner: Anthony Matt and I set up the site for John's fans; I hope they enjoy it. I think the best part may be the bibliography. I post weekly, not monthly, by the way. I'm currently posting the notes he kept in 1967, which he eventually turned into *The Mothman Prophecies.*

John Keel made some truly deep and lasting friendships and positive impressions with many different people, inspite of the rocky relationship that he often had with mainstream Ufology. There were those who got what he was saying and writing. His words resonated especially with those who said that they had personally encountered, glimpsed, or investigated the alternative reality that the mainstream crowd seemed unwilling or psychologically unable to acknowledge. When author Andy Colvin, who grew up in West Virginia, met with Keel at the Mothman Festival in 2003, he told Keel that his book *The Mothman Prophecies* had had quite an impact on him and helped him to better understand his own strange experiences. "I really aimed that book at people who had had experiences," Keel explained. "I've heard from thousands of them since. They know that they're not crazy."

Michael Grosso, Ph.D.

Michael Grosso, Ph.D., is a scholar, teacher, author, and painter, whose interests span psychical research, metaphysical art, the parapsychology of religion, and, primarily, philosophy. He is another one of those people who knows the alternative truth for he too has experienced it. He received his Ph.D. in philosophy, and studied classical Greek, at Columbia University, and has taught at City University of New York, Marymount Manhattan College. He has published books on topics ranging from life after death to the mythologies of the end times. He lives in Charlottesville, Virginia. He is the author of *The Man Who Could Fly: St. Joseph of Copertino* and the *Mystery of Levitation*.

Michael Grosso knew Keel quite well also and spoke at his New York Fortean Society. I was fortunate to interview him too.

Brent Raynes: You have pointed out how pioneering researchers like John Keel and Jacques Vallee (who Keel used to joke he was a "ghost writer" for), made the controversial connection between UFOs and the paranormal, noting parallels with fairies, elementals, angels and demons. You've explored a great deal of similar terrain. In addition, I read in one of Keel's newsletters for the New York Fortean Society that you gave a talk there in May of 1988. You described some of your own UFO sightings, personal precognitive dreams, and a haunting situation.

Can you share with us the impact of Keel's work on your own studies and journey into the unexplained, and tell us some about your own experiences and the effects they have had on the evolution of your own understanding and theories about what seems to be going on?

Michael Grosso: I might begin with the first time I ever met John Keel. I came late to where John was speaking and I was immediately struck by his presence, a little bell rang in my head, announcing that here was someone entirely unique. Eventually I discovered he was in public on the grumpy, off-putting side. But I also noticed that when we spoke on the phone—and we had some long conversations—his manner was entirely relaxed and friendly.

John alerted me to the complexity of the UFO experience, especially the possible religious connection, and he also injected a healthy dose of skepticism, even contrarianism, into our talks.

Here let me describe my own UFO experience.

It was April 23, 1971, about 11 p.m., a perfect clear night in Greenwich Village, New York, in my apartment on the top floor (sixth) at 14 Bedford Street, with my girlfriend, listening to John Coltrane's "The Father, the Son, and the Holy Ghost." I go to the window and see before me a cluster of dazzling lights in the sky jigging back and forth in apparent rhythm with Coltrane. Jane comes to the window, sees same; lights do their dance for us, then shoot straight to the dome of our Lady of Pompei, about three blocks north; stays motionless, pulsing light (at us, it seemed); then, bolts away north and vanishes over the Empire State building. Jane and I then went up to the roof and ran into Louie, young guy interested in Coltrane—he saw what we saw, noted its noiseless character, and a pattern in the lights, pyramidal.

Three of us saw the thing. Its trajectory in space was more cartoonish and surreal than physically credible. I would call it a close encounter of a telepathic kind. *It* seemed to know we were listening to the Father, the Son, and the Holy Ghost, and proved it by flying to the dome of Our Lady of Pompei, where it pulsed and beamed at us, and vanished. I don't believe it was a vehicle from outer physical space, more like a tearing open of physical space and something bleeding into our reality.

Brent Raynes: Over quite a few years now you've delved into a full spectrum of controversial subjects. Like Keel, you perceived many potential interconnected aspects of such high-strangeness reports as out-of-body experiences, near-death experiences, poltergeists, and apparitions, and levitation. UFO close encounter and contact experiencers have a marked overlap with many of these phenomena. And there are many more categories of experience than what I've just mentioned, of course. The landscape is an immensely vast and enigmatic one.

Would it be possible for you to take a stab at articulating an abbreviated description of the "big picture" that you perceive?

Michael Grosso: Well, a stab it will have to be. Yes, I am interested in a wide spectrum of phenomena, in part because they seem like scattered clues suggesting some large albeit unknown dynamic—or single source. Another reason I'm curious about the spectrum of phenomena is that all my life I've sporadically experienced a range of events that leave me in no doubt that we inhabit a universe (multiverse?) much stranger than most of us can imagine. The percentage of dark matter and energy is analogous to the percentage of dark, unknown consciousness, in my opinion.

The essence of the big picture I would infer from the facts of my experience is the primacy of consciousness. This of course is not a fashionable view, neither for science or religion. The big picture I'm working on revolves around a taxonomy of PK, the whole ensemble of psychophysical interactions. Types of PK range from normal voluntary use of our bodies in all our activities to the abnormalities psychosomatic medicine to the supernormal realm of levitation, materialization, bilocation, projection by perfume, extraordinary healing, light phenomena, bodily incorruption, etc.

The culmination of mind over matter is mind over bodily death, and again we have a typology of survival evidence. (Here too I have some direct evidence) In short, there is a spectrum of evidence that points collectively to the next possible step of human evolution. The evidence may also be pointing to postmortem continuity, which is at least consistent with the irreducibility of consciousness to brain process, i.e. if consciousness preexists the brain, as William James suggested once, why not postexist the brain. I'm partial to Bergson's suggestion that the universe is a machine for the creation of gods.

Brent Raynes: Mainstream science continues to resist serious examination of any purported claims or evidence of anything paranormal. Speculations related to quantum physics give me hope

45

that perhaps we're finally making genuine inroads into what has for so long been dismissed as fantasy and pseudoscience. Do you think we're finally making some real progress here, or do we still have a painfully long, long way to go?

Michael Grosso: I think the ratio of the receptive to the unreceptive to supernormality is pretty much as it was since the dawn of the scientific revolution. There is always a minority at odds with the denser, more conservative mainstream. Yes, there are signs in various quarters of an awakening—the awakening to animal consciousness is also good news. But is any of it strong enough to stop the juggernaut of power-structures currently rushing us toward a triple-pronged apocalypse? I doubt it, but who am I to say what miracles might happen?

Every human psyche contains a divine spark, but unless we light a conflagration, it won't amount to much in the form of human benefit.

Three trends are at work in the world today converging towards nuclear war, climate catastrophe, and unsustainable economic inequity. No way to stop or reverse these trends, which are interactive and accelerating: they will have to work themselves out.

In my opinion, nothing radically creative is likely to occur unless the entire system is uprooted and forced to reinvent itself. Something like the near-death experience of world civilization may be the only hope on the horizon, an idea I touch upon in *The Final Choice: Death or Transcendence?*

Brent Raynes: What other projects are you working on?

Michael Grosso: I'd like to spend more time painting, which I think of as a form of materialization. It affords me the purest of pleasures. I also want to spend more time on what is really a new branch of science, the parapsychology of religion—especially my favorite topic, the parapsychology of apocalypse.

Credit: johnkeel.com
Tim Beckley (right) and John Keel (left) clowning around with a
rubber frog presumably pretending it was from one of those classic
and mysterious episodes of alleged frog falls from the sky, as well
as fish, snakes, etc.

Timothy Beckley reminisced:

John Keel was a good friend of mine. We both resided in
Manhattan's Murray Hill district. Ate at the same deli. Even went
to see a couple of movies together. Keel didn't drink so we would
part company for our individual evening's entertainment. I was on
the board of directors of the New York Fortean Society, which he
founded in the 1970s. In fact, the meetings were held just a few
doors down in a building that was torn down ages ago and is now a
vacant lot. Keel didn't like to be called a UFOlogist. He was
admittedly picky about who he hung with, not wanting to tarnish
his reputation. He thought the ET hypothesis was meritless. He
was among the first to lump together all manner of weirdness,
including UFOs, cryptid creatures (i.e., even Bigfoot), ghosts – all
of which pretty much can be labeled as what we today call
"Fortean Phenomena." That all-inclusive term is named after
Charles Fort (1874– 1932) who for all intents and purposes started
the discussion when he said humans were but pieces on a cosmic
chessboard and were being controlled by some outside influence.
Keel didn't identify with the term "Matrix" because it was still

early on. But he did believe there was what he called a "Superspectrum" in existence all around us and that openings (he called them "window areas") allowed a wide variety of otherworldly denizens to hop back and forth before taking the midnight train back to Magonia.

On the back cover of his book, <u>The Eighth Tower</u>, we learn that: "There is a single intelligent force behind all religious, occult, and UFO phenomena. Strange manifestations have haunted humans since prehistoric times. Beams of light, voices from the heavens, the 'little people,' gods and devils, ghosts and monsters, and UFOs have all had a prominent place in our history and legends. In this dark work, John Keel explores these phenomena, and in doing so reveals the shocking truth about our present position and future destiny in the cosmic scheme of things. Are we pawns in a celestial game? "In the Orient, there is a story told of the seven towers. These citadels, well hidden from mankind, are occupied by groups of Satanists who are chanting the world to ruin. Perhaps this is just a story; perhaps there is some truth behind it. But what if there is yet another tower, a tower not of good or evil but of infinite power? What if all our destinies are controlled by this cosmic force for its own mysterious purposes? And what if UFOs and other paranormal manifestations are merely tools being used to manipulate us and guide us toward the cosmic role we are fated to play? Perhaps, after all, we are not independent beings but are instead the creations and slaves of the eighth tower."

Utilizing Keel's own words, we start to get a better picture of what he is trying to convey to us: "This is a hypothetical spectrum of energies that are known to exist but that cannot be accurately measured with present-day instruments. It is a shadowy world of energies that produce well-observed effects, particularly on biological organisms (namely people). This superspectrum is the source of all paranormal manifestations, from extrasensory perception (ESP) to flying saucers, little green men and tall, hairy monsters."

Others who have broached the UFO topic with similar views would include, of course, Dr Jacques Vallee, Paul Eno and probably yourself to a large degree.

Former New Yorker Valerie Schultz, today a MUFON (Mutual UFO Network) state director for Maine and New Hampshire, recalled for me her early exposure to Keel. She stated: "My husband and I had gone to a UFO seminar at a high school in the village and John Keel was a guest speaker. John Keel had said he had decided to create a new Fortean Society and it was around the 40th anniversary of Kenneth Arnold's UFO sighting in 1947. We became Charter Members on September 19, 1987. The monthly meetings were held in Manhattan at 7 East 30th Street. Some of his guests were Whitley Strieber, Antonio Huneeus, Zacharia Sitchin and Timothy Beckley. The meetings were always excellent and very informative! Those were really fun days!

"At those wonderful Fortean Society meetings we always found John Keel to be very approachable and easy to talk with. Mr. Keel had a great sense of humor and he was always cracking jokes. He signed my copy of' *Disneyland of the Gods* this way – 'For Valerie

– Fortean extraordinary and discriminating book buyer. All the best.' We loved listening to John Keel discuss his world travels and investigations. I was fascinated by his theory that UFO's, psychic and Fortean phenomena are related! He used the word 'ultraterrestrials' to describe what we would now say are entities or extraterrestrials and felt that they have been interacting with us on this planet for a long time and keeping watch on us. However, he didn't feel they came from other planets but were more related to the earth itself and to mankind."

"Being a member of John Keel's Fortean Society in New York City opened my eyes to all things unusual! It taught me to have an open mind and think outside of the box."

Sandra Martin, Keel's former literary agent.

"John Keel was one of my favorite authors," Sandra Martin, a former New York City literary agent told me. As his literary agent, she negotiated a sale for his book *The Complete Guide to Mysterious Beings* (1994) to Doubleday. They frequently met for lunch.

Martin jokingly but affectionately referred to Keel, artist and psychic Ingo Swann, who is best known for his role in the remote

viewing field, and Polish born parapsychologist Dr. Alex Imich --
all three residents of the Big Apple -- as grumpy old men. "I used
to say with love and affection how I have these three grumpy bear
authors. They were really adorable but were consistent in always
voicing the negative side of everything," she said with a hearty
chuckle. "They were dedicated to their life work and trying to
move the field forward. A lot of the grumpiness was not having
mainstream researchers, nor public acknowledgement of their
particular field validated – although they did not strive for that, but
I know it made an impact. They seemed to be between two worlds:
either worshiped by fans, or totally ignored." All three men were
dear friends and clients, and all three were serious-minded,
pioneering, original-thinking researchers who struggled to bring
clarity and progress to their vision of the paranormal world.

Martin told me she felt motivated to help writers such as Keel
because she believed so completely in the work they were doing.
"Mostly I sold self-help books, consciousness, spiritual and New
Age books. Every now and then an editor would ask me, 'Are you
really interested in all of that weird stuff,' and I'd have to go, 'Yeah,
I really am.'"

We talked about Keel's large fan base. "I think it's because he was
such a great writer," Martin said. "That's what drew me to him. He
was just an extraordinary, talented and multi-disciplined kind of
writer. He could write anything!"

For the motion picture production of *The Mothman Prophecies*,
Keel read the scripts under consideration by the studio. "He would
call me at the office to complain bitterly about how they were
'butchering my story,' and would reject most of them."

"After a few years of this, he called and said, 'Sandra, I finally got
a really good script for *The Mothman Prophecies*. Well, let me
preface this first. None of the facts about my life are true. They
made me married.' He went on. 'All of these things that were
totally not true,' but, he said, 'They were true to the heart of the
story. They were true to the things that happened and didn't
exaggerate.'"

"He was laughing on the phone. He was so happy. I hoped that the movie would stay true to the screen play, but that rarely happens."

Martin said Keel approached things with great caution and looked out for his friends. For example, there was one occasion where someone billed as an extraordinary psychic was going to give a public demonstration. She and Keel were invited.

"John and I decided to go together because, even though I am totally and completely interested in all of these phenomena, I am such a skeptic in so many ways – mostly because I sat there at my desk listening to people that were trying to pitch me a book and sometimes it was just something – I hate to even say this phrase, but something they just made up at that moment. So I became really discerning about the field, and I think that's one of the things that John Keel liked about me because both of us were coming from the same point of view. My reputation was based on the manuscripts I agented or published myself – they had to be valid and had to have merit."

"John picked me up in a taxi and we went downtown. It was a big event. The press was there and the place was packed. It was set up in a circle of chairs. John and I, because of who he was, were sitting right up front so we could see the psychic in action and so everybody could see we were there."

"The psychic was given an introduction and then he began this demonstration of psychokinesis (mind over matter). He had a match box and he was holding it like a foot apart between his hands and it was floating in the air and he was doing all of these things with his hands, sort of conjuring this energy. While I was watching mesmerized, John Keel grabbed my hand, and while pulling me up said to me, 'We've got to get out of here!' and we just shot out the door. I was confused, 'What? What? What's going on?'"

"Outside, safe on the street, John says, 'Sandra, I can take you down to 23rd Street and teach you that magic trick in five minutes.

That guy isn't the real thing and I don't want anybody taking my picture with him and I don't want anybody taking your picture with him.' So we left. John was always really protective and understanding of what I was doing."

The gathering had been held at the home of Ingo Swann, and the supposed "psychic" had been brought there by parapsychologist Dr. Alex Imich. I'm not sure if this happened after this event or not, but Doug Skinner recalled a time that he and Keel met with Dr. Imich to discuss magic and the paranormal. "John tried to tell him that some psychic phenomena were simply magic tricks, which was not what Dr. Imich wanted to hear," Skinner wrote me. "John was a lifelong magic buff and thought investigators should know some of the basics of sleight-of-hand."

Returning again to the mysteries at hand presumed to be genuine, Martin had more to say. "Our world is complicated. Science hasn't caught up or maybe it is way out in front of us about these fields – we just don't know. In the 1990s, physicists were discovering and acknowledging multiple dimensions and who knows what else. Being on the leading edge is a dangerous place. Trying to bring to the mainstream information about how extraordinary the human spirit or soul is happens to be very threatening to many institutions and they fight back. I had a long and exciting career selling manuscripts on new consciousness research, spirituality, spirits and ghosts, UFOs and conspiracies. John Keel was one of my 'go to' experts to ask about questionable manuscripts. A good man."

In his first book *Jadoo* (1957), detailing his dangerous travel adventures from Egypt to Singapore, Keel exposed quite a number of fake miracle workers who posed as yogis, fakirs, snake charmers and what he called the jadoo artists. The fake New York psychokinesis show was not his first encounter with such human tricksters. In his travels he had learned many clever secrets like walking on water, the Indian rope trick, poking long steel needles through flesh, being buried alive and surviving it, and even how to temporarily cause a snake known as the *naje haje* to become paralyzed and temporarily rigid, until thrown down upon the ground – the same trick, Keel was told, that was used by Moses to impress the Pharaoh.

On the flip side of this though, Keel came away from his adventures in the East with a genuine feeling that some things might not be explained in a conventional way. In India, a young oracle sat cross-legged before a huge Buddha statue, putting on a special demonstration for Keel on summoning ghosts. Within a short time, Keel noticed the flame of a lamp waver and then extinguish. Then something loudly thumped on the roof of the small temple they were in. Then a small stool moved toward him from one of the corners of the temple. "I passed my hands all around it," Keel wrote. "There didn't seem to be any threads or mechanisms of any kind. It was just a plain three-legged stool. It moved on to another corner and stopped. Later I examined it carefully but couldn't find any sign of trickery." A revered lama named Nyang-Pas gave Keel an impressive demonstration of telepathy, picking up specific things that Keel was thinking of. Keel also heard stories from the people of India of the legendary Yeti, and he even came across the creature's apparent footprints and heard what were said to be Yeti vocalizations.

Keel was well respected in the magic community. Often on Thursdays Keel and Martin would go for lunch at Manhattan's Edison Hotel, where a group of old magicians would gather to talk magic. Keel would always join in their conversations, introducing Martin as his agent. Ben Robinson, described by the *New York Times* and others as a master magician, wrote an article about Keel for *MagicTimes.com* in 2002, which is posted on his website www.illusiongenius.com. "Keel is best known to magicians for his 'autobiography' written at age 27: *Jadoo*," Robinson wrote. "It is one of the first western books to tell the story of Indian street magic. The author befriended many *galli galli* men [name of street performers in India], and those who performed feats no longer seen, such as the instantaneous appearance of many small birds from under a basket. ...A book of original tricks he has on a shelf has never been published."

Years ago, I had read John Keel's *Jadoo,* describing his heroic, death-defying, real-life adventures trekking from Egypt to

Singapore. However, that wasn't the whole story, as gripping and exciting as it was. There was also a love story, involving a German girl named Lite who for several weeks stayed with Keel in Egypt. Sadly, Keel struggled to make their relationship survive in the midst of a writer's severe financial dry spell. His writing career wasn't going well at the time, and he tried unsuccessfully to obtain a local job there in Egypt. In the end, while there was just enough money, Keel went with Lite to Alexandria where she got on a boat to head back to her home in Germany. In a revised 2013 edition of *Jadoo,* published by Anomalist Books, Lite's story is finally included. She is called Ingrid in the chapter Keel had initially intended to be used but could not without a written release. In the new version there is a small picture of Lite and Keel in an affectionate embrace with the words, "This book was written for Lite who lived part of it and suffered all of it."

Their parting certainly seemed like a sad and touching end to this part of *Jadoo.* When they parted in Alexandria, she looked at him and cried, "We'll never see each other again. Before, I was sure we would...but this time..."

"For a long moment I stood looking down into her sad, freckled, loving face, thinking of throwing her bags off the boat, scooping her up and taking her back to Cairo," Keel wrote. "Later, a thousand times, I wished I'd done that."

It was not quite the end, however. Skinner said that while Keel stayed in Barcelona after his year-long trek through the Orient, and was writing the book that would become *Jadoo,* he was joined there by Lite once again, and after that she even joined him briefly in a return to New York City. "He said New York was too much for her," Skinner recalled. He wasn't certain if Keel, at that point, regretted their separation or not. However, Keel once remarked to Rosemary Ellen Guiley that the days with Lite were some of the best times of his life.

Keel dated many women during the 1960s. A 1976 photo of Keel and a woman in Sweden was supplied to me by Hakan Blomqvist. Skinner thought it was a lady named Arlene Stadd, whom he was seeing around that time. Blomqvist wasn't sure who she was.

Stadd would have had things in common with Keel, as she was a longtime television writer and had written scripts for shows such as *Hawaii 5-0* and *Love, American Style*. He was planning to join her in Los Angeles in his later years, but before that could happen she died of a stroke on February 5, 2001, at age 70.

Sadly, Keel has also left us as well. I am reminded of a gentleman and author who, a few years ago, before his own passing, remarked how with each person's death a library of rich and unique knowledge, stories, and information is lost to us forever. Thankfully with John Keel, this is not the case, and we are left with a thought-provoking collection of books and articles by which much of his library, so to speak, is still preserved. But I must admit, as I reviewed much of his writings, both personal and published, watched videos of some of his presentations, and interviewed his old friends and acquaintances, I missed terribly the days when I could pick up the telephone, and say, "Hey John, I have a question…"

I sure wish that I had asked him more questions.

"I am sure that Keel is now in the *Disneyland of the Gods* delighting all with his rich repertoire of strange tales," Phyllis Benjamin warmly noted with humor in her tribute. In that same issue of the *Fortean Times*, Doug Skinner reminisced on Keel's legacy and on the "wild" books he left behind for us. "I suppose we'd have to call it Keelian: outrageous, scary, mischievous, dramatic, funny, and a bit dodgy. Even if you didn't believe all of his tales, or agree with all of his interpretations, he kept you engaged. His ideas were a major (and, in my opinion, healthy) influence on all of us poor souls who puzzle over the unexplained. I still find *The Mothman Prophecies,* among its other qualities, one of the best caveats to the perils of rooting about in the shadowlands."

FOUR
KEEL'S UPS AND DOWNS

While John Keel was concentrating on his UFO research and field investigative work from 1966 to the early 1970s, the mainstream ufologists found it extremely difficult to wrap their minds around his findings and ideas. Conservative ufology was dominated by the extraterrestrial quest for "nuts and bolts" hard evidence, while Keel maintained that we were likely dealing with deceptive intelligences from a "parallel world." He had trekked through some 20 states and befriended more than 200 contactees (those who claimed direct interactions with the intelligences behind the UFOs), which was not something many so-called serious ufologists did back then. For example, the mainstream civilian organization known as NICAP (the National Investigations Committee on Aerial Phenomenon), based in Washington, D.C., begun back in 1956 by retired Marine Major Donald E. Keyhoe, took a dim view of anyone claiming alien "contact." In a lecture, Keel recalled the tone of the times: "If you came in with a UFO story that had a memory lapse in it they said that must be a hoax and they'd just dismiss it." Keyhoe had attacked the famous contactee George Adamski of the 1950s as an opportunistic charlatan and had a similar distaste for many others who described similar encounters with benevolent "Space Brothers" (and Sisters) from Venus, Saturn, and so forth. Another prominent organization was the Aerial Phenomenon Research

Organization (APRO), founded in 1952 by Coral and Jim Lorenzen in Wisconsin (soon afterwards relocated to Tucson, Arizona). APRO did investigate "occupant" reports so long as they conformed to the behavior of alien space scientists who came to our planet to collect rock and soil samples and check out our military installations and nuclear sites. The "Space Brother" stories were frowned upon by them as well. The Lorenzen's initially had a hard time wrapping their minds around the 1957 sexual breeding account of a Brazilian farmer named Antonio Vilas-Boas, who claimed an alien abduction where he had sexual intercourse with a female entity. However, it was carefully investigated by one Dr. Olavo Fontes of Brazil's National School of Medicine. Dr. Fontes took the case very seriously and, of course, as time went on more and more similar accounts would emerge and become regarded as credible, as the Boas case had become. Boas later became a respected Brazilian lawyer and for the rest of his life continued to stick by his story.

In a *True* magazine article published in February 1967 entitled "Never Mind The Saucer! Did You See the Guys Who were Driving?" Keel touched upon the reports of entities associated with UFO encounters worldwide, adding that most magazines "would not touch contactee stories." He tapped into an aspect of ufology that many researchers had neglected. "A few weeks after the magazine came out, the editor called me," Keel recalled. "He said he had something to show me. And he waved his hand towards the corner of his office and there were about six mail bags. He said, 'This mail is for you, Keel.'" There were thousands of letters, many from people claiming UFO abduction and contact experiences, including "memory lapses for long periods of time."

Keel advanced the idea that the intelligences behind the UFO displays could be conducting psychological mind games with us. Instead of being a new phenomenon, which seemed to be the case when the "flying disk" sightings were first noticed in 1947, the manifestations represented variations on anomalous occurrences that had been chronicled in previous centuries throughout the world. Through the years, he wrote extensively on the close resemblance between UFOs and elementals of occult literature, which he preferred to call "ultraterrestrials." He argued that the paranormal was an important but neglected component of UFO close encounter and entity cases.

While Keel spent a great deal of time writing and talking about his ultraterrestrial/elemental theory, he confessed in his *Fate* magazine column, "Beyond the Known," in April 2002: "With me, the ultraterrestrials were only one possible explanation of certain weird phenomena. I never actually said that it was the only true solution to anything – just speculation."

Keel stated time and again that he wanted to introduce professionalism into this field. "When I got into the business publicly in 1966, I was immediately appalled by the utter irresponsibility of the UFO groups," Keel wrote me in 1970. "I reviewed all the UFO zines of the past 20 years that I could locate. Keyhoe's attacks on Adamski, for example, were emotional, groundless and slanderous. Coral was fond of presenting gossip and rumor and unchecked speculation as fact. Many of the most coveted 'cases' of the 1950's had, in fact, never happened but have been repeated so often that they have become 'fact.' If you read *FSR [Flying Saucer Review]* you know I have been openly questioning many of these cases and trying to straighten this mess out."

"Although numerous newspapermen, editors, and scientists strongly advised me to have nothing to do with the UFO buffs I decided to try to introduce professional integrity into the field. The result is rather obvious: the buffs have labored to turn me into some sort of controversial mystery man. I had incredible problems with teenaged buffs in particular. But others, who should know better, such as Ralph Rankow and Hynek, have also circulated ridiculous, totally unfounded claptrap about me."

It is clear that Keel's ideas and findings were in such sharp contrast to those of the ufologists who dominated the field and that few in the ufological mainstream took him seriously. It was extremely frustrating for him to struggle to get his ideas, evidence and points across to a resistant audience. Keel was in a state of depression over it much of the time. If one asked him how he was doing, he'd invariably reply, "Suffering and struggling." It was as though a cloud hovered over him I was told, making everything look bleak. Some friends chose to distance themselves from him. A few years before his passing, Keel scribbled in a note to me, "Religions are merely a method to reach down to us and keep us confused. We are skidding to the end and we'll never know the ultimate truth."

During a phone conversation with Keel, in which we had been discussing Virgin Mary miracles and apparitions, I asked him outright if he had ever stumbled upon any evidence that there was a benevolent, positive force behind any of these occurrences. "I know in a lot of what you've written you keep referring to the demonic elements – the deceptive and manipulative elements of the phenomenon," I said.

"Vallee has also tried to write about that," Keel replied. "He doesn't know enough about the subject." Then Keel answered my question. "No," he began. "In all of these years, I've never seen a positive side to it." He said that in the late 1960s and early 1970s he tried to make his position on this clear. "I sent out a form letter back in those days saying that I had concluded that it was all sort of against the human race, that whoever – whatever is doing all of this doesn't have our interests at heart. I think Vallee came to the same conclusion. Even with the angel visitations and all, they always turn sour so it's a little scary."

The UFO literature is a strange concoction intermixed with the languages of "nuts and bolts" science, metaphysics, mysticism, parapsychology, and quantum physics. It's difficult for participants in the UFO field to agree on everything because the matter can be subjectively approached from so many different directions. It makes for a TOE (Theory of Everything) seem impossible. One report has an anomalous object visually observed and tracked on radar, appearing to be a solid physical craft while another has something that flies straight into a hillside like the hill was a cloud instead. It's these kinds of reported variations that makes analysis and interpretation of the UFO phenomenon very challenging.

"There have probably been more books written on UFOs, I would guess, than any other subject," Timothy Green Beckley, known by many in ufology as "Mr. UFO," told me in an interview. "I mean, there are just thousands of them. Even the Library of Congress, at one point, put out a bibliography of UFO books."

Tim was indeed correct. I pointed out to him that the bibliography was mentioned in John Keel's *UFOs: Operation Trojan Horse* (1970). Tim said that the compiler of the bibliography, Lynn Catoe, had been a "good friend" of John Keel's! Tim recalled that in the 1960s he had been giving a lecture at a Congress of Scientific Ufologists conference in Parma, Ohio, when both John and Lynn entered the room and sat in on his presentation together.

Regarding the bibliography, Keel had written in *Operation Trojan Horse*: "Recently the U.S. Government Printing Office issued a publication compiled by the Library of Congress for the Air Force Office of Scientific Research: *UFOs and Related Subjects: An Annotated Bibliography*. In preparing this work, the senior bibliographer, Miss Lynn E. Catoe, actually read thousands of UFO articles, books, and publications. In her preface to this 400-page book she states:

"'A large part of the available UFO literature is closely linked with mysticism and the metaphysical. It deals with subjects like mental telepathy, automatic writing, and invisible entities, as well as phenomena like poltergeist manifestations and possession. Many of the UFO reports now being published in the popular press recount alleged incidents that are strikingly similar to demonic possession and psychic phenomena which has long been known to theologians and parapsychologists.'"

"That's the closest that you could actually get to the government making a statement about flying saucers," Tim quipped wryly. "It's in an official book printed with taxpayer money."

After that conversation, I couldn't help but wonder how deep was the relationship between Keel and Catoe. They both strongly noted the correlation between UFO literature and mysticism, demonic possession, and various aspects of psychic phenomena such as telepathy, poltergeist manifestations and automatic writing. Catoe's extensive bibliography had been requested by the Air Force Office of Scientific Research (AFOSR) to help brief Dr. Edward U. Condon and his UFO research committee at the University of Colorado on popular ufological literature. I can't help but wonder if the Air Force saw this as something that might have helped persuade the Condon Committee to release the Air Force from the PR responsibility of investigating UFOs since it overlapped into so many other areas that would be outside of their jurisdiction. Interestingly, Keel wrote in the *Flying Saucer Review* in 1969 that Air Force investigators had startled UFO witnesses and enraged ufologists by gently implying at times that perhaps witnesses had undergone a "psychic experience" rather than a physical one.

I soon had my answer about the relationship between Keel and Catoe. According to Keel's long-time friend Doug Skinner, "John dated Lynn Catoe for a few months in 1968," he wrote. "They broke up when she wanted the relationship to become more serious. I don't think they investigated cases together."

Keel was a technical advisor to the Library of Congress from 1968 to 1969, which would have afforded him the opportunity to meet Catoe. I imagine that the two shared interesting conversations on the UFO/paranormal "can of worms," as Keel liked to call it. They both delved extensively into literature that covered so many of the same reported psychic, metaphysical, and spiritual phenomena.

Interestingly, in chapter 17 of *The Mothman Prophecies,* Keel describes an unidentified woman connected with the U.S. Air

Force and the Colorado UFO Project who had arranged to spend a weekend on Ivan T. Sanderson's farm in rural New Jersey to go through his extensive UFO files dating to the 1940s.

Skinner confirmed to me that the woman was in fact Catoe.

Catoe was followed by a suspicious character driving a panel truck. Traveling on the New Jersey Turnpike, she noticed that when she turned off onto country roads to head toward Sanderson's home, the truck also turned off and remained behind her. She stopped at a gas station and the truck pulled in behind her. A man in neatly pressed coveralls and shined shoes got out and approached her, stating that he had been watching her tires from behind and thought there was a bad lump on one of the back tires. She looked and could see nothing wrong, at which point a gas station attendant appeared and the man got back in his truck and drove off. After she left the gas station she continued on until she stopped at a small restaurant for a snack. As soon as she got out of her vehicle the stranger again appeared. "I'd really better have a look at that tire," he exclaimed. Before she could protest he crawled under the rear area of her car. After about two or three minutes, he re-emerged stating, "I guess it will be okay. Where are you going?"

She decided to forego the snack and proceed on to her destination. When she arrived at Sanderson's farm, she immediately told him what had happened. Sanderson called Keel, who suggested that Sanderson go have a look underneath her car. Meanwhile, Keel switched on his tape recorder and began questioning Catoe about what had happened. Then Sanderson returned and reported that on the bottom of the gas tank there were "three big globs" of putty-like material in an equidistant triangular arrangement. Keel advised calling the police in case the "globs" might be "plastic explosives." The police arrived and took the material with them. Sanderson theorized that the putty was possibly used to secure antenna wires of a small electronic homing device.

In addition, Catoe described a sign on the truck that was from an appliance company in a nearby town. However, when the police later checked there was no such company in that town.

The phone connection had been very clear. Keel had tape recorded their conversation. He found it very odd though that every time Sanderson spoke on the tape he could be heard very clearly, but whenever Catoe spoke there was heavy static drowning out her voice, even though there had been no static heard by any of them during their conversation. Interestingly, this sort of problem with recording phone calls became a difficulty after this. "Whenever a contactee or mystery voice would call, the tape would just contain static," Keel wrote. "I switched to another, better recorder but the problem persisted. Even portions of conversations with Mary Hyre were drowned in static when she was discussing some of the more mysterious events in Point Pleasant."

Keel often had a feeling he was being watched. Perhaps someone was concerned about the relationship between Keel and Catoe and what they might share and uncover. Was someone concerned that the two might collaborate and influence public attitudes on the UFO issue that might require more monitoring?

While mainstream ufology generally shied from things paranormal, in addition to Keel certain people connected with the government seemed interested too. For example, New England ufologist Raymond Fowler, in his book *The Watchers* (1990), wrote that in 1968 he learned about a joint Air Force and NASA study of psychokinetic (PK) subjects. An Air Force employee working with the project told one of these PK subjects that information on persons demonstrating good results was sent to the CIA in Washington, D.C., and that the CIA suspected a connection between psychic phenomena and UFOs.

In the early 1980s, I knew a person who was deeply involved in parapsychology, who suddenly retired from the field. While I cannot go into details because of the sensitive nature of our conversation, I will state that this person, who was working on psychokinesis with other parapsychologists from coast to coast, learned from a member of the secret service, "we've got a list of you people."

"That's why I got out of active research," this researcher (who also studied UFOs) told me.

Abductee Betty Hill was present during one of this researcher's successful PK experiments. Fowler suspected that the CIA may have been using the Air Force/NASA psi project to locate "unsuspecting amnesiac abductees" for "special study."

Remote Viewers and UFOs

In 1995 it was big news when major media outlets such as *CNN* and *Newsweek* revealed that, over a two decade period, $20 million had been invested in a joint project of the Defense Department and the CIA to employ and study 16 "remote viewers." A decade earlier, in 1985, physicist Russell Targ and experimental psychologist Keith Harary disclosed details of a remote viewing program at Stanford Research Institute (SRI) in California in their book *The Mind Race* [1984]. The authors said the government had been supporting a "multi-million-dollar program" at SRI to experiment with remote viewing techniques. The media took little notice of the book.

French born scientist Jacques Vallee, author of a number of books on UFOs, discovered that many gifted remote viewers also had UFO experiences going back to their childhoods. Beginning in 1971, Vallee was asked to assist the Parapsychology Research Group in Palo Alto, before they joined with SRI. "When it turned out that many of their subjects had experienced UFOs, they brought me into the project on a strictly confidential basis to document that aspect of the problem," Vallee told me. We were both giving talks at a UFO conference sponsored by the Association for Research and Enlightenment in Virginia Beach,

Virginia, in December 2005. This organization was founded by the late "Sleeping Prophet" Edgar Cayce, who had a heavily documented history of exceptionally accurate psychic readings. "Edgar Cayce himself had mentioned that some of his gifts came after an incident when he was a teenager," Vallee told his audience. "There was a globe of light and inside the globe of light there was a figure that he took to be a lady who asked him what he wanted. He said he wanted the power to help people, to heal, and after that incident his life started changing. That is a fairly common occurrence among people with special psychic gifts." In our interview, Vallee told me that the phenomenon of UFOs was "far larger than current speculation" allowed. "It raises questions about consciousness, about the nature of reality, and about human history on the earth."

Many UFO contact experiencers strongly identify with these "psychic gifts" and with the life and work of Edgar Cayce.

"As a life-long alien abductee, I can attest to the validity of the psi/UFO connection," Bret Oldham told me. "Throughout my many years of research I have often interviewed other alien abductees who had returned from their experiences with some form of psychic ability that was not present before these events began. Another common theme was an increase in paranormal activity that centered around the particular individual and/or their house. Many abductees and experiencers also gravitate toward the healing arts just as Cayce did, especially of energy healing. This also coincides with an increased awareness of these new found abilities after an alien contact event."

"My first abduction event happened when I was only five years old and soon after I began a life filled with spirit contact. I could often hear them, feel them and sometimes even see them. I also had an innate ability to use energy healing even though at the time I had no idea why. Since those early years, I have refined these gifts and use them to help others both in this plane of existence and in the spirit world. I now firmly believe that those who are taken by these beings, whether they are indeed

66

extraterrestrial or they are ultraterrestrial, are being taken using dimensional portals. This process changes our vibrational frequency causing it to speed up to more closely match that of the spirit world and perhaps other unknown dimensions. This shift somehow opens up these psychic abilities in the individual being taken. Case after case the findings are the same. The correlation of psi and UFO's is undeniable."

Uri Geller, Terrified Scientists, and the CIA

One of SRI's most controversial and interesting test subjects was the famed Israeli metal bending psychic Uri Geller. Reportedly the CIA had requested and paid for the tests done on Geller at SRI. Less well-known were the experiments conducted by a small group of physicists and engineers at the Lawrence Livermore National Laboratory, a secret nuclear weapons facility a short distance from SRI. Some were reportedly nervous about testing Geller's purported PK abilities at this site because the movement of a few grams of nuclear material by only a few centimeters could either set off or sabotage a nuclear device.

Soon after the experiments began, strange and disturbing events were described by the scientists and their families. Some reportedly saw something like the apparition of a miniature flying saucer hovering in various rooms, or a six-inch ball of light rolling down a hallway, items flying through the air; giant birds walking through the gardens at one of the scientist's home. One physicist and his wife saw an apparition of an arm with a hook instead of a hand appear in the air at the foot of their bed. The scientists also recorded a strange metallic voice.

The recorded voice occurred in a makeshift lab shortly after an infrared camera had captured, for several seconds at a time, inexplicable patches of radiation high on a wall, whereupon a tape recorder then picked up the strange, unintelligible metallic voice that no one heard at the time. A CIA contract manager was called in to listen to the tape. Though there were few recognizable words, this person was quite surprised to hear the code name for an unrelated top-secret project that he was certain none of the personnel at Lawrence Livermore had any knowledge of. He was also quite puzzled over the claims of the scientists when he talked with some of them himself, as they were emotional and even weeping as they told their stories. They all held high-security clearances and were known to be very psychologically stable.

Sandy Nichols (L) and Bret Oldham (R), both who have described alien experiences, attempting in this picture to obtain "electronic voices" – both spirit and alien.

Geller himself seemed quite puzzled by the Lawrence Livermore events. "They're always bewildering, strange, mysterious (experiences), but they would never hurt anyone," he told me in a phone conversation. He felt that what happened was something that he had "nothing to do" with. "But for those credible, quite prestigious scientists to see such phenomena is just mind blowing," he concluded.

While I and others have found John Keel's investigative field work and research a worthwhile avenue to further pursue, his writings have often been criticized for bouncing too far outside the court of acceptable reason and logic. Many times this criticism is leveled by those who find his ideas of a terrestrial origin for the UFO phenomenon and the paranormal components of it to be a very disturbing notion.

Sometimes these criticisms have been aimed at occasional inaccuracies cited in his published conclusions or personal observations, as, for example, a particular incident reported in *The Mothman Prophecies.* In the chapter entitled "Purple Lights and April Foolishness," Keel described some skywatching that he and Mary Hyre were doing and of some of the unusual sightings that they had near Point Pleasant. In one instance, on April 3, 1967, he noted how the moon was supposed to rise in the sky at 1:59 a.m., but that it still hadn't done so when he departed the hilltop at the conclusion of the skywatching around 3:30.

"The 1967 *World Almanac* says (after the proper corrections for latitude and longitude are applied) that an observer in Parkersburg, West Virginia, should expect the moon to rise at about 3:33 on the morning of April 3," noted UFO skeptic/author Robert Sheaffer in a letter to researcher Allen Greenfield back in 1976. "Allow about 15 minutes for it to rise high enough to be seen. Keel says he expected it to rise at 1:59, and that he left at 3:30. So there's no mystery here. The only thing it proves is that John Keel can't read an almanac, and that he rushes off into print with absurd statements, without first checking them out."

I checked it myself and Sheaffer was correct. You can confirm this yourself online at the U.S. Naval Observatory's Astronomical Applications Department at: aa.usno.navy.mil/data/docs/RS_OneDay.php

Keel should have double checked that one. He admitted that he wasn't happy about writing *The Mothman Prophecies,* and unfortunately he rather hastily pulled his material together to do it. He explained how he had last written about Mothman for *Saga* magazine and England's *Flying Saucer Review* around 1968, after which he wrote me that he had "dropped the whole matter and went on to other things."

Then in 1973, his agent wanted him to write up "the full Mothman story for a small but prestigious publisher."

"I balked at the whole idea but they talked me into it," Keel wrote. "I had saved a suitcase filled with clippings, affidavits, memos and my daily journal from that period, so I started to assemble the book reluctantly. When the book was published in 1975 it laid a big egg. It only sold 50 copies in all of West Virginia! I finally got a total of $202 in royalties from it...including the paperback edition!"

That must have been a heavily packed suitcase, for Keel informed me that he could have gone on and written six books total on UFO and Mothman-related matters. "Unfortunately, there was little interest on Madison Ave. in the 60s and there was no place to publish any of my findings," Keel added. "In addition, the hardcore UFO buffs, NICAP, APRO, et al, fought bitterly against things like mutes, abductions, lost time cases, etc. They chose, instead, to attack me and accuse me of making it all up."

Keel took another hit to his credibility from skeptics due to his investigations into a controversial case in 1967 involving Tom Menteleone, a 21-year-old psychology major who was in his senior year at the University of Maryland. Tom said that on December 10, 1967, at about 1:15 a.m., he was headed home to Adelphi after visiting with his parents in Baltimore, when a white egg-shaped craft blocked the highway ahead. He came to a stop and next noticed two tall men dressed in silver-blue coveralls standing near the craft. One of them, with a broad grin on his face, approached Tom's Volkswagen and struck up a conversation with him in perfect English. He introduced himself as Vadig and asked Tom where he was from, where was he going, what sort of things he enjoyed doing, and so on. You know, standard interview questions that ET's routinely ask of earth motorists that they stop along deserted highways in the middle of the night.

Keel commented that he was initially quite skeptical and cautious of this account, suspecting it was "some kind of put-on." The West Virginia contactee Woodrow Derenberger (who said he was contacted by Menteleone after being on a Washington, D.C. radio program) was on Keel's suspicion list, too, with a similar story about a landed craft on a highway, and a grinning man-like alien who introduced himself as Indrid Cold from the planet Lanulos, and quizzed Derenberger with odd questions. Keel wondered if the two might be in on it together -- or else Menteleone might be doing a paper for college on gullible UFO buffs. However, after interviewing Menteleone, Keel came away impressed with the story, calling it "one of the most puzzling contact stories in my files."

Menteleone confessed to ufologist and writer Karl T. Pflock that he never expected the story to go as far as it did. He had heard Derenberger live on Washington's WWDC radio and called in. He told Derenberger, "I want you to know that I know you are telling the truth," adding, "I've been to Lanulos too."

In his article "Anatomy of a UFO Hoax," in the November 1980 edition of *FATE* magazine, Pflock declared, "Tom's story is 100 percent pure, unadulterated baloney."

Menteleone told Pflock that by the time Keel arrived at his apartment for his interview, in late March or early April 1968, Menteleone had already been interviewed by several people in the UFO field. Keel interviewed him quite carefully for some two hours, had really done his homework, and initially seemed skeptical, asking many penetrating questions. "I had to be fast on my feet," Menteleone told Pflock.

However, toward the end of the interview Menteleone decided to add a new tale that he had not told any of his previous interrogators: a Men in Black encounter with the driver of a "brand new" black Buick. Keel jumped up from his chair allegedly exclaiming, "That clinches it! You have just revealed to me important information that is not available to the public. There is no possible way you could have known about this unless it really happened to you. As a matter of fact, I investigated a case in which the same car was seen about three weeks ago in Warrenton, Virginia, very close to here. This is conclusive evidence that they have been working in this area."

However, Menteleone reportedly knew nothing of the MIB subject prior to this interview and said he made up the Buick story on the spot. Keel said that prior to that revelation he had figured the story was a "college prank," which he had expected to expose.

In a further cautionary statement in the letters section of the *FATE* February 1981issue, Pflock remarked: "That it served to make an outlandish tale credible to an experienced investigator like Keel should be a lesson to us all."

As for the Woodrow Derenberger story, Keel stated that from the beginning he was cautious about Derenberger, a complex character, but felt his story nonetheless had some substance. In an interview with author Andy Colvin [2003], Keel pointed out, "he was scared enough to go the police. Nobody's going to go to the police with a bogus story. They might come to you or me with a bogus story, but they're not going to go to the cops."

Derenberger, age 50, was a sewing machine salesman. He lived in Mineral Wells, West Virginia with a young wife and their two children. On November 2, 1966, a rainy night, he was driving home in his panel truck from Marietta, Ohio. He was alone on the highway when a UFO "shaped like the chimney of a kerosene lamp" landed in the highway in front of him. A man, a little less than six feet tall, with a dark complexion, slightly elongated eyes, and a big grin walked over to him and asked Derenberger to roll down his window. He did, and the stranger spoke to him using telepathy. He said his name was "Cold" and that he came from "a country much less powerful" than the United States. Their conversation was brief, but before he left he said he'd be back.

He did, and Derenberger's wife and children said that they too met "Cold" and some of his alien team. Mrs. Derenberger was scared of them. Cold and his team also visited Dr. Alan Roberts, a West

Virginia psychiatrist who had worked with Derenberger as well as other contactees in the area.

Derenberger claimed he could telepathically summon UFOs to appear. Keel reportedly was among the people who witnessed this. "These lights would suddenly appear in the sky when he would concentrate," Keel told Colvin. "It has to be a form of psychic ability."

Keel found two other men who had "identical incidents" that same night, which they had reported to the Parkersburg police. When Keel tracked them down for details, they confirmed what had happened but stated that they didn't want their names used. There was a report of a Mrs. Frank Huggins and her two children who said that they stopped their car to watch a UFO soar low over the highway just minutes after Derenberger had said his UFO had left. A young man alleged that an object hovered over his car, shining a blinding light down on him. People came forward and described seeing a man speaking to the driver of a panel truck that was stopped on the highway.

There seemed to be a good deal of supportive testimony confirming that something unusual had been going on in that same area around the same time as Derenberger's encounter. Of course, as every investigator also knows, not all so-called "witnesses" are truthful. That Keel got taken in by Menteleone should not be an indictment against him and his overall contributions on this particular investigation. Keel investigated many high-strangeness situations that too many in the ufology mainstream had chosen to ignore over the years. All of us strive to judge witness credibility as best we can and often we must rely exclusively on witness testimony in the absence of hard evidence. Misreading subjective testimony is a common hazard in the UFO field.

Yes, it happened to Keel, but it could have happened to any other UFO investigator.

"With an obvious knack for romanticism and a propensity to embellish for the sake of dramatic impact, we must wonder how far Keel took things at times," wrote Ken Gerhard in *Encounters with Flying Humanoids* (2013). Gerhard cited Keel's account of the November 25, 1966 Mothman testimony of Thomas Ury, who saw a "manlike" being shoot straight up into the air like a helicopter -- but Ury himself later revealed this detail was untrue. Ury didn't describe the creature as "manlike" at all, but rather like a gigantic bird. Jeff Wamsley interviewed Ury years later for his book *Mothman...behind the red eyes,* and learned that Keel had never interviewed him. Instead, Mary Hyre had interviewed Ury.

Ury told Wamsley that about a month after the story she had written came out, he went by her office in Point Pleasant and told her jokingly, "Mary, I ought to shoot you."

He said, "When I first saw this giant bird, I never stated that I watched it take off straight up in the air from the side of the road like a helicopter. The only time I had ever mentioned a helicopter was to Mary Hyre, and I told her that when I first saw it out of the corner of my eye (which would have been about a quarter of a mile from Route 62 over to the river bank). It reminded me of something out of an Arnold Schwarzenegger or Sylvester Stallone movie where the silent helicopter rises up over the treetops."

Technically, this inaccuracy was not entirely Keel's fault, but there did appear to be the embellishment of it being manlike instead of a large bird. As for his style of "dramatic impact," Keel had a solid reputation as both a successful and professional author and journalist.

I had heard criticisms directed at Keel for errors in his material during my teenage years. I wrote to him in 1970 about this matter, to which he replied that many errors attributed to him were actually done by typesetters, copy editors, and printers who often felt that his material was too long and needed to be reduced, and took it upon themselves to do it.

"You must realize that many of the errors in my books and articles are typographical errors over which I have no control," he wrote. "I did catch the 'New Salem' error in Strange Creatures [something I had pointed out to him…author] but, for some reason, many of my changes in the proofs of both books were ignored. Typesetters frequently get names and dates (especially dates) wrong. Some of the errors that got into *Operation Trojan Horse* were outrageous…'invisible' appeared as 'visible,' completely reversing the meaning of one sentence, etc.; 1848 comes out 1488, names and places were misspelled or juxtaposed."

In Keel's privately circulated *Anomaly* newsletter (No. 5, October 1970) he straightened out several published errors. "On page 46 of *Strange Creatures From Time and Space* we briefly mentioned how Mr. Orland Parker was attacked by a giant snake while horseback riding near Kenton, Ohio on June 9, 1946," Keel wrote. "This story has been mentioned often in various articles and books, such as Brad Steiger's *World of the Weird,* page 86 (Belmont paperbacks, 1966). Now we have received a letter from Mrs. Orland Packer (not P-A-R-K-E-R) – offering more details. Mr. Packer is still alive but has been crippled since the incident. The snake, described as having 'a flat head and a diamond shape on its back' first struck the horse 'in the side and took off a patch of hair.' It then nipped Mr. Packer in the heel. He 'finally had to have his heel cut out as it would not heal,' Mrs. Packer states. 'He was on crutches for two years…His fever would rise till he would almost go out of his head. Then after he broke out in sweats where you could wring water out of his clothes, I changed his bed several times a day so I know,' she continues. 'Several other people in that community had seen similar snakes. This was not identified as a boa constrictor.' The Packers now live in Forest, Ohio."

"Another case discovered in both *World of the Weird* and *Strange Creatures* (pages 84-5 in *World,* page 47 in *Creatures*) concerned the celebrated monster wave around Lebanon, Pennsylvania in 1946. A former resident of Lebanon, Curtis Sutherly, sent us the following report: 'I checked the microfilm files of the Lebanon, Pa. Daily News for more info and found, to my disappointment, only a small AP item from Lebanon, Indiana! The incident never took place in Pennsylvania at all! I hope this bit of info may help set the record straight.'"

"Finally, in *FSR [Flying Saucer Review]*, May-June 1970, page 11, we mentioned the disappearance of the French dirigible 'Dixmude' in 1923 and suggested that someone should research the incident. Our source was an aviation encyclopedia and we lacked the time to look up further details. However, it turns out that Mr. Lyle Gaulding of the International Fortean Organization was way ahead of us. His article, 'Mysteries of the Airship Age,' appeared in the Spring 1967 issue of the *INFO Journal* (pages 22-25) and carefully summarized the Dixmunde disaster. (Yes, our encyclopedia even spelled the name wrong!) The body of the airship's captain, Commander de Plessis, was found by fishermen off the island of Sicily on Dec. 29, 1923. No trace of the other 51 passengers was ever discovered."

"All of this proves, again, that despite our backbreaking efforts to be accurate, we can and do make mistakes. Lots of them."

Gerhard noted that Keel, in his contact with early Mothman witness Linda Scarberry and her parents, Mabel and Parke McDaniel, had told them how to best place crucifixes around their home for protection. That sounded odd to Gerhard since Keel was a life-long atheist. When I visited the McDaniel home in May 1976, Linda told me about an incident where the apparition of a man appeared in her bedroom. The "man" lit a cigarette and as soon as its light illuminated a crucifix on the wall, the apparition vanished.

Why indeed, I wondered, would Keel have told the family to place crucifixes around in the house?

Paranormal investigator Timothy Frick of Maryland and a frequent visitor to Point Pleasant offered me this answer: "I've got the lo down on John Keel, Linda Scarberry and the crucifixes. During the 2003 Mothman Festival, my brother John and I spent eight-plus hours talking to Keel, and among other things, we asked him about Linda and the crucifixes. He told us the reason he suggested Linda put crucifixes around her house was because if she had faith in the Christian religion and believed the crucifixes would help, then they would. Keel used the phrase 'placebo effect,' implying that Linda's belief would be the trigger mechanism, not whether or not he, himself, believed it would work."

I asked others for their critical thoughts on Keel. One respected ufologist wrote, "I spoke with him a few times on the phone and had lunch with him twice. My impression was that he would stretch things to make a point. For me, that is not a huge problem, although it isn't my style."

"He may also not have really realized that he was doing it. The important thing was the ideas he put into the field and the lateral thinking he showed as an important part of looking at the anomalous."

Oh, what a night!

I was a young 15-year-old living on a hilltop in Hallowell, Maine, when I thought a squadron of UFOs might be invading our skies. It was about 7:30 p.m., Eastern Standard Time, October 4, 1967. Myself and neighbors were gathering outside to witness various large and bright lights appearing in the southern sky. It sure was a very strange sight!

That very same night, about 8 p.m., Keel was driving along the Long Island Expressway and found himself being followed by a "large brilliant sphere." When he arrived in Huntington he saw cars parked along the road and citizens and police officers out in a field looking up at strange lights. Four other spheres had joined the one that Keel had felt had been following him (*Operation Trojan Horse*, 1970).

However, that night a rocket had been launched from Wallops Island, Virginia, to conduct high atmospheric barium plasma experiments. Did Keel witness this NASA missile test? If he did, he made no mention of it that I'm aware of. However, in his privately distributed newsletter *Anomaly* (#7), published in the Fall of 1971, Keel wrote a well-researched report of such launches and said they were often mistaken for UFOs. He did not speculate that his Long Island sighting in 1967 may have fit that category though.

"Early on the morning of October 5, 1970, a gigantic greenish sphere cast an eerie glow over the entire northeast," Keel wrote in his *Anomaly*. "At 6:10 a.m., radar operators at the Canadian Armed Forces Radar Base near Sheerwater, Nova Scotia, studied their scopes in bewilderment. 'We made contact with a solid, stationary unidentified object,' Base Air Traffic Control Officer, Captain R. G. H. McKendry said. 'The object was motionless and stayed that way for about 10 minutes. That's pretty unusual.' He estimated the hovering whatzit was at an altitude of 2,500 feet, about seven miles north of the base."

Keel noted that about 45 miles northeast of the radar installation, a 16-year-old in Truro had just left his home in a car when he saw a multicolored object "as big as a bungalow, trailing white smoke and emitting a high-pitched whine." His mother saw it also, saying it made a sound "like a kitten being killed." Meanwhile, some railroad workers in Kentucky saw a bright greenish disc bobbing in the sky; a Vermont woman reported "a beautiful red saucer with a green band around it" which she was sure "landed on a nearby mountaintop"; and in Tice, Florida, another woman saw an orange object with a tail which she estimated came within 1,000 feet of the ground, and then just disappeared.

Keel heard from 22 witnesses of that event. As mentioned, the NASA installation at Wallops Island was responsible. "Strangely, many of these reports were accompanied by the same bizarre details often found in unexplained UFO sightings...weird sounds, odd maneuvers, and even radar 'angels' and aberrations," Keel wrote. "These were highly subjective impressions translated into reality by the witnesses' minds." Even the radar at the military base in Nova Scotia was "apparently befuddled" by the barium cloud experiment. Keel pointed out that the Wallops Island tests show us too that "most witnesses, even trained observers like pilots, military men and police officers, can greatly misjudge distance, size and speed when they don't know any of the characteristics of the object they are watching."

Keel said the Max Planck Institute for Extraterrestrial Physics out of Munich, Germany, had begun such experiments back in 1966. A German team, headed by a Dr. Reimar Luest, had been working with NASA at Wallops Island, using Javelin and NIKE rockets to launch payloads of barium, sodium and other chemicals some 300 to 600 miles above the earth. Keel added that the German scientists had at that time "quietly spent the past five years lighting up the skies from Scandinavia to Australia with a long series of experiments designed to study the earth's erratic magnetic fields."

Keel also said the Air Force had been doing similar experiments, pointing out how they had done a barium cloud launch from Florida's Elgin Air Force Base in January 1967, which resulted in "a massive wave of UFO sightings." Other Air Force launches had been done in Alaska and South America. In the 1960s there was once a special base on Easter Island that conducted "atmospheric tests," about which no information was available.

One time the space scientists got a bit of karmic payback for causing false flying saucer alarms. Keel described a puzzling case reported on January 5, 1965, when Dempsey Bruton, Chief of Satellite Tracking, along with several others at the Wallops Island NASA rocket station observed a bright yellowish-orange object of circular appearance that appeared soon after the launch of an Arcas rocket. Bruton estimated that the unidentified object was traveling at around 8,000 miles per hour. He filed a report with the U.S. Air Force, who dismissed it and stated there was "no evidence of any superior technological development."

Over the years, there have been other reports of rocket scientists, engineers and technicians witnessing UFOs in conjunction with US rocket launches. Keel thought these launches, along with other activities of our space program, were often under intense scrutiny and surveillance by someone – a mysterious someone.

He cited one incident that was over the top. In the summer of 1966, some teenagers were firing homemade rockets from a field in Virginia. After reaching an altitude of about 3,000 feet the rockets would descend back to the earth dangling from a parachute. In less than 24 hours, five adult witnesses claimed they saw a circular object with an eerie glow around it land in the very same field that the teenagers had been launching their homemade rockets!

Nova Scotia's Shag Harbor lights

Meanwhile, back to October 4, 1967. The famous UFO "crash" off the coast of Nova Scotia's Shag Harbor was reported on the very same night I, Keel and many others watched funny lights and colored "clouds" in the skies. It was certainly a night filled with reports of a lot of odd lights from many different locations - some that can be explained by the barium rocket experiment. In some cases, the directions and times in those reports don't fit the scenario that a "dark object" estimated at 60 feet in length crashed into the ocean near Shag Harbor around 11:25 p.m. Atlantic Daylight Time (10:25 p.m. EST). Whatever the "dark object" was that came down onto the ocean water and floated on the surface for a time, it certainly wasn't a distant display of barium clouds. When local fishermen got to the scene, prepared to rescue possible airplane passengers, they found only a mysterious yellow "glittery, shiny foam," not like regular sea foam, on the surface of the water. Reportedly six or seven naval vessels, both Canadian and American, positioned themselves over the submerged object for seven days afterward, until they were diverted by news of a Russian submarine that was closing in and threatening to penetrate the 12-mile limit off of Shelburne. Divers from the ships were taking photographs of the object, plus another unknown object that had joined the first one. The initial submerged object had drifted out to sea, going northeast along the coast and around Cape Sable Island. It came to rest over, of all things, a magnetic anomaly detection grid feed at the mouth of Shelburne Harbor to a secret submarine detection base at Shelburne.

Government secrets?

Chris Styles, a Canadian UFO author, talked in person with an experienced ex-navy diver who was involved in the underwater survey of the Shag Harbor anomaly but was reluctant to talk publicly, saying he didn't want any trouble. He did share that the divers brought up from the bottom large chunks of a foam-like material, some of which decomposed as they brought it to the surface. Styles was surprised by this, as he had only been aware of the fishermen and Mounties reporting a yellow foam floating on the surface of the water after the object had gone under. Styles followed up with a phone call to the diver and tried several approaches, hoping to shake loose additional details. His attempts failed, and he only made the diver more and more angry with his questions. Finally, the man angrily declared, "I don't know what it was that was down there, and I don't know where it came from. But it didn't come from this planet, I can tell you that! Now don't call back!" The man slammed the phone down.

Obviously, the Shag Harbor story has a few extra anomalous wrinkles in it that make this story more complicated and mysterious than just the one single barium-bearing rocket launch from Wallops Island that night.

Dark Object (2001), written by Don Ledger and Chris Styles, is a detailed description of this intriguing case. However, I could find no reference in it to a barium cloud launch. I contacted Brock Zinck of the Shag Harbor UFO Incident Society in Nova Scotia and found that he had never heard about the barium cloud rocket launch that night. He was interested in knowing more, so I forwarded my documentation to him.

Near the beginning of *Dark Object*, the story of Captain Pierre Guy Charbonneau and his co-pilot and first officer, Robert Ralph, flying a Douglas DC-8 (Air Canada Flight 305) at about 12,000 feet above southeastern Quebec, makes me think of the barium cloud launch. What they saw was to the south. It appeared to be a large rectangular orange-colored object with a string of smaller lights trailing behind it. Suddenly, at about 7:19 p.m. Atlantic Daylight Time, which would have been about 6:19 p.m. Eastern Standard Time, there was an explosion near the object. A big white ball-shaped "cloud" turned red, then violet, and then blue. Two minutes later, bigger and higher up in the sky, there was a second explosion, an orange colored, pear-shaped "cloud" which also faded to blue. Around this time the smaller lights broke free of the rectangular object and danced around the clouds like fireflies. The declassified report from the Ballistic Research Laboratories, Report No. 1459, of the Aberdeen Proving Ground, Maryland, released in December 1969, stated that the rocket launched at twilight October 4, 1967 released three barium clouds, the first around 64 miles altitude, the second at 116 miles, and the third at 140 miles.

I believe the Canadian pilots saw this launch, though the sighting seemed a bit earlier than the time the *Kennebec Journal* gave for my strange "cloud" sightings in Maine and the time Keel gave for what he saw on Long Island. Perhaps there was more going on that night at Wallops Island or NASA than what has been released to the public. What came down in Shag Harbor that night at a 45-degree angle, with a whoosh or whistling sound, a flash of light and a bang, happened close to 11:25 ADT (10:25 p.m. EST). This was much later in time than the Wallops Island launch.

Captain Leo Howard Mersey was piloting his fishing boat in the waters near the southern tip of Nova Scotia when around 9 PM ATD (8 EST) when he and one of his hands with him on the bridge observed an object with red flashing lights low over the water. Their radar showed that something was indeed there, some 16 miles northeast of his boat's location, which was the wrong direction for Wallops Island. The object eventually lifted into the air and passed over his boat. One of his crew members picked up reports on the radio of people on shore seeing UFOs. He filed a report with the Royal Canadian Mounted Police.

It certainly was a busy night. Were there other launches that night that have yet to be declassified? Or was it as a retired weapons technician with the Canadian army had told Chris Styles? In 1970, while serving in the military, the technician had seen several large glowing orange spheres one evening on nearby Cape Sable Island. He was curious what was going on in the area, and, having heard of the Shag Harbor incident of 1967, he wondered if the spheres had anything to do with the nearby Baccaro Radar Station. He questioned Colonel Calvin Rushton, who matter-of-factly told him that the Shag Harbor incident in 1967 involved a UFO that was tracked by NORAD. It had entered our atmosphere over Siberia and made a half orbit around the earth before splashing down into the bay off of Shag Harbor, where three Royal Canadian Mounties along with others watched it float and then sink beneath the water.

Why did an MIB-type Air Force disinformation agent try to drink Jell-O?

In chapter two of Keel's *The Mothman Prophecies*, "The Creep Who Came in from the Cold," Mrs. Ralph Butler of Owatonna, Minnesota, reported that following a wave of UFO sightings in that area, she was visited by a mysterious Major Richard French who claimed to be with the U.S. Air Force. He wore civilian clothes and had long black hair, which seemed inappropriate for an Air Force officer. He drove a white Mustang.

Major French engaged Butler in a normal, fluent conversation – that is, until he complained of stomach trouble. She offered him some Jell-O, thinking that might help. "Did you ever hear of anyone – especially an air force officer – trying to drink Jell-O?" Mrs. Butler declared. "Well, that's what he did. He acted like he had never seen any before. He picked up the bowl and tried to drink it. I had to show him how to eat it with a spoon."

The case has become a MIB classic. The man wore a gray suit and shoes that looked brand new. He a pointed chin and olive complexion. "Richard French was an imposter," Keel wrote. "One of the many wandering around the United States in 1967." However, there really was a Richard French, who said he worked with Project Blue Book as a UFO debunker in the 1950s. In 2013, he testified at the Citizen's Hearing on Disclosure in Washington,

D.C., that in one case off the coast of Saint Johns, Newfoundland around 1952, he observed two submerged UFOs and small alien beings who appeared to be doing repair work.

Noted UFO researcher and author Micah Hanks sees this revelation as significant because it shows that in 1967 a Richard French was doing "precisely" what French claimed in 2013 that he had been doing for the Air Force, engaging in disinformation and skeptical downplaying of the UFO phenomenon. Is he still following through with that earlier assignment? Some ufologists have wondered if he may have used details from the similar Shag Harbor case to spin this other story. "All things considered, I, too, find this to be a compelling theory," Hanks said.

However, we really don't know for certain whether or not the real Richard French had visited Mrs. Butler up there in Minnesota or not.

Who was the other Jell-O-drinking MIB?

Dr. Jacques Vallee describes in his book *Confrontations: A Scientist's Search for Alien Contact* (1990), his investigation in northern California of a small lumber town known as Happy Camp, which had only one bar and one cafe. From 1975 to 1977, the town's people seemingly experienced a bizarre series of UFO-related events that included humanoid being encounters, poltergeist activity, a "huge bird," and more. One day early in 1976, a peculiar stranger showed up at the cafe. Though it was the middle of winter, he wore no coat, only a strange-looking shirt. He was pale-skinned with Oriental eyes, and his face bore a constant odd, grimacing smile. He ordered a steak dinner but didn't know how to use a fork and knife. He also left without paying. To top it off, Vallee added this: "Among the peculiar things he did during his extraordinary dinner was a brave attempt to drink Jell-O out of his glass."

Noctilucent Clouds

John Keel was also intrigued with high altitude, luminous noctilucent clouds often said to be glowing an electric blue, that have produced many spurious UFO sightings. He lamented that the Soviet Union had taken the lead in investigating them. The Russians had discovered in the mid-1960s that the clouds reflected radio and television waves. I wrote about this phenomenon in my book *Visitors from Hidden Realms* (2004), wondering if the clouds were tied in with some South American UFO reports. "They generally seem to appear in the mesosphere some 50 to 85 kilometers up," I wrote. "Space station astronaut Don Pettit had spent several weeks studying them from space. 'We routinely see them when we're flying over Australia and the tip of South America,' Pettit stated in an interview. These mystery 'clouds' first appeared in 1885. Gradually they seem to be spreading out and becoming more commonplace. One speculation is that they're some sort of high-altitude clouds being seeded by meteorites entering the atmosphere, while another theory suggests that they may be the byproduct of the Industrial Age. No one seems to know for sure."

Keel noted that the U.S. Air Force had launched instrument laden rockets into these "clouds" from several bases in Alaska, but that the results of their experiments were not released to the public. In an interview with Don Ecker for *California UFO* (Vol. 4, No. 4, 1989), Keel stated: "The basic mystery is that there are funny lights in the sky which move around by themselves. No reputable astronomer, no scientist has ever really examined these moving lights. If I were to be put in charge of a real UFO investigation, the first thing I would do is fire rockets into these lights with instruments, and see what they're composed of, what the energies are."

Ecker then asked, "Do you think the intelligence behind the lights would allow that?"

Keel replied, "It would be interesting to find out."

Keel said that some scientists speculated that these "clouds" might be related to the Air Glow Phenomenon. "Astronauts orbiting Earth have seen and photographed spherical glows on the dark side of this planet," he once wrote (Phenomenon, 1988; editors John Spencer & Hilary Evans). "These spheres are sometimes arranged in neat formations, like rows of soldiers. This phenomenon is rarely seen by ground observers..."

Ball-lightning

Keel said ball lightning could certainly also produce UFO reports. Few laymen realize that lightning and ball lightning both sometimes travel from the ground up to the sky, which could account for some reports of luminous spherical UFOs launching off into the sky from the ground.

For a researcher and author who many saw as too far out and woo-woo, Keel certainly explored many possible natural and man-made explanations that could better help the ufologists separate the proverbial wheat from the chaff – possible solutions that few in the field had adequately addressed.

FIVE
JADOO, VOICES AND UFOS

Dan Drasin

Dan Drasin became a good friend of John Keel's back around the time Keel began investigating the numerous and very anomalous events that were going on in and around Point Pleasant, West

Virginia. He even joined Keel in West Virginia to acquire firsthand information about what was going on there back in 1967, and even saw some odd things in the skies there himself!

When I got an opportunity to interview Drasin personally, I jumped at the chance.

To begin with, let me tell the reader a bit about Drasin himself. Drasin was born and raised in the New York City area. He now resides near San Francisco, California. His broad interests include the arts, sciences and humanities. He originally intended to pursue a career in industrial design, but after meeting documentary film pioneers Albert Maysles, D. A. Pennebaker and Richard Leackock in the early 1960s he became their apprentice and never looked back. Following five semesters at Pratt Institute, Harvard University and the New School, Drasin began a career in independent filmmaking and media production that has now spanned over five decades. Films he has produced or photographed have earned over two dozen international awards, notably his short 1961 documentary *Sunday,* which was widely acknowledged as one of the first social-protest films of the 1960s. *Sunday* is part of the permanent film collection at New York's Museum of Modern Art and was recently restored and preserved by the UCLA Film and Television archive.

Here's our interview:

Brent Raynes: As a young film producer in 1967, you accompanied Keel to the Point Pleasant, West Virginia area to film some of the testimony of the Mothman and UFO witnesses. Can you share with our readers how this came about?

Dan Drasin: I'd just had my first UFO sighting, and mentioned it to a friend who, as it happened, had just seen an ad for a talk John was giving. So I attended the talk, buttonholed him afterward, and we soon became friends.

Brent Raynes: What sort of stories had you filmed, and what were your thoughts on what was going on and being reported at that time?

Dan Drasin: Unfortunately, I never got to the point of doing any actual filming. I met a lot of witnesses in Point Pleasant (most of whom are surely deceased by now), collected a lot of information, and wrote up a proposal for the Public Broadcast Laboratory -- a weekly news/features program that ran on PBS stations. The proposal *almost* got funded but ended up being rejected at the last minute for reasons that were never explained.

Brent Raynes: What was it like working with John Keel?

Dan Drasin: John was a unique character, two steps ahead of the culture. He was pretty fearless and often sallied forth where angels feared to tread, though he did carry a small pistol while exploring the spooky old abandoned power plant in the TNT area, just in case the Mothman showed up unannounced! I liked John a lot.

Brent Raynes: Did you and your film crew have any anomalous experiences?

Dan Drasin: On one of my visits I carried a simple, silent 16mm movie camera (sound cameras were hard to come by, then). On some nights I'd drive alone into the TNT area -- never completely out of sight of the main highway! -- and sit on the hood of my car watching the sky. On one occasion, I saw a dim, diamond-shaped cluster of round, multicolored lights cross the sky, but my film wasn't sensitive enough to capture them.

One evening John and I saw a bunch of strobe-light flashes in the sky, south of Point Pleasant, that seemed to come from nowhere. There was no aircraft that would have explained them.

I think John wrote in *The Mothman Prophecies* about the incident where he and I and Mary Hyre were up on a hill south of town one afternoon [he did, in chapter 10 - author]. The sky was cloudless, except for one very oddly perfect, puffy little cloud that looked as if it had escaped from a children's storybook. In the distance, we all saw something that looked like an ill-defined UFO, which proceeded to head straight for the cloud and entered it. Then, out the other side came a small, twin-engine plane, headed in the same direction. We could even hear its engines. That was quite a head scratcher.

Some weeks after my last visit to Point Pleasant, I was at home alone in my New York apartment, sitting at my desk. Suddenly, the air around me seemed to be filled with "sparkles." I can't say whether or not I actually saw them with my eyes, but it felt as if I were taking a bath in soda water. It felt good -- sort of tickled. This lasted maybe a half a minute, and then suddenly ended. A half-hour later the phone rang. It was Park McDaniel calling to let me know that Mary Hyre had passed away a half-hour earlier.

Mary, by the way, was profoundly psychic. When we first met, she immediately said she felt that we had some kind of connection -- presumably in a previous life.

Brent Raynes: I see you're working on a film project dealing with mysterious electronic voice phenomena (EVP) evidence from around the world. How much of this goes back to your work with John Keel and those early experiences in West Virginia?

Dan Drasin: My work with John was part of a chain of influences that actually started in my early childhood, when I experienced many precognitive dreams and was fascinated by reports of UFO sightings. During my teen years -- the 1950s -- I was a devoted listener to a late-night New York radio host named Long John Nebel, whose studio guests included many of the classic early UFO contactees, researchers, and authors of books on paranormal issues. Later I'd experienced a number of UFO sightings of my own, and in general became increasingly curious about what was going on behind the curtain of mainstream awareness. My interest in afterlife research began mainly with my exposure to the books of Robert Monroe, a businessman turned out-of-body explorer. My interest in EVP and ITC was sparked mainly from my meeting Mark Macy in Boulder, Colorado, where I lived for a few years in the early 1990s. At first I was quite skeptical about ITC, but was intrigued enough by that and other aspects of afterlife research to follow it up in the early 2000s by joining up with co-film-producer Tim Coleman. Together Tim and I traveled across the US, and to England, Scotland and Spain, shooting several documentaries about afterlife research. In 2009, we went our separate ways, with Tim going on to complete his film *The Afterlife Investigations* (which centers on the Scole Experiment), and me finishing *Calling Earth*.

Brent Raynes: After nearly half a century of exposure in thought and investigative activity related to unexplained occurrences, from Mothman to apparitions to the EVP experience, what might be your personal impressions and thoughts about these phenomena? Why we should seek to investigate them further, and what we may ultimately learn from them that may be of value to humanity?

Dan Drasin: Well, this is a huge question. But I think it comes down to our recognizing that our understandings about the true nature of life and consciousness are pretty much in their infancy and there is so much more to learn and to be. I think the main thing keeping us from participating in this greater reality is fear.

Brent Raynes: What do you hope that people will take away from your documentary *Calling Earth*?

Dan Drasin: Above all, I hope that *Calling Earth* helps to allay individual and collective fears about what lies beyond our physical existence. If we can perceive our bodies as temporary (albeit purposeful) dwellings, we'll begin to see death not as a fearful or spooky affair, but more as a gateway to limitless possibilities. EVP and ITC are important because they provide the kind of objective evidence that science needs in order to feel comfortable tiptoeing outside the box of its materialist worldview.

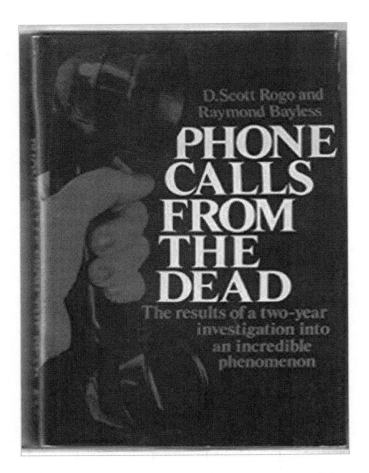

Published in 1979, this book was written by two of the psychical field's top researchers, D. Scott Rogo and Raymond Bayless.

Phone calls from the dead

Keel investigated communication with the dead, including the phenomenon known as "phone calls from the dead," in which a living person gets an unexpected call from the Other Side. There were too many cases to ignore – but was it really the dead doing the talking? John was not so sure.

I encountered phone calls from the dead in one of my own case investigations.

In 1975, Dr. Schwarz put me in touch with a husband and wife UFO investigative team who lived a short distance outside of Cincinnati, Ohio. They were serious-minded ufologists who had covered many amazing cases, particularly during the 1973 UFO wave, some of which are detailed in Len Stringfield's *Situation Red: The UFO Siege* (1977). They also had experienced quite a number of strange paranormal episodes and had seen UFOs themselves.

"It happened at 4 a.m.," Geri began, the wife of this investigative team, as she described her most remarkable encounter in July 1973. "I had gotten up to give the baby her bottle. I went downstairs to warm the bottle in a glass and running hot water over it for a few minutes. All of a sudden, I had this urge to go upstairs to our bedroom and look out the window. When I came to the window this huge saucer-shaped object was hovering above the telephone wires. The craft covered the entire parking lot. The windows were long rectangular (shaped). I could see the fine ridges which reminded me of stainless steel."

The following year, Geri began to see a strange being that would materialize in her home. "He seemed solid enough but he disappeared at will. He had high cheekbones, blue eyes, a high forehead. His hair was white and stood high, which could have made his forehead seem higher. He had square shoulders and stood about six foot two. His silver suit looked very soft and seemed to be in one piece. He gave me the feeling of being very old but appeared to be only in his fifties. He projected peace and love with the smile of an angel. He comes whenever there is going to be a flurry of sightings."

I spent quite a bit of time with the family and got to know them well. Dr. Schwarz met Geri's mother during a visit in September 1974, as did I during my many weeks visiting with the family during the summer of 1975, and we both considered her quite credible and sincere. Geri told Dr. Schwarz that her mother had had one of those curious "phone calls from the dead" experiences, and so he proceeded to interview her too. Over a year earlier in 1973, on a January evening, Geri's mother received a phone call from her favorite Aunt Lorraine.

"She was four years older than I," the mother told Dr. Schwarz. "We were like sisters. We talked about different things we had done in the past, places we had been together, just sort of reminiscing. I was home alone. This went on for about half an hour, but when I hung up, I thought 'It was Lorraine! But she's dead. She was killed instantly in an automobile accident six or seven months ago!' I even get chills now, talking about it. In fact, I was so upset, I dialed her number but nobody answered."

1973 was certainly a busy year. In another case, on two nights back to back, October 9 and 10, 1973, an 18-year-old woman in Jacksonville, Florida said that around 9 PM she had seen a disc-shaped craft approximately 25 feet in diameter with a row of white lights encircling its outer rim that pulsated together. It was at tree top level. On October 9 she was walking on her way home. She looked at it in dumbfounded shock and then took off running. The next night she had stepped into the backyard to feed her small dog when she noticed the dog was agitated. It was looking upwards, and when she followed the dog's gaze, she saw the same object flying overhead from south to north that she had seen the night before. She was nervous and shaken, and went into the house, sat down and tried to collect her thoughts. She decided to call the police and report what she had observed. The operator tried to connect her but had difficulty doing so. It took the operator about

15 tries before she succeeded. After the young woman told the police what had happened, they asked if the UFO was still there. She rushed outside to take another look, saw it coming back from the north, and then got back on the phone and told them it was still there. Unfortunately, when the police arrived there was no sign of it.

I read about her experiences in the *Jacksonville Journal* on October 11. The sightings were a short distance from the Jacksonville Naval Air Station. I contacted the witness, who agreed to be interviewed. Her name was Donna.

I and Ramona Hibner, a fellow investigator and UFO experiencer herself, arrived to interview Donna on Saturday evening, October 13. Ramona asked the witness if she had had any psychic experiences, and initially she replied no. However, within a short time she remembered something odd, and then another odd something came to mind, and as she pondered further, more and more unusual memories of a paranormal nature surfaced. One of the memories she recalled was in fact a phone call from the dead. It concerned a close male friend of hers who had drowned. About six months later she received a strange call. A voice sounding just like him and claiming to be him spoke to her. The voice said he was coming over to visit her. She began crying and told him he could not do that. No one showed up. "I have dreams that come true millions of times," she added, mentioning how she had foreseen the death of Martin Luther King. We both felt she was sincere about these experiences. She appeared to be quite shaken. Ramona, who was half Cherokee and pretty psychic, felt the young girl's half-Cherokee and half-French ancestry might have been contributing factors to her psychic awareness.

"There are now many cases in which the voices of deceased persons have seemingly called up their loved ones on the telephone, just as the metallic-voiced space people have been phoning researchers and reporters around the world," John Keel wrote in *Operation Trojan Horse*. Keel also was aware of many cases where mediums, as well as telephones, radios, and tape recorders would pick up voices of the dead, or even alleged space people, though he was quite skeptical that any of these voices were who they claimed to be.

"There are marvelous mimics who can imitate any voice on the telephone," Keel told me. "It is all so damned unbelievable that most people finally throw up their hands and quit the whole business." He described how a friend of his had obtained a tape recording of the voice of George Bernard Shaw coming through a medium. The man had been dead for some 30 years.

"We can't believe a damn thing that comes through," Keel wrote. While it might sound like that person's voice and use their favorite expressions, Keel was skeptical, believing it was likely someone or something imitating a particular person. "We're going to find that electronically, we can communicate with whatever this force is," Keel added. "It's a very mischievous force."

Did John Keel contact me from the Great Beyond?

After Keel had passed in 2009, I attempted to reach him electronically. I have several recorded examples of a voice coming through a digital AM radio uttering, "John Keel," and a good number of other examples of intelligent, interactive responses.

Was it really John Keel, or just something or someone pretending to be him? Whatever the case, I am convinced that there is a real phenomenon here. I keep an open mind on a variety of possibilities.

I and others I have worked with have found that we can get interactive responses when we request our guides (commonly called technicians) to connect us with spirits of the departed or possible extraterrestrials.

For me, the EVP journey began in earnest in 2010, when UFO contact experiencer Bret Oldham, also a paranormal investigator, introduced me and others, including UFO contact experiencer Sandy Nichols, to an EVP device commonly known as the "ghost box." Ghost boxes use radio sweep to generate background noise that is believed to facilitate the manifestation of spirit voices. Ghost box technology was developed decades ago in Europe and was popularized for paranormal investigations in the mid-2000s.

I admit that initially I was quite skeptical. But one night in particular proved to be my turning point, when we did two sessions with the box at Sandy's home in Thompsons Station, Tennessee. It was July 3, 2010, the one-year anniversary of John Keel's death. I asked the group if they would mind me reaching out to him. They thought it was a great idea. So much happened that night I could no longer deny that something quite anomalous was occurring.

We asked to speak to John Keel and a male voice

quickly said, "John Keel"! The first and last names were clear. (This happened again on other dates.) Bret asked the "box" what Keel now knew about Bigfoot, a subject he had been quite interested in while on this side of the veil. Again, almost immediately a male voice declared, "Smuck Bigfoot, see?" Soon this was followed by two voices that said, "See," as though acknowledging the presumed "Keel" voice. Those are just a couple of examples of the activity we had that night. There were quite a few. I even asked what Keel could tell us about Jadoo and a voice clearly replied back with the same word, saying what sounded like "Jadoo, eh?" All this was recorded on our digital recorders. The "ghost box" was hooked up to two stereo speakers. We obtained some nice recordings.

I quickly repeated the Jadoo question. Immediately what sounded like the same voice replied, "Into the fire, into the fire." That seemed appropriate enough if you're talking about black magic! Then a few seconds later, the same voice said, "Teach me outside."

As I thought about it later, "teach me outside" could have referred to Keel's preferred mode of learning. He was well-known for his extensive research and his ability to devour many, many books. However, his real passion was clearly his taste for travel and adventure. As he wrote in his 1957 book *Jadoo,* Keel had a burning desire to "go around the world, to see India and get a first-hand look at the celebrated feats of the fakirs, to explore the Himalayas, to investigate the fire-walkers of the Pacific Islands."

"Jadoo" is a Hindi word from India meaning black magic or sorcery. The book describes Keel's fascinating journey, often on foot, from Egypt to Singapore, during which he endured great hardships and dangers to seek out the truth surrounding tales of magic and mystery in the East. Keel was a skeptic who practiced the sleight-of-hand variety of stage magic, and he sought to learn the deceptive tricks of the trade, such as "X-ray vision" and the legendary rope trick that fakirs used to fool the tourists. However, he came to believe that telepathy was real from his encounters with lamas in remote regions of India. He was especially impressed by the great lama named Nyang-Pas, who read his thoughts. He also felt that there was something to the stories of the legendary Yeti as well.

A little over a month before the "Jadoo" reply on July 3, 2010, a small group of us, which included Sandy and Bret, investigated two haunted homes that were close together and owned by the same family, near Clifton, Tennessee. The date was May 22, 2010, and there was a good amount of apparent paranormal activity. We got unexplained "voices" on regular digital recorders alone plus real-time "electronic voices" through the ghost box that were interactive with us and gave intelligent answers. Twice through Bret's ghost box we recorded a clear voice saying, "John Keel." One young man present claimed to have once seen a Bigfoot nearby, and over the years people there had heard something striking tree trunks in the woods nearby (something commonly reported in areas where Bigfoot are encountered). When Bret asked Keel what was causing the knocking sounds, a voice replied, "A monster." This was interesting, because Keel lumped all cryptids into the "monster" category. I later showed Bret the first letter I had gotten from Keel in October 1969, where he referred to a book he had coming out that was an "encyclopedia of 'monsters'" and featured accounts of Bigfoot, lake monsters, Mothman, and so on. The book was entitled, *Strange Creatures From Time and Space.* The first sentence of Chapter One read: "No matter where you live on this planet, someone within two hundred miles of your home has had a direct confrontation with a frightening apparition or inexplicable 'monster.'"

On September 28, 2012, one of the principals in the Clifton case stopped by our house, and my wife Joan and I did a ghost box session to try and reach her father on the other side. At one point we got "John Keel" again, who I hadn't heard from via the ghost box in a while. But the real wild card of this session came when I asked this woman's father what he did on the other side. "Do you go back to school?" I asked. Suddenly we heard (and recorded) "Jadoo."

This was interesting too because her husband I learned had used "black magic" to do curses on people he was upset with and used an oujia board and made voodoo-type dolls. I was shown a board with a circle on it, with a place for yes and no responses, and a pendulum with a key and some coins, which would be given to those he cursed. Her son said he had once seen a possible Bigfoot with two other hunters, also had been suffering spells where he'd wake up paralyzed, seeing a dark, evil figure nearby, often inches from his face. He said it had a deep and creepy voice and that this would always happen at 3:33 a.m. Even if he was in another time zone! It was just a black figure, he said, with "no features to it whatsoever." Other family members would awaken at this same hour as well, and his sister was suffering with the temporary paralysis too.

I speculated that this area near Clifton might be what Keel called a "window," a location that seems, for one reason or another, to have more than its fair share of strange activity. For example, a short distance down the road, my daughter Chandra and I had interviewed a family who had experienced a series of psychic events. Two sisters said their car had been followed by a large triangular UFO that they could see through the sunroof of the car. When they slowed or speeded up, it adjusted its speed and kept pace with them. A little further down the road from their home was a place where, in the late 1920s, a farmer and his wife and kids saw an angel appear while they were outside one day. "My great-grandmother and her children were down past the house at the barn working in the garden," a descendent told me. "She turned back to see what the kids were making noise over and she saw it. It was an angel. It looked like a human. It was full-sized, dressed in a flowing type garment. It had wings and long golden tresses that were curly and very shiny. It was beautiful and bright. The angel was fluttering in the air about head high. She said it came so close to them that they could see its fingernails and toenails. It had no shoes on. My great-grandfather turned and ran toward the house to get a gun and my great grandmother said, 'Stop, you can't shoot it, because it is a heavenly being.' They went on about their business and left it alone. They were not afraid of it."

Across the Tennessee River was a small unincorporated site called Point Pleasant! Now there's a funny coincidence.

In one of the two haunted houses we had investigated, where the "black magic" practice had been described happening years earlier, I learned that there lived a man in this house who in 1969 had become something of an international sensation. He had been severely burned by a mysterious underground fire on a nearby farm that had continued burning for seven years! I spoke with Flora Mae Davis, a former columnist for Waynesboro's *Wayne County News,* who lived close to where this had happened and who first broke the story, which was carried by United Press International and appeared in the *Stars and Stripes* and various foreign newspapers. She told me there were the remains of an old iron furnace on the farm that had been destroyed at the beginning of the Civil War when Union gun boats shelled the area as it cruised up and down the Tennessee River. During the Mexican War this farm had been used to make cannon balls. The property was then owned by Solomon H. Baker who had about 100 slaves, a brick kiln, the iron furnace and a tannery. Davis believed that he used charcoal to fire the furnace and that there had been a great deal in the ground there. "There was enough charcoal out there to have furnished all of the charcoal grills in the country for years if we had realized it," she said. "This charcoal was what burned." There were wet water springs in the area where an oily film was noticed. Between World War I and II oil prospecting had been going on in the area, but it was found that there wasn't enough oil in the ground to be profitable and so those operations ceased. But somehow something (lightning?) had sparked and ignited the underground charcoal.

I couldn't help but wonder if the apparent "John Keel" spirit was drawn to our Clifton investigation because it had a mix of "black magic," "monsters" (one with "wings," with Point Pleasant nearby), poltergeist activity, a Bigfoot sighting, a possible dark paraphysical entity, and UFOs reported in the area. And, last but not least, Keel's very close friend and colleague, the Scottish born zoologist Ivan T. Sanderson, had actually written about the Clifton man who was burned from the underground fire! (See *Fate* magazine, January 1978.)

Sometimes it seems like a very small world.

After that I was off and running. I soon acquired my own ghost box and began recording sessions in my home and on investigations, including haunted sites. There were some bewildering incidents. Myself, Bret and Sandy had been hearing a voice repeatedly saying either something like "Enik" or "Enoch" on different occasions. I decided one day to find out which name was correct. A voice replied, "Enoch with an O."

After each session, we'd request that the spirits stay on their side and let us know when we could "clear the session." We'd listen for a voice to say "clear," at which time we'd turned off the ghost box. But on one occasion a voice stated, "This cannot clear. This is energy."

Most of the time we'd get only a meaningful word or two, but sometimes, as described in the above two paragraphs, we'd get an actual sentence or two.

I have discussed with and shared some of my audio with various researchers and scientists, some of whom are looking into quantum physics as a possible answer to such manifestations. Jon Klimo, Ph.D., a retired professor of psychology, thanked me for the audio files and information I had shared with him and described his own deep interest in ITC (instrumental transcommunication) and the EVP (electronic voice phenomena). Klimo had been funded by the Vanguard Foundation of San Francisco for three years to support his own research into this subject. In an article in *UFO Magazine* in 2001, he expressed his strong desire to initiate an effort to "record extraterrestrial as well as human spirit presence." He added, "At least some of these extraterrestrials appear by their feats to be inhabiting a set of dimensions, levels or kinds of reality other than our own physically-based one, and by visiting us they seem to lend a cross-world or interdimensional quality to our experience."

Keel and Professor Walter Uphoff, an American parapsychologist, noted that one of America's earliest EVP researchers was UFO contactee George Hunt Williamson, a follower of George Adamski for a while. However, Uphoff failed to mention Williamson's UFO background in a report to Harold Sherman, the founder and director of ESP Research Associates Foundation. The report appeared in Sherman's book *You Can Communicate With The Unseen World* (1974). Williamson claimed that in 1952 he and others established communication with UFO beings through a ham radio operator. One night, a UFO was seen hovering over the ham radio tower. The "voices" over the radio knew things that the group was talking about in the radio shack when the microphone wasn't even turned on. Keel described how back in the 1950s, amateur radio operators started receiving mysterious voices that they couldn't explain over their ham radio sets. Some of these voices would claim to be from outer space. "Ham operators in flap areas have cautiously reported all kinds of manifestations, including the materialization of entities in their radio shacks," Keel wrote in *Our Haunted Planet* (1971).

SIX
IS DJINN THE OZ BEHIND THE CURTAIN?

"These creatures, the Djinn of the Muslim religion and the elementals in the Buddhist religion, reportedly can materialize and dematerialize, and so can our Western culture's abducting creatures," California's ufologist Ann Druffel explained to me a few years ago. "They shape-shift in various forms, they delight in harassing and traumatizing human beings. They reportedly abduct human beings. They reportedly abduct human beings and transport them long distances in a matter of seconds. And the Djinn, the elementals, and our own abducting greys [have taken] a sexual interest in human beings down through the millennia. In every major culture of the world, and in many minor cultures, they all have these same folkloric stories, and even religious and philosophical texts in some of the countries talk about this 'third order of creation,' as the Muslims call it. They aren't angels, they aren't devils, they aren't human beings. They're something in between that share our world with us in a hidden state."

The word "Djinn" originated from the Arabic word *junna,* meaning "hidden from sight." The Djinn prefer to remain hidden and mysterious. According to Muslim tradition these beings are often disruptive spirits who leave illness, insanity and accidents in their wake. However, sometimes they may provide kind services for humans who know how to bind and control them. According to Muslim tradition the Djinn are composed of smokeless fire (plasma?). Islamic scholars teach that the Christian Devil was a Djinn named Iblis (meaning despair). Whereas Christianity depicts the Devil and demons as fallen angels, the Djinn are beings who act in devilish ways but who possess free will and have a shot at redemption.

"The Djinn supposedly have a group identity, much like a bee colony," Dr. Greg Little wrote in his *People of the Web* (1990). "Note that Whitley Streiber's *Communion* relates that he likened his alien abductors to insects with a group consciousness."

The late British researcher Gordon Creighton, editor of the highly respected *Flying Saucer Review,* delved deeply into the possible UFO/Djinn connection. He pointed out that the Djinn were supposedly composed of something that in the Arabic language translated as "essential fire" or "smokeless flame." After a 1983 article that Creighton had written exploring this possible connection, a leading Iraqi scientist wrote a letter to him explaining that he felt that it was quite plausible that the Djinn were real and were composed of some form of plasma-type energy that modern science had yet to fully understand. A number of UFO and paranormal authors have seriously pondered that some UFOs and some beings may be plasma forms of energy. *LightQuest: Your Guide to Seeing and Interacting with UFOs, Mystery Lights, and Plasma Intelligences* (2012), by British author Andrew Collins, is an excellent exploration of the potential UFO/plasma link.

Greg Little, who wrote the introduction to Collins's book, has long pointed out that UFOs often appear to be composed of plasma energies that "frequently assume an intelligent form and shape and display an interactive intelligence with their observers." Both authors had been greatly influenced early on by the writings and theories of John Keel regarding UFOs and beings as temporary intelligent energy forms. On the ghost front, plasma energy may explain some apparitions. Joshua P. Warren, in his book *How To Hunt Ghosts* (2003), states that "it seems ghosts often materialize in a state of plasma." Warren was once on a national radio show and a caller wanted to share an unusual experience. The caller said he worked at a haunted neon-light factory, and on one occasion a glowing woman in loose garb appeared. "As the apparition lingered, neon bulbs around her brightened," Warren said. "This is what happens to a neon tube when subjected to a stream of charges. After only a few seconds, the specter disappeared. The neon bulbs blinked out..." Warren went on to speculate that a "ghost" might "use electrical charges to create a temporary physical form," perhaps even manipulating "electrical fields and charges to gain access to our world."

Rosemary with John Keel

Rosemary Ellen Guiley is an acclaimed and prolific author with numerous books under her belt – and she'll no doubt be belting out many more yet! She's the author of such noteworthy and thought-provoking works as *The Encyclopedia of Demons & Demonology, The Encyclopedia of Angels, Monsters of West Virginia, The Encyclopedia of Vampires and Werewolves, and The Djinn Connection,* to name but a few. Her range of knowledge and insight into the realm of the paranormal is truly impressive and far reaching.

I did an interview with Rosemary wherein we discussed the Djinn, UFOs, and the paranormal.

Brent Raynes: You travel widely, you've written numerous books on the paranormal, you have worked as a writer and editor for *Fate* magazine. You're obviously a busy gal! How did you become interested in the paranormal and what are some of your major accomplishments in the field?

Rosemary Ellen Guiley: Like many people in this field, I became interested in the paranormal in childhood. There were a variety of influences: paranormal experiences; an intense interest in astronomy; a voracious reading habit that focused on the paranormal, occult, horror, science fiction, mythology, and mystery; dissatisfaction with the "answers" provided by organized religions; and a desire to explore and experience the Unknown.

My work focuses on the how and why of extraordinary experiences ranging from the mystical to the fearful. The paranormal has always existed for me, so I have no need to "prove" it. You believe in it or you don't, and it's usually an experience that makes you a believer, no matter what science and religion have to say about it. I look for patterns of experiences throughout history that illuminate what we are experiencing today. In particular, I have helped to introduce Westerners to the Djinn, supernatural beings who are active in all our paranormal experiences, and to the presence of interdimensional portals, thin spots between dimensions. The books I have written have provided explanations of all kinds of paranormal topics, experiences and phenomena.

Brent Raynes: In your studies, you identify the supernatural beings of the Muslim religion, known as the Djinn, as actual earth-based intelligent beings who live in a nearby parallel dimension to us and who often engage in deceptive activities. In fact, you feel that they are shapeshifters, as tradition claims, and that they (the Djinn) have a role in what we call "alien abductions."

Can you share how you arrived at this observation and what are some of the major points you feel should be made on this subject?

Rosemary Ellen Guiley: I just followed the threads of my research and fit puzzle pieces together, to mix a couple of metaphors. Shadow People led me to both ETs and the Djinn, and the evidence for both Shadow People and the Djinn is present in abduction literature going back decades.

We need to reexamine abduction experiences, as well as most (if not all) of our paranormal experiences to take into account beings like the Djinn who have been operating below our radar. I cannot say that the Djinn account for everything, but I believe they play major roles, and for purposes we have yet to uncover.

Brent Raynes: You have even used a ghost box to try and communicate with the Djinn. Do you feel you've been successful, and isn't that something considered a little risky?

Rosemary Ellen Guiley: I have gotten numerous communications from entities who identify themselves as Djinn. Are they who they say they are? Proving so is difficult if not impossible. That applies across the board to all communicators, including the dead.

Brent Raynes: You have mentioned that you feel that you may have communicated with the late John Keel - I believe, in of all places, Point Pleasant, West Virginia. Can you share with us details of what transpired?

Rosemary Ellen Guiley: It was during ghost box sessions conducted with a group of researchers. We all meet up in Point Pleasant several times a year. We asked "John" for some personal opinions, and I'll leave it at that. The voice that came across the ghost box sounded like John.

Brent Raynes: You truly believe that the ghost box is a device that does allow one to communicate with intelligences from another dimension, correct? You have even heard people's first and last names - including your own as I recall?

Rosemary Ellen Guiley: I have heard my own name (first only, first and last, and first, middle and last) as well as the names (first, first and last) of other researchers present at various sessions. I consider the ghost box an intriguing device that delivers communications that are hard to explain naturally. However, I readily acknowledge that it is a controversial and unpredictable device, and we have to consider that there is a trickster element. In most cases, we can't prove who we're talking to, but have to take the evidence at face value. As with all tools for spirit communications, the natural mediumistic ability of users and others present can influence results. Living humans are the biggest wild card of all when it comes to spirit communications.

Brent Raynes: You have mentioned that you also are working on videotaping procedures whereby the images of communicators may be captured in addition to their voices.

Rosemary Ellen Guiley: I have yet to undertake any formal image research of my own. It's on the list! There are many researchers all over the globe who are, and have been, researching the reliable transmission of images of the afterlife and other-dimensional realities. Like voice communications, the images are difficult to prove, but are often hard to explain away. There have been formal forensics done on some images to match them to images of people who have died. Some of this research is described in *Talking to the Dead*, the book I co-authored with George Noory.

Brent Raynes: You personally knew John Keel, and my impression is that your own studies were probably influenced quite a bit by his investigations and research. Can you tell us a little about what meeting John Keel was like for you, major areas that you came to agree with him on, and any areas where you may have parted company?

Rosemary Ellen Guiley: Meeting John was like meeting other professionals in field – if you're out doing your work, you are going to have interaction with many others involved in the same pursuits. I attended many of his Fortean meetings when he had them in New York City, and we also got together for dinner in Manhattan periodically. We both participated in other Fortean events and conferences. My favorite photo of John is one I took of him standing in front of Stonehenge during a crop circle excursion in England.

John's perspective on the paranormal was way ahead of others, and he influenced the research of many people. He zeroed in on the trickster element, and on "ultraterrestrials," beings who come from other dimensions rather than our reality or other planets. He understood the interconnectedness of phenomena, something I also saw very early in my own work. However, John opined that we are just being manipulated by some cosmic Trickster force, and that paranormal phenomena are generated in order to spawn certain beliefs, and to keep us endlessly chasing our tails in circles. I do believe we are often manipulated, but I believe in a cosmic order that transcends that to wholeness and balance.

One thing I especially appreciated about him was his emphasis on multi-disciplinary approaches to understanding the paranormal, UFOs and other phenomena. I have taken this approach throughout my career.

Brent Raynes: Who else in the field of paranormal studies have influenced you?

Rosemary Ellen Guiley: I have to rephrase the question to, "Who else has influenced your thinking?" Not all of them are in the paranormal. The nine encyclopedias alone required extensive reading in many disciplines. Literally, thousands of sources have gone into my work over the years. I have had a deep appreciation of many streams of philosophical, spiritual and religious thought. I cover so many topics that I would have to list influential people in every one of them. In terms of UFOs, Jacques Vallee has been of importance to me, along with Keel.

Brent Raynes: What directions do you hope to see manifest in the future of this field?

Rosemary Ellen Guiley: I would like to see researchers give themselves a broader education on what's going on around them in other fields. The paranormal is not a pie chart of neat little slices. Phenomena bleed from one area into another.

Brent Raynes: To a newcomer, what advice might you impart?

Rosemary Ellen Guiley: Look for natural explanations first. Establish a daily practice of meditation and embrace your natural psychic ability. The paranormal is largely a subjective psychic experience. Read and study to gain a foundation of knowledge.

End of interview.

In the book *Phenomenon: Forty Years of Flying Saucers*, edited by John Spencer and Hilary Evans (1988), there were chapters by many leading figures in the UFO field, including one by John Keel, entitled "The People Problem." In it, he wrote: "The landings, abductions and contacts and general tomfoolery are primarily part of a very ancient, very well observed phenomenon that has spawned all of man's belief systems. It has no more basis in reality than the popular Arab belief in Djinns. The manifestations behind these systems have a purpose that has been deliberately hidden from the human race for thousands of years."

I asked Rosemary to respond to Keel's statement. She replied: "From the context of our reality, the Djinn are quite real, as real as any other entity or being we have encountered throughout history. They are not fantasy. I agree with Keel's statement that the manifestations behind popular belief systems 'have a purpose that has been deliberately hidden from the human race for thousands of years.' There is some mysterious Oz behind the curtain that orchestrates the confounding phenomena we experience. From the Middle Eastern point of view, that Oz is the Djinn, a disturbing enough idea, that one race of beings accounts for everything in our paranormal panorama. Even more disturbing is the idea that there may be something else even behind the Djinn, manipulating all our concepts of 'reality.' Whatever it is, whenever we get close to exposing it, it artfully shape-shifts away."

It's all such an extraordinarily complex and enigmatic puzzle. Perhaps someday we'll be able to expose all of the hidden components to this thing, and hopefully when that day finally arrives, the ultimate outcome will be a good one.

SEVEN
JOHN KEEL AND SWEDISH UFOLOGY

Hakan Blomqvist was born in 1952, in the beautiful Swedish city Karlstad, the City of the Sun, according to local tradition. He undertook university studies at Stockholm University: History of Religion, Philosophy and Ethnology, retiring as a librarian for the Norrköping Public Library in 2016.

A large part of Hakan's spare time is devoted to volunteer work at Archives for the Unexplained (AFU), formerly Archives for UFO

Research, a foundation of which he was one of the founders in 1973. He is chairman of the AFU board and also board member of the national organization UFO-Sweden. For many years, Hakan has been a student of the Theosophical/Esoteric Tradition and literature. He is the author of *UFO in myth and reality* (1993), *UFO Contacts in Sweden* (2009), *A Travel in Time. The History of UFO-Sweden 1970-2010*, 2010), *Return of the Gods, UFOs and the Esoteric Tradition*, (2013), as well as hundreds of articles in magazines and newspapers.

Below is an interview I had with Mr. Blomqvist:

Brent Raynes: During our initial and brief correspondence in 1978, you were mystified by the psychic component of the UFO phenomenon. In fact, you wrote me then: "There are many striking similarities between UFO humanoids and the devas, elementals and fairies described in the occult literature. It's like some energy zeroes in on certain individuals under certain conditions." Are you still on the same page, so to speak, as you were back then? How may your thoughts have evolved?

Hakan Blomqvist: Yes definitely. There is a psychic component in almost all the close encounter and contact cases I have investigated. Sometimes the witnesses develop psychic abilities after the initial UFO experience. That there is a close connection both historical and in regard to phenomena between encounters with UFO humanoids and fairies has been obvious since the publication of Jacques Vallee's classic *Passport to Magonia* in 1969. Many books have since been published following in the Vallee footsteps. UFO-Sweden has published sightings of leprechauns in various publications as field investigators now and then stumble on witnesses who recount not only UFO observations but encounters with the little people. I presented one of these very intriguing reports, the Helge Eriksson case, 1931, in a blog entry.

The writings of Jacques Vallee and John Keel made mainstream ufologists aware of the close resemblance between some UFO entities and the devas, nature spirits and elementals described in folklore and religion. According to the esoteric tradition, devas and nature spirits are a parallel evolution to man living at different levels of the multiverse. In the coming centuries we will, according to the esoteric tradition, become more conscious of each other's existence and be able to cooperate. The reappearance of The Fairy Investigation Society is an interesting cultural phenomenon pointing in this direction. I have for some years in my blog and latest book argued that the Esoteric Tradition as formulated by Helena P. Blavatsky, Alice Bailey and Henry T. Laurency constitutes the best and most interesting multiverse paradigm and theory to explain the multitude of intriguing phenomena documented by many researchers.

Brent Raynes: You also are interested in burial mound sites, ley lines, and so-called "window" areas. Have you found any connection in your country with these ancient sites and paranormal and UFO activity?

Hakan Blomnqvist: This is an interesting theory, but I have not personally been doing any research into this issue. UFO-Sweden field investigators have documented cases in specific flap or window areas but as far as I know found no definite connection between mounds or ancient sites, possibly with one exception in Vallentuna, Sweden.

Brent Raynes: In 1978, a good friend and colleague of yours named Ake Franzen of Stockholm corresponded with me for a while. In October 1969 he spent nearly four weeks in Point Pleasant, West Virginia, meeting with many major notables in the legendary Mothman saga, among them Mary Hyre, Connie Carpenter, Marcella Bennett, Linda Scarberry (who he became romantically involved with I learned later), Linda's parents, plus many more. He arrived with a letter of introduction from John Keel that he felt "opened almost every door in Point Pleasant" for him. He had helped Keel with research for a chapter that appeared in his *Operation Trojan Horse* on the Scandinavian "mystery plane" flap back in the 1930s.

You investigated a case in Sweden of a couple who had had hundreds of paranormal experiences and that during a UFO flap on the night of October 30, 1965, they saw "several small humanoids floating around their car." You added, "The creatures had big, hypnotic red eyes, just like Mothman." Did they appear to be self-luminous I wonder? That story always fascinated me. In addition, you said that the **woman in this case was a clairvoyant and that when out in nature she would often see "the little people." Do you still feel that these experiences indeed may be interrelated?**

Hakan Blomqvist: Yes, there are similarities between Mothman and the small creatures observed by Sture and Turid Johansson in October 1965, a case I have documented and mentioned in one of my blog entries. In a taped interview, Sture described the incident: "When we arrived at the place we were told to visit those entities were already there but we did not observe them until we had parked the car. It was not totally dark but twilight. We noticed them first over the field and then they came very close to the car, about 50 centimeters. We believe they were five or six, between 1,25-1,50 meter with large heads and shining eyes. The eyes were red, phosphorous. The entities didn't walk but floated around in straight lines. I wished for all my life that another car would come but no one showed up. After some time the entities disappeared over the field and then it was like a saucer tried to land on the car. Our whole car shook and the radio screamed in the back seat. We took cover below the dashboard."

My theory is that Mothman and entities observed by Sture and Turid were elementals. Elementals was a favorite term of John Keel who interpreted most entity encounters as elementals. But Keel never studied the scholarly Esoteric Tradition as far as I know. Elementals are simply mind creations, made consciously by those who know how and unconsciously by religious devotees of all faiths. A form of multiverse robots - good, neutral or evil.

An interesting example of thought-creation is given in *Conjuring Up Philip: An Adventure In Psychokinesis,* by Iris M. Owen and Margaret Sparrow. A group of parapsychologists in Canada decided to try to create a fantasy entity named Philip. George and Iris Owen were well known parapsychologists interested in poltergeist phenomena. The group succeeded in creating an entity they could communicate with and who caused several paranormal phenomena. The famous traveler and author Alexandra David-Neel gives a very vivid description of how she created a fantasy monk, a *tulpa*. This mind-creature became so physical that a visitor took it for a live lama.

In 1976, Sture began his life as a trance medium travelling all over the world together with his wife. He became quite famous and celebrities like Shirley MacLaine and Dennis Weaver visited their home in Sweden. Sture also figures in the 1987 miniseries *Out on a Limb,* starring Shirley MacLaine.

My late friend and ufologist Åke Franzén visited Point Pleasant in 1969, interviewing about 30 Mothman witnesses and visiting observation sites. Åke didn't just become an ordinary ufological field investigator in Point Pleasant. During his stay he fell deeply in love with one of the main witnesses, Linda Scarberry. He later had plans to emigrate to the U.S. but couldn't find a job. Åke became a good friend of local reporter Mrs Mary Hyre and also several of the local Mothman witnesses and Åke and Mary often went together by car during field investigations. One of the things Åke noticed in 1969 was that several of the witnesses suffered from post-traumatic stress. Linda Scarberry showed the scars she had on arms and legs. After the experience she had suffered from shock and was hospitalized. One morning she woke up at the hospital with arms and legs badly scratched. At AFU we have preserved the correspondence (many love letters) between Linda Scarberry and Åke Franzén.

Brent Raynes: American researcher and writer Andrew Colvin said that John Keel would show MIB witnesses "racial profiling" pictures and that the majority of these people identified their MIBs as resembling Laplanders – looking like people from Northern Sweden. I know that John Keel later visited Sweden, and that he was interested in the early "mystery airplane" stories and phantom submarines, but I wonder if he engaged you and your colleagues in any questions regarding this MIB aspect?

And, of course, overall what was it like to have John Keel visiting with you and your colleagues? Did he shed any light on anything for you?

Hakan Blomqvist: I regard John Keel as one of my mentors in our fascinating underground field. To me, John Keel and his books opened up a new world with his knowledge, humor and suggestive language. I corresponded with Keel in the 1970s and 1980s and also had the good fortune of having him as a guest in my home when he visited Sweden in October 1976. We were a small group of ufologists who gathered in my small one room apartment in Sundbyberg discussing all aspects of UFO and paranormal phenomena for a couple of days. I was especially interested in hearing of his experiences and theories regarding the Men in Black (MIB) phenomenon and the very physical UFO and contact cases. Keel was intrigued by this aspect and convinced there were aliens among us. "I'd really like to get one," was his comment. In my copy of *Operation Trojan Horse* he wrote: "For my good friend Håkan Blomqvist – the secret to the UFOs is on page 321." Last page in the book is 320. Typical John Keel Fortean humor. After a lifetime of travel and study of UFO, Fortean and paranormal phenomena, Keel reached the conclusion shared by many researchers into these areas: we live in a multiverse inhabited by a variety of diverse intelligences. I agree with his view.

Brent Raynes: You've been involved in Sweden's UFO museum for many years now, the AFU, Archives for the Unexplained. Can you tell our readers some about this significant part of your ufological journey?

Hakan Blomqvist: I wouldn't perhaps describe it as a museum but rather archive and library, but we have plans for a regular museum. Our start in 1973 was a very humble beginning, an informal working group. Three young lads, Kjell Jonsson, Anders Liljegren and me decided we wanted to do serious UFO research. In 1974, Kjell Jonsson began building a UFO lending library in his small one room apartment in Södertälje. Starting with two bookshelves and 300+ books, the library expanded steadily until we moved to our own premises in Norrköping in 1980 and also changed our group to a formal foundation - Archives for UFO Research (AFU), later Archives for the Unexplained. Today we are the world's largest UFO, Fortean archive and library with 13 premises and between 15 to 20 people working at the archive on a daily basis. Collections to AFU are coming from all over the world. Hilary Evans donated his entire archive and library to us. We have the *Flying Saucer Review* archive and presently we are waiting for the archive of *Borderland Sciences Research Foundation* (BSRF) coming from Eureka, California. Our ambition is to be a sort of world heritage for our subjects.

Brent Raynes: In your years of memorable UFO investigations and research, have you had any notable experiences yourself that you might recall for us?

Hakan Blomqvist: I´ve never had any UFO observations but several paranormal experiences. In the beginning of the 1970s I participated in a meditation group run by Sture and Turid Johansson. We did some experiments in distant healing. One evening, I decided to try sending a ball of energy to my girlfriend who had a cold and lived a few miles away. I didn´t mention the experiment to her but did the concentration and visualizations necessary for the healing and then sent a ball of energy to her. The next day, she called me to relate a curious experience last evening. She was trying to fall asleep when suddenly a ball of light appeared in her room, silently floating into her body. She was not afraid but in the morning her cold was better. Whether I created this "UFO" is impossible to say but the coincidence is fascinating. I associate this experience with the balls of light created by the so-called Kahunas of Hawaii and often mentioned by Riley Crabb.

Brent Raynes: I was just reading through Raymond Andrew Keller II's *Venus Rising* and saw your comments that the early 1950s contactee movement had ties to the Theosophical Society. Author Paul M. Vest had been approached in the early 1950s by a mysterious Bill (also known as Mr. Wheeler by others) who provided a list to Vest of contactees in southern California. Vest followed up and reached these people, who verified that they had been in touch with this man. Orfeo Angelucci's wife told Vest that the man had given her the "creeps" because he seemed to know everything about them, and she found him frightening. In Vest's interview with "Bill," he discovered that he seemed to have a great deal of knowledge about Theosophy. According to Keller, you suspect that a secret esoteric group may have had a hand in trying to promote the early contactee movement. Would you care to comment further?

Hakan Blomqvist: Glad you asked this question. In my latest book, *Return of the Gods: UFOs and the Esoteric Tradition,* I advance a rather heretic theory regarding some of the first generation physical contactees, partly based on my research on Swedish contactee cases. This theory makes me something of a heretic among "scientific" ufologists. Here is a summary you may use:

The esoteric intervention theory

Perhaps the most controversial part of my writings is a variation of Jacques Vallee's esoteric intervention theory. I have advanced the theory that some of the physical contactees of the 1950s were involved in a cultural influence test. An experiment implemented by a group of benevolent aliens, earth based or extraterrestrial, a group with access to "vimana" technology. This test was done in co-operation with the Higher Intelligence Agency, the custodians of the ancient wisdom, using a new type of phenomena attraction as they used in spiritualist phenomena in connection with the founding of the Theosophical Society in 1875.

A brief summary of my arguments for seriously considering this theory follows:

1. Many years of investigating and documenting physical contact cases have convinced me that some individuals (very few) have actually met and communicated with "aliens" from somewhere.

2. In spite of their faults and personality idiosyncrasies there is circumstantial evidence that the following contactees were involved in a cultural and psychological test: George Adamski, Orfeo Angelucci, Daniel Fry, George Van Tassel,

and Howard Menger.

3. The contact experiences of journalist Paul M. Vest indicates that the test was a carefully orchestrated plan by this benevolent group.

4. The message or information presented to these contactees is a somewhat simplified version of the Esoteric Tradition with basic ideas such as: a multiverse reality, reincarnation, universal laws for the evolution of consciousness, Earth a quarantined or "prison planet," man not alone in the universe, etc. In order to detect and understand the similarity in ideas between the contactee messages and esotericism a thorough acquaintance with the works of Helena Blavatsky and Alice Bailey is required. Few ufologists have this background.

5. The "hidden hand" similarities between the outbreak of spiritistic phenomena in the 19th century and UFO phenomena in the 1940s and 1950s. In the Esoteric Tradition this hidden hand is the planetary guardians, the custodians of the Ancient Wisdom (scientists of the multiverse) using "phenomena" to expand the worldview and consciousness of man, a form of education through astonishment.

6. The assertion, in the 1930s and 40s, by Alice Bailey's teacher the Tibetan D.K. that "extraplanetary beings "stand ready to intervene" and "offer their help at this time."

In Chapter 7 of John Keel's *UFOs: Operation Trojan Horse* (1970), "Unidentified Airplanes," Keel provided details on the "forgotten Scandinavian flap of 1932-38," involving curious "ghost fliers" who were presumably unidentified. He described how a Swedish researcher named Ake Franzen (1936-1995) had been most helpful to him in uncovering details of this wave of early sightings, how Franzen had retrieved more than ninety detailed reports from the Stockholm newspapers of the 1930s and had tediously translated them into English for him.

Swedish ufologist describes his visit to Point Pleasant

In 1978, as stated in the interview above, I had both the pleasure and honor of briefly engaging in an exchange of written correspondence with Ake Franzen, then a resident of Stochholm. Mr. Franzen had traveled to the United States to visit Point Pleasant in 1969 to learn firsthand what the Mothman controversy was all about.

In a letter dated May 26, 1978, Franzen wrote me:

"Hi Brent,

My name is Ake Franzen and I'm a member of A.F.U. and I am also a very good friend of Hakan Blomqvist. I've heard from him that you belong to the few of us that really are seeking the truth behind the curtain of the unexplained.

It's a fascinating task to try to reveal just a little of the giant jigsaw which lies in the Twilight Zone. I've tried several times to do it but it seems to be more complex when you try to dig.

Nevertheless, in 1969 and 1970, I tried to get as much information about the Mothman as I could get. This birdman of Point Pleasant took, at that time, all my interest, and I decided to investigate the whole case.

I started from scratch, almost. The only person I had been in contact with was John Keel and he told me a lot about research and the difficulties I had to face in a foreign country. He gave me also a letter, which later on opened almost every door in Point Pleasant for me. You see, I think I got this help from him partly because I had been helping him with a chapter in his book, *Operation Trojan Horse.*

When I started my research work I had in mind it could be a hoax and if it turned out to be, I had to take the whole thing then as a pleasant holiday. But to my astonishment I found out that there was more behind that than I could have dreamed of. I met Mary Hyre, at the time a reporter for the *Daily Messenger,* and she was that person through which everything in Point Pleasant circulated. Through her, I got a lot of names of witnesses around the area and also a lot of help with transportation. I also met Linda Scarberry and her parents the McDaniel's, Connie Carpenter, Marcella Bennett and a lot of others too. I stayed almost four weeks the first time and a little less the next time.

I can tell you Brent, the stories about the Mothman they told me convinced me that something strange was going on."

In his second letter, dated September 9, 1978, Franzen also wrote:

"For myself, West Virginia's Mothman was the first case that turned me on. Before this I was the passive reader of UFO books and other publications. So I wrote to John Keel and asked for more details about Mothman and his appearances. I got a nice answer and an inquiry about helping him with material about the ghost fliers over Sweden in the 1930s.

I decided to try to get to the bottom of the Mothman story, to see if there was any truth behind it. So after eight months I had saved enough money and started my journey to the distant exotic Point Pleasant.

And in October 1969 I began my search for the winged creature. I also had plans to buy a net of some kind to catch him but soon abandoned those plans. Late on the evening of my first day in Point Pleasant, I knocked on the door of the *Athens Messenger* and I stepped in to my first meeting with Mary Hyre. She was indeed a nice person and we got to be really good friends at once. She was also that person who everything of interest in Point Pleasant circled around.

Mary introduced me to the McDaniel family and they in turn told me about others. And I was lucky. Just a couple of days before I arrived in town another person had come too. She had lived with her husband in Ohio, but she had taken her baby Danny and left the misery behind. Linda Scarberry.

Next day I was invited to dinner in the McDaniel home and it turned out to be an unforgettable evening. A lot of fun and also serious talk. Mrs. McDaniel told me her story about the grey shape over Tiny's and the visiting of the mysterious Mr. Brown with his needled socks. And later on they told me about a very strange story. It was only Linda and her mother in the house and they were sitting in the living room when suddenly somebody was moving on the front porch and the door opened. But nobody entered. Instead the sound of steps was heard. Both Linda and Mabel got very terrified and were sitting almost paralyzed. The steps seemed to take a turn to the kitchen and then to the bedrooms. A few minutes later the sound came back in the living room, the door out to the front porch was opened again and closed.

Almost the same story has been told to me by a Swedish couple, years later, so there must be something to it. Later in the evening, we took a trip to the Power Plant, a really eerie place in the TNT area. That time nothing unusual happened, but some weeks later when we visited the Plant again, something strange happened to me. It was Mary, Linda, Connie Carpenter and me. When we were standing with the car on the small road beside the Plant they suddenly refused to leave the car. My intention was to explore the building, but Linda and Mary told me not to go in, they could feel that something was wrong. I must admit I got scared, but my curiosity was a little stronger so I got out of the car and approached the ruin. It was then when I noticed the change. Earlier, when we had been there before, a lot of noises was heard from all directions. A bark for instance from a dog nearby, crickets in the grass and a lot of different sounds from the woods. But now it was complete silence! Not a single sound from anywhere. I can't understand it because there should be something! Well, I continued through the opening in the building, where it had been a door one time in the past. I searched with my flashlight around the walls and the inner room, but found nothing. But the whole time the air felt thick in a strange way. On my return to the car, Linda screamed that something was moving in the ruin and I turned my body. But there was nothing to be seen and I came back to the car. Mary and Linda told me that my hair had been raised when I turned my back to them and it's possible but I didn't feel it. But both Mary and Linda had seen something move in a windowless window in the building after my search. I can't explain that either, but my opinion is that both of them are able to see things others can't.

I had also several meetings with Marcella and Connie and they told me their stories, which you already know of. They have, Mary,

Linda, Marcella, Connie, and Mabel, something in common. They are highly sensitive persons and perhaps very susceptible for this sort of experience. Linda even suffered from hearing heartbeat sounds from the cellar now and then. Louder and louder until they suddenly disappeared.

Perhaps our enigmatic friends from the Twilight Zone need sensitive people to make themselves known. We discussed these and other explanations many times, but as usual it can only be speculation, as you know.

Another thing that I found interesting was the highly developed children. Marcella Bennett's daughter Tina and Linda's Danny. They did start to talk very early and could follow adult conversations easily. They learn new things very quickly and appeared more elder than their real age. Perhaps it's nothing important, but you can never know.

EIGHT
PAUL ENO ON GHOSTS, UFOS, AND THE MULTIVERSE

Paul Eno is best known as the elder of the father and son co-hosts of the CBS Radio and WOON 1240 AM and 99.3 FM Boston/Worcester/Providence drive-time show "Behind the Paranormal," with an estimated three million listeners.

Paul was one of the first paranormal investigators of the early 1970s, while he was studying for the priesthood. His early mentors included parapsychology pioneer Dr. Louisa Rhine, Fr. John J. Nicola S.J. (technical advisor for the film *The Exorcist*) and legendary ghost hunters Ed and Lorraine Warren. Paul graduated from two seminaries but was expelled from a third because of his paranormal work, with less than two years to go before ordination. He went on to become an award-winning New England journalist and the author of six books on the paranormal and two on history.

Two of his books, *Faces at the Window* (New River Press 1998) and *Footsteps in the Attic* (New River Press 2002) are considered classics of paranormal literature. Several of his cases are famous, especially the Bridgeport poltergeist outbreak of 1974, which made headlines all over the world, and the ongoing Litchfield County, Connecticut, paranormal flap, subject of the 2015 book *The Haunted House Diaries* by William J. Hall.

Early on, Paul found that many ghost cases, if thoroughly researched, turned into UFO cases. This led to theories and methods that go way beyond the classic spiritualist interpretation of the paranormal and involve previously unsuspected connections among ghosts, cryptids and UFOs.

Paul has appeared on the History, Discovery and Travel Channels, and he and his son Ben have lectured all over America and in Europe.

Brent Raynes: Paul, please share with us some information about yourself and how you became so deeply involved in the field of the paranormal.

Paul Eno: The starting point was the most traumatic event of my life: At the age of seven, I witnessed my father's suicide. I was a second grader at a Catholic school, where we were taught that if you did things like eat a hamburger on Friday, miss Mass on Sunday or commit suicide, you could go to hell. My dad was a wonderful, kind man. How could he have gone to hell? One of the good nuns got me through all that.

I entered the seminary, back when you could still do so at the tender age of 14. I still wondered about my father, and I also wondered about the stories of ghosts one encounters in every culture. Couple that with my exposure to the Roman Catholic doctrine of "purgatory" – a theoretical state between heaven and hell – and I had the question that actually prompted my research:

Could ghosts be souls stuck in purgatory?

In late 1970, I found a place to test the theory: the long-abandoned and overgrown "Village of Voices" in Pomfret, Connecticut, about 60 miles from where I lived near Hartford. In three expeditions there in 1971 and 1972 – all involving other seminary students, a historian and a photo expert – we experienced apparitions, along with the voices and sounds of everyday life, right down to the sounds of metal farm implements.

All this made me question not only purgatory but just about everything else. These people didn't seem to be dead at all, never mind in purgatory. It was all so physical. How could these even be spirits? Were there "spirits" of farm tools, wagon wheels, cows, horses, dogs and other things we heard?

Maybe "ghosts" had more to do with the nature of time than they did with death.

Meanwhile, I was taken under the wings of four different paranormal "legends" as the 1970s continued.

One was Fr. John J. Nicola of Washington D.C., whom I met through my brother, a priest who taught in Washington. Fr. Nicola was a Jesuit priest and probably the greatest expert on exorcism of his day. He was the technical advisor for the film *The Exorcist* (something he regretted) and was involved in the original case. This gave me the theological perspective on the paranormal, which is NOT taught in the seminary.

Then there was Dr. Louisa Rhine of Duke University, with whom I corresponded and eventually met. She and her husband, Dr. J.B. Rhine, were the founders of modern parapsychology. Thus I was exposed to the scientific perspective on the paranormal.

Finally, there were Ed and Lorraine Warren, probably the founders of modern pop "ghost hunting." Lorraine read something I wrote about the Village of Voices case, liked the purgatory idea, and I ended up quite close to them personally, while working with them on cases from 1972-1978. By Ed and I had an outwardly amicable parting and went our separate ways. Thus I got the popular, hobbyist perspective on the paranormal.

My personal opinion today is that all three perspectives are wrong.

I continued through other cases into the late 1970s in confusion about what I was actually dealing with. In 1979, I encountered the "ghost" of someone who wasn't even dead, with multiple witnesses and work with the girl herself and the people who had seen her in their house 120 miles away.

That did it. I started looking into the physics of time, found out that (according to most physicists, at least) linear time as we experience it doesn't even exist, that there are almost certainly many parallel worlds with versions of ourselves and others who might have died here and not there, and with entirely different laws of physics.

That was the beginning of the "multiverse" theories that my son Ben and I use today. And the results have been astounding.

In 1976, I was still in the seminary, about two years from ordination. But the faculty was fed up with my paranormal research and threw me out. I ended up a newspaper and magazine journalist!

Brent Raynes: You, along with Rosemary Ellen Guiley, were interviewed by Tim Beckley and Tim Swartz for their radio show, *Exploring the Bizarre*. You talked about your investigations of a haunting/poltergeist situation in Connecticut, and an up close and personal entity encounter you had that was more than mere ectoplasmic, whispy stuff. Can you tell us about that?

Paul Eno: You must be referring to my experience on the evening of the second day of my involvement in the Bridgeport, Connecticut poltergeist case of 1974. Our assumption was that we were dealing with "demons."

Ed and Lorraine Warren had left the house to do a TV interview and I was left there with the 10-year-old girl, the parents, a neighbor and a reporter. We were all in the living room and could feel a powerful energy forming down the hall in the kitchen. As this energy grew, four faint, gauzy figures came down the hall and into the living room.

I put the girl behind me because I knew they were after her. One came and stood right in front of me. Instinctively, I pushed toward it and I felt physical resistance. I even felt bone structure, though it didn't seem human. This was a physical being.

This was my first lesson in how not to deal with "parasites," as we call them today. As I became angry that it was after the girl, it fed on the anger and got stronger. The energy became so powerful that I pulled the family out of the house, then called the Warrens. Fortunately, the police had pushed the crowds back to each end of the street and we didn't emerge into a mob of curiosity-seekers.

Brent Raynes: What other significant personal revelations have happened to you in the field?

Paul Eno: One result of adopting a "multiverse" view of the paranormal is that all sorts of connections between seemingly unrelated phenomena have become apparent. Why do so many people who have UFO encounters also report ghost and/or poltergeist phenomena in their homes? Why are cryptids often seen in areas of UFO activity? Being aware of the multiversal process (energy, objects and even inhabitants coming and going – sometimes intentionally – across the "branes" or boundaries of parallel worlds, usually in a very physical way) completely transformed paranormal concepts and experiences for me.

On a very personal level, there is much that I never spoke publicly about until recently, primarily because it made me look like a psychic or medium, which is not what I do, and I don't think those people "get it" anyway. But since becoming aware of the constant interactions in our multiverse, if that's what it is, there have been a number of interesting encounters with what might be called "neighbors" from parallel worlds in the course of my paranormal work and my son's. These would have been grossly misinterpreted as spirits or ignored completely under the standard, narrow spiritualist theories.

Brent Raynes: Where has your research and investigative work taken you?

Paul Eno: Instead of spirits of the dead or trying to prove the existence of the soul or some kind of afterlife, the paranormal seems to provide a panorama of a rich, elegant and intimately connected series of all possible worlds where versions of ourselves, and everyone and everything else – alive or dead - exist in all possible forms simultaneously. This makes death (as in the absence of life) impossible and our usual understanding of just about everything, including the paranormal, impossibly narrow and completely inadequate.

Brent Raynes: Although this may be outside the usual area of your exploration and expertise, your friend and colleague Rosemary Ellen Guiley has tackled the alien/Djinn question quite extensively in recent years, and the UFO/alien encounter experiencers all seem to possess heightened paranormal profiles. Many times they report that following their "alien" encounters they notice the sudden appearance of psychic sensitivities. These could be poltergeist episodes, seeing ghosts/spirits, telepathy, clairvoyance, clairaudience, psychokinesis, premonitions, etc. Have you come across any of this in your own work/studies and do you have any thoughts or insights on it?

Paul Eno: This is precisely what follows from what I've said previously. Every phenomenon you name could be explained by routine multiversal interactions. My son and I expect this in our research. So when called in on a case, we never look at just one house or family. We will study an entire area, sometimes for years. One of our original cases of this type began in Litchfield County, Connecticut, and is the subject of William J. Hall's 2015 book *The Haunted House Diaries*. The case is ongoing and keeps getting bigger.

UFO researchers are becoming vividly aware of these connections, and we have been consulting with several prominent people when they run into this in their own cases. We are also in demand as speakers at UFO conventions.

Brent Raynes: What would you like people to know about the paranormal?

Paul Eno: That nothing in it is what it appears to be. Also, that they should forget everything they think they know about it because it's the first day of school.

Brent Raynes: What do you hope that your work, and that of your colleagues in this field, will ultimately achieve?

Paul Eno: First, I hope that we're right about this multiverse approach. One never knows, and a large dose of humility is essential before attaining any true knowledge. But assuming that it is correct, we would hope for an expansion of understanding about who and what we really are and what our ultimate destiny can be.

Brent Raynes: Your research and investigations run parallel to much of John Keel's work. Did the two of you ever meet?

Paul Eno: I was just getting started in the paranormal field while John Keel was in his heyday, and I'm sorry to say that I never met him. More's the pity, since we had similar backgrounds: journalists with an insatiable interest in the supernatural. Along with Jacques Vallee and the late, great Brad Steiger, John pioneered the idea of parallel worlds and "window areas" as answers to paranormal mysteries. This forms the basis of my work today. Without John's contributions to the field, we might still be back in the paranormal bronze age.

NINE
WINGED "MONSTERS"

In 2007, an informant told me of "birdman" sightings by his brother, who lived in the desert community of Chaparral, New Mexico, and a neighbor, who had a close encounter with the winged anomaly.

On the evening of Sunday, September 30, 2007, my informant, cell phone in hand, visited his brother's next door neighbor to help me get the low down on this man's incredible account. The neighbor is a truck driver who speaks only Spanish, so my informant acted as an interpreter. Back and forth we went between English and Spanish.

The incident occurred sometime between 2 and 3 a.m., either in early August or late July 2007. The man was outside and was about to smoke a cigarette when he heard a commotion in the tree nearby. He flicked his lighter, and that's when he saw the winged creature.

"He thought that it was coming toward the dog to attack it, but the dog went in back of him and started barking really, really loud," my informant stated. "That's when he looked up and that's when he saw it." A tree nearby was swaying back and forth "like there was a windstorm." I asked about feathers, as I had been told that the creature had them. "He said he didn't see feathers on it." I asked about eyes. "He didn't see the eyes. You know what he did

131

say? He had a tiny head, big fanged teeth, and sharp claws on his hands."

"It made a horrible sound, kind of like a – he can't even describe it – it was like a squealing but a really, really loud – I guess like a squealing and a hissing at the same time," the interpreter said. "When he saw the creature it made that noise. He was so shocked that he kept trying to turn on his lighter and he kept doing that motion."

"He didn't think the creature saw him until he started lighting his lighter. It came down the way an eagle comes down when they're landing."

"With his front legs up in the air?" I asked.

"Exactly. And his hands were close to his chest."

"How tall?" I asked.

"Six feet or more. It was pretty big."

I asked how long this event went on.

"It seemed like it lasted a long time but it might have been five or six seconds. When it was coming down and was low to the ground it stopped in mid-air when it saw the lighter flickering. It turned around flying."

Then it landed on my informant's brother's garage roof and sat briefly "in a squatting position."

"It turned around and looked at him again, like the way an owl tilts its head, and made that same sound and took off flying really, really, really fast" in the direction of nearby mountains.

On September 28, I talked with my informant's brother about his sighting, which occurred around 5 a.m. on September 14. He and his wife were outside their home talking. He was lying on the back of his car looking at stars and watching a light move in the sky when he saw a form go through the air. It looked to him like it was about 30 to 50 feet high and close to his outside light, which was on a pole. "It didn't have any feathers," he said. "It looked like somebody hang gliding. The wingspan was pretty big, about a good 15 feet, from side to side."

"I told my wife, 'Look, look…Look at that!' The only thing she saw was a black cloud, but I saw it real good because I stood up and I looked toward it. I was following it. I followed it for about three or four seconds…" He felt his wife was in denial "because she's so scared of that thing, of people talking about it," referring to others in the area who had seen it.

My informant, who holds a responsible position with the judicial court system of El Paso, Texas, wrote me: "The only reason the neighbor told my brother was because his kids and my brother's kids get together at my brother's house to play and they stay up late. The neighbor said, 'As crazy as it may sound' and then proceeded to tell him what he saw. He said, 'I'm only telling you this because what I saw has the capability to take a child or two.'"

Someone else in Chaparral contacted me with details of two more strange cryptid incidents. One involved a friend who was riding in a car with another person one night when they encountered a mysterious entity. "It was walking on its hind legs and was super tall with blood shot eyes!" my informant wrote. "Everything went slow motion as it looked at them."

This informant described her own experience that she had shared with her brother. They were inside their home when a huge shadow appeared in the room. The lights dimmed, and then a bright light filled the room. Her brother turned pale and declared that something was in the window.

"I could see this seven-foot tall white thing covering its eyes trying to look into the window," she said. "It didn't have a face but I know its eyes were black. My brother couldn't move because I guess he couldn't believe what he was seeing, so I grabbed his hand and we ran out of the room. It was gone by the time we had courage to go back."

The Birdman of Madisonville

Much closer to home that same year I learned of another interesting location, right here in Tennessee. It too sounded like what Keel frequently referred to as a "window" area, a location with a good bit of anomalous and recurrent traffic.

"We called it the Birdman of Madisonville," Mark Boring, editor of the *Monroe County Buzz* of Madisonville, Tennessee, said. He had been "fairly skeptical" of it when reports first surfaced. A local radio station mentioned it and made fun of it.

Mark explained that nearby there is a ridge known as the Hiwassee Knob and how back in the late 1960s and early 1970s young people used to gather there near an old fire tower and build bonfires.

"As I remember, the first time there were 10 or 12 kids who reported there was a bird-like creature," Mark said. "They didn't say a whole lot more about it, but then it got my interest and that of a couple of my buddies, and so we started going to the bonfires and traveling around. One day a buddy of mine and I were driving in the knob area and actually caught a glimpse of something, a huge bird that was too big to be a regular bird. Its wings were outstretched, and it was soaring into the woods. Then some other people spotted it on the ground and chased it. They said it ran like a man."

"I saw it again flying over the knob. There were several more sightings, and another buddy of mine took a picture of it on top of the town water tower, but he has since disappeared somewhere in the wilds of Utah and I guess has taken the picture with him."

"A mother and some children saw it, and of course it terrified them. These sightings happened from about 1964 or 1965, until 1971, 1972 or so. I left to work in New Orleans in 1970 and people that I communicated with told me that they saw it. I came back and went to work in Chattanooga around 1972 or 1973. There were a few more sightings, but by 1975 nobody saw it or talked about it. For a 10-year span there were about two or three sightings a year."

I asked about a report that someone shot the creature with an arrow.

Mark replied, "Yes, and there was a guy who shot at it with a pistol too. The guy who claimed to have shot the birdman said he took part of a foot off. Someone who said they were from the Smithsonian looked him up and asked to take the piece. He never heard from them again."

A lot of this metamorphosed into legend, you might say, or into the realm of a tall tale. Some of it we have told time and time again and so it has taken on an aura of a tall tale. My boys just laugh at me now when I talk about it. Not many people believe that this 'birdman' happened. Some do. When we mentioned the 'birdman' in the paper recently, the lady who has a restaurant next door to my office came over and said, 'I remember that. I had forgotten all about it.' You know, we're looking back at 30 years or so."

I asked Mark how big it appeared to be. He said, "Six or seven feet. Like a tall man. Some of the people said it was at least seven feet. You don't really get a chance to stand there and measure the 'birdman.' You see it and it just looks like a huge creature."

I asked Mark to estimate the wingspan of the bird he had seen and he replied that his had maybe a six or seven foot wingspan. This must have been a smaller one than what others had reported.

Originally I had contacted Mark simply following up on a report of crop circles that had appeared on a local farm in Madisonville in May 2007. A Jeff Wilson from Ohio's Independent Crop Circle Researchers Association had visited the site with a team and reportedly removed over 1,500 samples that had unnatural elongation of wheat nodes and "expulsion cavities" on the stems of some of the wheat. Similar odd characteristics have been reported at other crop circle locations around the world. "We now have enough scientific evidence to conclude that this formation was not man-made," Wilson was quoted. Mark admitted being initially skeptical of the crop circle business, though he had been approached by locals reporting UFOs too. However, he didn't want to put those stories in his paper and sound like *The National Enquirer*. He felt the crop circle story had "pushed the bounds of reality" enough. "We just wanted to keep things on a reporting basis rather than on a sensationalistic one."

Mark told me that around the time of the crop circle event there had been three credible witnesses reporting a UFO in the area, the description of each witness matching pretty much. None of them wanted any publicity, for the usual reasons. For fear that people would think them crazy. A few weeks later, Mark put me in touch with one of the witnesses. This woman told me it was her first UFO, how it had bright blue lights on it, and how a local businessman had seen the same thing while also driving down a local section of Highway 411. She said it was a week later, on a Friday night. It was a dark night. The object had bright blue lights on it, the lights appearing to encircle a circular or oblong object. She pulled over to the side of the highway, she said, and rolled down her window and turned off the car engine. It was just over the trees, at one point may have been hovering, and then it moved directly over her car, passing very quickly overhead. She said it covered the whole two lanes of the southbound highway. There was no sound that the witness could hear coming from the object.

About two weeks later, she heard about the crop circles.

"I don't know what the hell it is" – John Keel

The people sounded credible, and the events quite strange, in a hauntingly familiar Keelian way. I called John Keel on October 10, 2007 and chatted with him about these large bird-like sightings, the crop circles, UFOs here in Tennessee and, of course, the New Mexico stories as well. I figured who better than the author of *The Mothman Prophecies* to discuss such weird and winged oddities? After I told him the story about the truck driver in New Mexico, John remarked, "But he saw the fangs?" I replied, "Yes."

"That's a great sighting," he said. "I don't know what the hell it is."

I guess we probably never will. That seems to be the way it goes.

Birdmen in the home

Tennessee has had other reports of Mothman-like creatures. On May 30, 2004, Sandy Nichols of the Alien Research Group in

Thompsons Station, Tennessee, and I were interviewing a housewife near Knoxville about her lifetime of UFO, alien abduction, and MIB experiences. She also shared a couple of intriguing Mothman encounters.

One happened years earlier while she and her family were living in a rural area of eastern Kentucky. She was home with her three young children who had gone upstairs to play. They came back down, pointing upstairs. She investigated and was shocked at what she saw. "It was big about seven feet in length, and it had wings," she said. "It was lying on the floor. It had these weird bug reflector eyeballs that looked like bicycle reflectors...You know, in a fly's eyes you can see those criss-cross things? Well, you could see those little criss-cross things when it moved slightly and the light reflected in those eyes."

Her initial reaction was one of being "horrified...It was like, 'Oh my God, I've got to get out of the house!'" Then she decided she wasn't going to let the creature think she was afraid, so she sat down on a couch and said a prayer while looking at it "in mortal terror." At some point she decided to leave the warmth of the house and step outside (it was February, and about 25-30 degrees outdoors). "So we [she and the children] ran out the front door and stood out there on that porch in the cold," she said. They were all barefoot. "Finally, I gave up, I was freezing to death and they were too. When we went back in the house it was gone. My husband was teaching at a community college at that time. When he came home we told him about it."

She was puzzled how such a thing could have gotten into the house and then somehow gotten back out. This sort of thing has apparently happened to a few others as well. Andy Colvin, in his book *The Mothman's Photographer II* (2007) interviewed a woman who had seen a Mothman creature hanging upside down from her bedroom ceiling "like it was a bat, with its wings tucked up. Its face was right against mine. It was black." For a moment, she turned away, and when she looked back it was no longer there. She said she wasn't scared of it but did want it to go away.

Russian born ufologist Paul Stonehill wrote of "flying man" stories from Russia in an article in *FATE* magazine (November 1992). In a community known as Petropavlovsk, a family who had been hearing strange noises outside their home at night discovered a strange creature underneath one of their beds. Initially the family threw slippers underneath the bed at the thing. It stirred and then a "very long trunk" came out of its nose and grabbed at their legs. Quite scared, the family began striking the creature with anything available. The children even sprayed it with household chemicals. The creature seemed to die.

"When it was brought out from under the bed, they discovered a creature that looked like a dog," Stonehill wrote. "It had very short bluish hair, two three-fingered paws, and strong wings, about a meter and a half in wingspread. The shape of the creature's wings reminded the family of a bat's wings. The creature's muzzle looked like a human face cast in plaster: an almost flat, clear face with small forehead, very large eyes, and a tiny lipless mouth. Instead of a nose, the creature had one triangular hole."

Fearing that they may have killed some state-protected animal, the family placed it in a ditch outside. Soon afterward it was nowhere to be seen.

Our Tennessee housewife, who lived in Bristol at the time of the next series of incidents, said she awoke one night to find a strange human-like being leaning over her, acting like it was trying to take her breath. She screamed and it disappeared through the wall near the window. She looked out and saw a large owl with glowing red eyes sitting in a tree. It flew away quickly.

She was convinced that a man in her town who possessed powerful spirit energies was attacking her psychically and could exert some control over her. "All the while that he was destroying my life, I felt ecstasy," she said. "I would have walked barefoot through fire just to experience that feeling.

"There were times when I just absolutely would burst out of my house at 3 o'clock in the morning. I wouldn't even know where I was going and I would wind up in the woods near where this man lived. A dark figure would be waiting. It had a long black robe, a pale face and huge wings, which I could hear flapping.

"I kept it from my husband because I thought to myself, 'He'll think I'm crazy for sure. Who has seen anything like that?'"

The day before the family moved out of the city the family gathered at a local park. The woman's husband told her to look up at the sky. She saw a clear bubble and floating inside it was the winged thing she had seen in her upstairs. Its legs were apart and its bat-like wings were stretched out. The bubble floated away over the city and disappeared."

The husband corroborated his wife' description, adding that it looked like a gargoyle or winged devil. "I had never seen anything like that before," he said.

That was the last time the wife saw the winged creature. Thirteen years later, her daughter saw something similar where she was living in Martinez, California. One night she was looking out of her window at the southern sky and San Francisco. She saw a rusty-red-colored creature with bat-like wings fly in circles over a Shell Oil company refinery. She watched it for an estimated five minutes. It glided quite a bit, occasionally flapping its wings. Finally, it flew off toward San Francisco. The creature seemed evil to her.

Synchronized steps

This family has had experiences with quite a variety of beings, including the extraterrestrials known as greys. In 1985, the mother, pregnant and suffering, had nightly visits from them Fed up, she decided to put an end to it. One night she was ready as three greys marched side-by-side in perfect unison into her bedroom. When they reached her bedside she leaped out and grabbed the grey in the middle by its the neck. It snapped, making a sound like a small twig breaking. The head lolled onto the entity's back. The other two greys held their disabled comrade up and began walking away backwards in unison.

Indiana ufologist Don Worley came upon a similar case where "a woman who had the ability to kick out at the beings in her bedroom, struck one in the face and broke his neck with a snap."

The odd marching of the beings is found in other cases as well, including one documented in 1978 by British author Andrew Collins. In September 1951, Sheila Burton was in her late teens and living with her parents in Brighton, East Sussex. She awoke early one morning to see a large disc-shaped craft land outside on the lawn. Next, three identical humanoid beings in one-piece silver suits disembarked separately out of three doors. They stood about 1.5 to 1.8 meters tall and had egg-shaped heads and pointed ears. The three walked in a straight line for about 20 paces, then stopped and walked backwards in a synchronized fashion. The odd trio re-entered the craft simultaneously, whereupon the large square doors shut. Then the saucer took off straight up and was soon out of sight. The whole bewildering event had lasted only an estimated 40 to 50 seconds.

"It was as if someone had hit the rewind button on a video machine, making the tape run backwards at an exaggerated speed until the gradually unfolding scenario had totally reversed itself," Collins noted. "Such absurd actions are not what one might expect of highly advanced extraterrestrial visitors who would presumably have crossed galaxies to be here, and yet Sheila Burton, who is a mature and sensible woman, appeared to be sincere and I found no good reason to doubt her testimony."

Following the Keelian "outside the box" line of thinking one tends to get a lot of things that "are not what one might expect." Mainstream "nuts and bolts" ET hunting ufologists have long been conditioned to seeing things in a very specific way. If the data gets to sounding too weird to them and not what they're specifically looking for then like the Air Force used to do they dismiss it simply as delusional or as a hoax.

On July 20, 2005, at approximately 10:30 p.m., my investigator friend Sandy Nichols, who had interviewed the Mothman witness with me in East Tennessee, claimed that as he was driving west along a narrow country road known as the Bethesda-Arno Road, near Thompsons Station, Tennessee, that he rounded a curve and saw a tall, slender humanoid form with what looked like "wings" standing near a seven-and-a-half-foot tall road sign. It was several inches taller than the sign. "The creature's arms were outstretched and attached to the wrist of both arms was dark webbing that extended downward and attached at the knees, and also was attached to the torso of the body directly at the underarm and extending downward to the knees," Sandy reported. The facial area was dark and Sandy was unable to make out details of it.

His car passed within an estimated seven feet of it. He quickly turned around and came back, but the creature was gone. He said there hadn't been time for it to disappear so quickly.

A few years later, on May 16, 2008, around 2:30 p.m., Sandy was driving south on Interstate 65 south of Nashville, approaching the I-840 exit, when he noticed something in the air emerging from a narrow valley and heading toward the highway. It was flying slowly east, about 150-200 feet off the ground. At first, he thought it was a small black crop-dusting plane or a large vulture; then he saw that it was a creature of some kind with wings instead. It came closer and "executed an almost perfect hairpin turn directly over the far right lane, picking up tremendous speed without flapping its wings. "At the same time its body tilted to the right and downward affording me a clear view as if I was above it," Sandy noted. Then he realized that it was yet another airborne creature with "the unmistakable characteristic shape of another 'Mothman' type creature." It disappeared from view in a few seconds.

Sandy noted: "The color of the creature's body was black, and from the neck down appeared as kite shaped; its head a rounded diamond shape and oversized. Its arms were extended outward; its hands at an 8 and 4 o'clock position away from its body on a horizontal line with its waist. A dark, solid web like material, similar to a bat's web, extended from both wrists along the arms to the armpits, then continued downward along both sides of the body past the waist to half-way between the knees and the feet."

In late July 2011, Sandy received an intriguing email from a person who claimed he had seen a Mothman-type creature over in Dickson County, Tennessee. He was about to leave on an out-of-state trip for a week, so Bret Oldham did a follow-up on the report.

Soon a certainly interesting and very unusual story emerged. The witness said the sighting had occurred about two to three years earlier, one morning at about 3:10 a.m. The location was about one mile north of Dickson, near Highway 48. Bret asked if the creature seemed to have noticed him. "Yes, in fact it did. Upon first sighting it, I thought it to be a hang glider out at night and I stared at it in order to discern its nature, but upon inspection it appeared as a large humanoid with a set of large wings on its back. About three or four seconds after I spotted it, it looked down upon me with large, iridescent red eyes and did so for about two seconds. Afterward, it looked straight ahead again and disappeared into thin air." The sighting lasted nearly eight seconds. The creature was "completely silent," and flew east to west. "Though hard to discern, the creature's wings looked roughly one foot longer on each side than its arms," he added. "The creature looked about seven to eight feet in height, so perhaps around nine to 10 feet, but this is just an estimate. All I remember is that its wings were bat-like and very large."

"The creature had well-defined arms and legs and a distinctly humanoid shape. The creature had a stark brown color to it that seemed almost iridescent, and because of this I could make out a silhouette. It was very muscular looking and had an almost chiseled appearance. Its hands appeared larger than a human. The hands appeared elongated and slightly claw-like, but large and vaguely human-looking. The feet looked human, but with claw-like protrusions where its toes may have been (similar to someone having overgrown toenails that were sharp in appearance)."

"Its head was bulbous and swollen looking. It was roughly one-half to three-quarters larger than a normal human skull. Its head had the likeness of that of a typical grey alien in shape. It was round but slightly oval in appearance. Honestly, the creature struck me as being overwhelmingly reptilian in appearance, with large leathery wings. I had previously heard of the chupacabras (not the hairless canine creature, but the reptilian looking humanoid sighted in Puerto Rico) and its appearance may be likened to that, albeit larger and more upright-looking."

The witness said he did not know of any similar sightings in Dickson County. He added, "There is a continuing saga of a type of hairy humanoid sighted in Montgomery Bell State Park (the "Werewolf" of Werewolf Springs) that Dickson residents have claimed to see repeatedly since the 19th century, though I've never seen this creature myself."

I was struck by the witness mentioning "typical grey alien" and "chupacabras," indications that he had been doing some reading about UFOs and reports of strange creatures. I wondered if he had had other paranormal experiences too, as some experiencers report, including some of the Mothman witnesses in West Virginia. I asked Bret to inquire about this and it proved to be the case.

"I am one month from 21 years of age, and I actually have had a very interesting life involving the paranormal," he wrote. "I started out roughly at the age of six not believing anything I could not see and being non-religious. I later on began to have a severe case of demonic oppression, and roughly all I remember was seeing/hearing things typical of haunted individuals, and a continuous emotional/mental dark haze that shadowed over me. I tried telling those closest to me some of the paranormal things I had experienced (poltergeist/telepathic communication of dark entities via dreams/seeing orbs of light move around/hearing voices audibly), but I was told it was imaginary, so that discouraged me from speaking out or seeking help of any kind, until one day. I thought I'd try to pray to God for help, and honestly, I did not know what would happen, nor expected anything to happen, but desperate enough to try. I came out of that experience feeling completely renewed and I became a Christian."

"My experiences ceased for a while but began to pick back up. I was about nine to 10 years old. Developing a prayer life helped me to heal from the more traumatic experiences in my earlier years and learning about spiritual warfare helped ward off these dark entities. I even began to have more positive spiritual experiences as well. Oddly enough, members of my own household had concurrently experienced some of the same things as I did, which I was not informed of until later in my life. Long story short, I have experienced phenomena ranging from being choked in my sleep (feeling a massive weight on my neck and chest similar to 'night hag') to what was already mentioned, to seeing fully physical manifestations of alien and fairy-looking humanoids (non-flying), and even four alien abduction attempts (note: I was not actually abducted, but they came so close that the final time they tried to abduct me I was dreaming I was levitating, then I proceeded to rebuke in Jesus' name whatever was trying to take me. Then I awoke (eyes open) and my body dropped back onto the couch I was sleeping on and bounced twice)."

"I do not drink or smoke, neither do I ingest any drugs or medications. I have never been tested for mental illness but have never been suspected of it or recommended for psychological exams. For a while I did have sleep problems out of fear of things like these happening to me, but from about 15 on my sleep schedule began to recover. My imagination is relatively sterile. I do not seek attention, nor do I make extraordinary claims without first thinking about the objectivity of said claims. I firmly do not believe that I suffer from self-fulfilling prophecy problems as I do not seek to have any of these experiences; they just happen. I also do not believe that all aliens are demons, but the things I have encountered were definitely of that nature (reacting strongly to exorcism/seemingly phasing in and out of physicality/appearing malevolent and attempting to invoke fear/harm/some of these entities appearing similar to grey aliens, albeit more reptilian in nature and tall). Though I can only speak according to my own experiences, I can say that what I believe has been influenced by supernatural experiences, not the other way around, and that the exorcising of said beliefs later on in life against entities that appeared has altered later experiences (such as stopping them in the case of negative manifestations/bringing about positive experiences). Furthermore, I understand that there is a more physical side to researching the paranormal, which I cannot provide much of aside from testimony, but my experiences have been largely spiritual/supernatural in nature."

Perceptions of strange flying humanoid beings, orbs of light, poltergeist activity, alien abduction attempts, and mysterious voices again presents the challenge of an objective and thorough researcher to document and ponder the entire mixed bag of elements as presented in this single case. It is easy to either outright dismiss the entire narrative as delusion or hoax, or to simply focus on only the parts of his testimony that are of interest to you and that relate to your specific field of inquiry. On the other hand, it is truly a genuine intellectual challenge to take a multidisciplinary approach and pursue the evidence trail wherever it may ultimately lead. Objectivity is the golden rule here and what these "experiencers" are reporting may be far more complex and perplexing than most researchers have realized.

"I no longer find them intriguing"

In 1993, Keel revealed to me in a letter: "Incidentally, there have been Mothman-type sightings in every part of the world. I no longer find them intriguing." He added that he had written two short articles on the subject in 1968, one for the British magazine *Flying Saucer Review,* and another for an American men's magazine called *Saga.* "Then I dropped the whole matter and went on to other things," he wrote. He noted that a few well-known authors on UFOs and cryptozoological matters such as Jerome Clark, James Mosley, Loren Coleman and Gray Barker "continued to promote Mothman for years." Then in 1973 his agent wanted him to "write the full Mothman story." He balked at the idea initially but was talked into it, and it became *The Mothman Prophecies.*

Keel knew that Mothman was not unique to West Virginia and the mid-Ohio River Valley; similar sightings in other locations had been reported through the years. Keel made reference to sightings in 1877-80 in Brooklyn, New York. Witnesses told *The New York Sun* and *The New York Times* they saw "a winged human form" with "bat's wings." It was black in color, and, according to one account, "wore a cruel and determined expression" on its face. In 1948 there were two cases of "birdmen" in Washington State. Keel compared these to Mexico's *ikals* (tiny black men who could fly); India's giant *garuda*; the Native American thunderbird, the Piasa, a winged dragon-like creature with red eyes and a long tail, in the lore of Native Americans along the Mississippi River; and the winged, red-eyed Jersey Devil reported in parts of Pennsylvania and New Jersey as far back as 1735.

"I continue to receive a great deal of mail about Mothman and things that have happened in West Virginia since," Keel continued in his 1993 letter. "Thousands of people have had extraordinary experiences all over the country which match the experiences of the people in Point Pleasant. They write long letters of appreciation after reading my book."

In the March 1976 edition of *FATE* magazine, Virginia Miller of Elmer, New York, wrote a letter saying that after reading a book review of *The Mothman Prophecies* she was reminded of an experience with a Mothman-type creature that her father had had, of all times, on Halloween night in 1974. They had not ever heard of Mothman until nearly a year after her father's own experience.

Her father was outside their house that night watching for overzealous trick or treaters when he felt a compulsion to go to the backyard where his daughter Virginia had recently had a miniature replica of Stonehenge constructed with cement blocks. Stumbling over a low garden fence, he fell to his knees, got up and approached the miniature Stonehenge. Suddenly, over nearby treetops, Miller was startled to see a human-like figure. A fellow researcher visited the Miller's and learned that atop its long neck sat a "large grotesque head" with a "turtle-like face" with "glowing eyes." It had a 9- to 10-foot wingspan, "leathery skin," and it was gliding down towards him. The creature came close and then suddenly veered back towards the woods.

Virginia felt that her father had been protected from the winged "gargoyle" because a friend trained in the ancient Celtic traditions

146

had blessed the site with an old Celtic blessing. Like the people chronicled by Keel, she and her parents were "plagued by various misfortunes for months" after the encounter. Like so many of the Mothman witnesses Keel had interviewed, my friend discovered that the Millers had a history of various kinds of psychic experiences.

There is a tradition that the veil between the worlds of the living and the dead [or whatever lurks in the spirit realm] is thinnest on or around Halloween. I am reminded of Hakan Blomqvist's case described earlier of how on the night before Halloween in 1965 a couple in Sweden reported seeing "several small humanoids floating around their car" that had "big, hypnotic red eyes, just like Mothman."

In addition, the couple had reported "hundreds of UFO and ESP experiences." Blomqvist noted, "The woman is clairvoyant and when out in nature claims to see the little people. The woman has also met an Adamski-type humanoid on a boat in Norway. He was wearing a one-piece uniform and gave her several predictions about the death of Martin Luther King and some personal things."

In the 1960s, a married couple who ran a motel in Knoxville, Tennessee, were visited they believed by a dark-clad MIB (Man in Black)-type stranger with jet black hair and a complexion that was "close to snow white." The odd fellow visited their motel office on April 4, 1968, the same day as Martin Luther King Jr.'s assassination. Shortly before the man's arrival that evening, the couple heard the news about King's death. It was one of the first things that they had talked about with this stranger. "Good! I hope he dies," the stranger responded irreverently. The man hung around and engaged the couple in some very unusual conversation during a rather lengthy visit. The husband was even reportedly asked how much money it would take to get him to run naked across the highway.

Keel received a phone call from someone [he didn't state whether or not he knew the identity of his caller] in January 1968 in which he was told King would be murdered on February 4. The civil rights activist would be shot in the throat while standing on a balcony in Memphis, Tennessee. Since the Silver Bridge collapse and other psychic predictions that had come true Keel took this message very seriously, and even attempted to contact King by phone to warn him. "I never got through," Keel wrote. "He was not assassinated on February 4, but on April 4, exactly as described to me four months earlier."

It seems like this prediction of King's assassination was being broadcast far and wide.

1968 was, from a paranormal perspective, an especially active year for the Knoxville couple. One time close to midnight, around the time of the MIB visit, they had a close encounter with an eight to 10 foot wide silent rapidly rotating red glowing sphere that hovered for about two to three minutes and discharged a ray of light to the yard in front of their home. Also that spring, around 1 a.m. one morning they saw in the vicinity of Knoxville's World's Fair site another hovering red glowing UFO that moved toward them. When it came within an estimated 200 feet they got in their car. They followed it for several blocks as it slowly moved through the area, until it executed a departure "at incredible speed."

During the same year they saw, on three separate occasions, grapefruit-sized, white glowing objects in their bedroom. "There was no way a reflection from an external source was the cause for it, plus the objects lit up the area where they hovered, as well as displaying motion," they said. "In addition, people just don't turn over and go to sleep when some mystifying object is hovering in the bedroom!" While the couple may not have realized it, with "experiencers" that's a fairly common complaint.

One morning around 1-2 a.m., the husband happened to be looking out a side window of their motel office when he observed a hairless "black as coal tar" humanoid figure a mere 14-15 inches tall. They stared at one another for several seconds and then the mysterious figure disappeared behind the office, not to be seen again that night.

The couple had had unusual experiences prior to 1968. One night in the spring of 1961, around 11 p.m., they and the husband's father observed a "giant bird" with an estimated 20-25-foot wingspan sailing low over the treetops.

The couple offered me their own theory for things like Bigfoot and birdman appearances. They explained that perhaps it was significant that Bigfoots were again and again associated with bad smells, and how rotten eggs (hydrogen sulfide) odors topped the list. They wondered if this was due to a hibernation process and that perhaps it was "suggestive of the fossil fuels such as crude, natural gas and coal."

"There is a significant number of pieces of evidence that certain creatures have survived protracted hibernation," they said. They recalled reading odd published stories of small creatures like a frog that had been sealed up that came back to life after being released from marble. They recalled another story of an unknown creature that was allegedly discovered by miners embedded in coal. Initially it was alive and lived a short period after it was removed from the coal. After awhile though it died and seemed to dissolve, leaving only a residue.

Though such stories sound outrageous, there seem to be sufficient documented accounts to lend credibility to this. Jerome Clark's thought-provoking book *UNEXPLAINED! Strange Sightings, Incredible Occurrences, and Puzzling Physical Phenomena* (2013) contains an excellent chapter entitled "Entombed Animals," that describes impressive accounts of frogs and toads trapped for years in stone, and even a turtle that impossibly (so it would seem) survived being entrapped in concrete. "Nothing about this phenomenon makes any kind of sense," Clark remarked, in conclusion. "It seems to defy not only natural but even any conceivable outlandish explanation. Of the phenomenon all we can do is to acknowledge that while it is entirely impossible, it apparently happens anyway."

In Keel's *Strange Creatures from Time and Space* (1970), he quoted from an article that originated from the *Illustrated London News* (England) of February 9, 1856, about a strange creature that came out of a tunnel construction near Culmont (Haute Marne), France. After men blasted an enormous block of stone, a large goose sized creature with "membranous wings" staggered out of the tunnel and into the sunlight, gave a hoarse cry and collapsed dead. It had a long neck, sharp teeth, and a bat-like appearance, and when its wings were spread, they measured nearly 10 feet and seven inches from tip to tip. The body was taken to a local naturalist versed in paleontology, and he identified it as an extinct prehistoric pterodactyl. The stone from which it had emerged was from a deposit estimated by geologists to be a million years in age.

The Knoxville couple were unaware of that account, which added weight they felt to their theory. Keel had a controversial theory of his own for the physical appearances of these huge "monsters" and their sudden changes to ghost-like forms and abrupt disappearances. "The poor slobs literally melt," he quipped, with a typical twist of Keelian tongue in cheek humor. But instead of pinning it down to the hibernation process, Keel saw these various "monsters" as temporary creations, the result of complex and perplexing energetic and chemical reactions. Perhaps they were the thought form creations of mischievous ultraterrestrials. "Modern witnesses often complain that the monsters -- and some UFOs -- smelled like rotten eggs," Keel wrote in *The Eighth Tower* (1975), noting that ghosts and hauntings like the legendary Bell Witch of Tennessee are often accompanied by these horrible odors.

"Some of our funny monsters remain in an area for several days and are seen by many people before they finally disappear," Keel added. "Token attacks on domestic animals occur throughout the period, because the monster is somehow replenishing its diminishing energies with earthly animal matter. But it is a losing battle, and the monster must ultimately melt away leaving nothing but a terrible stench behind."

I found what I thought might be an interesting connection to Keel's ideas about "monsters" being temporary forms. In *Saga* magazine's *UFO Report,* Winter 1975, it featured an article by B. Ann Slate, "The Amazing UFO Discoveries of Peter Hurkos." Hurkos was a Dutch psychic who was extensively studied and authenticated by American scientist Dr. Andrija Puharich. Hurkos was famous for his psychometry ability where he would hold objects in his hands and was somehow able to provide accurate information about them.

In this instance, Puharich presented Hurkos with 20 sealed

envelopes containing various items related to alleged UFO evidence, such as bits of metal, ash, glass, soil samples, chemical compounds, and photographs, to see what he might be able to reveal using his documented powers of psychometry. One envelope held a picture of a large three-toed Bigfoot plaster casting sent by ufologist Stan Gordon, who had come across a number of these odd prints in his home state of Pennsylvania.

"Because of the mounting evidence and eyewitness accounts, it was Gordon's opinion that there might be a connection between UFOs and the hairy giants roaming the area," Slate wrote. "When Hurkos lightly touched the unopened envelope containing the print, he almost shouted his response. 'No! No! It is not complete!'"

"We asked if he meant the photograph had been improperly taken or if something within the envelope had been faked. We were in for a shock!"

"'This is not a trick photo. This is an alien!' the psychic announced with conviction. 'When other planet people die, it is not like our bodies decompose. They [the aliens] dry up, like powder, like flour! This creature from the photo is in the process of drying up but is not dried up completely!'"

"Hurkos ripped open the envelope and looked at the photo. He reached for a pen and rapidly drew two other toes on the print."

The psychic's explanation sounded very Keelian!

TEN
TIMOTHY FRICK, A MONSTER SLEUTH

Timothy Frick (left) and John Keel (right) enjoying lunch and conversation at West Virginia's Mothman Festival in 2003.

Timothy Frick of Cumberland, Maryland, is a writer, cryptozoologist, and an MIB impersonator (who the MIB may have impersonated!). Well, they say that imitation is the sincerest form of flattery. Tim read *The Mothman Prophecies* in 1991. "We have a monster in our neighboring state of West Virginia," Tim thought at the time. "That's pretty cool." The book ignited within him an intense curiosity about Mothman. "The Internet came along in the late 1990s and I studied up on cryptozoological creatures on the Internet. It was very interesting."

"I am an aspiring writer," Tim said. In 1985 and 1986, he created several fictional vampire characters and decided to present them in a comic book. "I created the characters and I wrote the stories, and I had to pay someone to illustrate them," he told me. "I paid like thousands of dollars to have a couple of issues produced and sold a handful of copies. That really didn't get me anywhere. I'm now trying to become a novelist, although I'm unpublished as far as that goes."

One day a friend called Tim and told him that West Virginia's Point Pleasant was having its first Mothman Festival in November 2002, on a weekend that would commemorate the famous initial encounters of two young couples, Roger and Linda Scarberry and Steve and Mary Mallette that started it all 36 years earlier on November 15, 1966. "It was the first one I went to," he said. John Keel was a guest of honor at the 2003 Mothman Festival, the following year. "I had dinner with him two or three times. I hung out with him and talked with him for a total of probably eight hours. He was a fascinating person and was very pleasant to talk with."

Over the years, Tim and John have become regulars at the annual Mothman Festival. They became good friends with the organizers and major players in the Mothman saga, mingled with the numerous and regular participants as well, and made some rather unique contributions of their own to these annual events. For the nighttime hayrides through the TNT area where Mothman was first seen, Tim and John created a life-sized figure of Mothman and rigged it on a pulley, sending it flying over the heads of startled and amused hay riders.

Tim and John also impersonate the Men in Black at the festival and have appeared in Mothman documentaries. Jeff Wamsley, author of *Mothman: The Facts Behind the Legend* (2002), co-authored with Donnie Sergent Jr., and *Mothman: Behind The Red Eyes* (2005), and a principle organizer of the festival, called them whenever a film crew came to town and they needed MIB actors. Recalling how it began, Tim said, "My brother and I got our first gig as the Men in Black for the Travel Channel in August of 2005. We didn't start appearing as the Men in Black at the Mothman Festival until two months later in September of 2005."

In August 2006, they played the Men in Black for the Sci-Fi (now Syfy) Channel, for a Mothman episode for *Sci-Fi Investigates*. Later they played the MIB for the Biography Channel. For all three networks, they flew their life-sized Mothman figure to be included in the filming.

Tim and John became close friends with Mothman witness Linda Scarberry. Often when they were in town and Linda was needed for an interview, Tim and John would provide her transportation. "She doesn't like talking about the Mothman a lot, because she said that she's afraid if she talks about it too much, it might bring it back," Tim said."

For Tim Frick and his brother John, it's not all just fun and games. They have a serious interest in the stories and the investigative work that Keel chronicled in his various articles and books. I asked Tim why he felt ufologists at the time didn't take Keel's work more seriously. "When it comes to UFOs there are two kinds of researchers," he pointed out. "There are the 'nuts and bolts' type where it's a physical craft from another planet, and then you have the kind like Keel who thought they're not just coming from another planet, they may be coming from another dimension. I think that a lot of people couldn't really wrap their mind around that."

For Tim it's more than personal. Not only has he confronted the eerie and unexplained in his own life journey (in fact, a number of times in Point Pleasant) but one puzzling incident has left the

MIB impersonator wondering if maybe the real MIB might have impersonated him and his fellow impersonator brother John!

"My brother John and I had visited a female friend of ours (Shirley) in northeastern Ohio back around midnight Friday, November 3, 2006," Tim recalled. "The following weekend, our friend sent John an email, asking if we had come back to her neighborhood since we had last visited with her, and John told her we hadn't. She then told my brother that a few nights before, probably Wednesday or Thursday night, while she was out walking her dog, a vehicle pulled into the church parking lot across the street from her house, and two tall guys got out. She thought that they were me and John, and she watched them until she noticed that they were watching her. This gave her the creeps, so she went back into her house and watched them from behind closed blinds. Shortly, another vehicle pulled into the lot, a man got out and talked to the two men who were already there (who, I remember, Shirley said were walking funny). Then the three people got into their vehicles and drove away. The following day, Shirley was checking out a baby monitor that she was planning to sell. There's something about baby monitors that allows them to pick up calls made by portable phones. What she heard was a conversation between two of her neighbors where one told the other that her (the speaker's) son had seen some suspicious activity in the church parking lot, so he pulled into the lot and asked the two guys what they were doing. Shirley then heard on the baby monitor that the two mysterious figures told her neighbor's son that their names were Tim and John, and that they were paranormal investigators. Well, whoever they were, it wasn't us. When my brother told me this story, I was blown away and said, 'Wow! We impersonated the men in black and now they're impersonating us!' Most people would be really freaked out by this, but I look at it like a badge of honor. The MIB posed as John Keel back in the 60s when he was investigating the Mothman sightings in Point Pleasant. Now they were posing as us. It's like Alan Bates' character Alexander Leek said in *The M333othman Prophecies* film. 'We noticed them, and they noticed that we noticed them.'

"Now I just remembered a small, but perhaps very significant detail regarding that trip. This particular occurrence happened the day after we visited and I had talked to Shirley in the church parking lot across the street from her house. (Actually, it may have been later the same day, since it was around midnight Friday that we were talking with her). After leaving her on Saturday (the date being November 4, 2006) we drove on to another city in Ohio and on the way there, we saw a white van with slightly shaded windows come up behind us, then pass us, and through the windows we could see three or four men in three piece suits (we didn't notice if any of them were wearing sunglasses). When the van passed us, we saw that the license plate number read 111L, and above the license plate were the words UNREGISTERED VEHICLE (there were no other identifying features on the van). Also the van stayed within sight of us for more than half an hour, either in front of us or behind us, and we passed each other several times."

"While all of this was happening, my brother and I were leery of the possibility that the people in the vehicle could be Men in Black, especially considering how unusual the license plate was, with the words 'unregistered vehicle' being above it. Also, the incident where the Men in Black impersonated me and my brother had not yet occurred (this would happen about a week later), and it is interesting to note that, at this point in time, my brother and I had played the Men in Black at the Mothman Festival twice, and appeared in one Mothman documentary as the MIB. We would go on to appear in three Mothman documentaries as the MIB; one on the Travel Channel, the Sci-Fi Channel and the Biography Channel."

Tim explained that he visualized alternate realities as being like guitar strings. "Imagine a guitar neck stretching out into infinity with an infinite number of guitar strings on it. Our reality is like one of those guitar strings and all of the other guitar strings are other realities, where something is slightly different than the way it is in our reality."

He then recalled the experience of another lady friend. "She visited some friends in Bakersfield, California and they were driving along and looking for a diner. They found a nice roadside diner and they went in. The people were very friendly and for her whole meal, including the drink, it was like $2.50. She said, 'Wow, what great prices! We need to come back here again!' So six months later she was back in the area and she was looking for the diner and she found out that it burned down back in the 1960s!

"I can't really prove it, but I think that it's possible that everyone, at any given time, could switch over into another reality, or into something slightly different, and then later on switch back," Tim added. "Of course, sometimes they might not switch back. I don't know."

Tim had a personal episode that relates to such a theory. "It was around 1:20 a.m. I tossed my nail clippers onto the coffee table and when I did this, the clippers hit a pen that was laying on the table, causing it to roll towards the edge of the table at a 45 degree angle. I saw that my wallet, which was about four inches from the edge of the table, was laying a few inches away from the rolling pen, and thinking I had to quickly stop the pen before it fell on the floor, I went to grab it. Before I could move an inch, however, I saw the pen on the other side of my wallet, rolling away from the edge of the table, at the same angle but reversed, as if in a 'V' formation. It was like I saw a ripple in the fabric of space and time, where I saw the result of my action without having done anything. That was definitely the weirdest thing I ever saw."

"Minutes before I had experienced this, my brother John had just finished telling John Keel's niece, Nicole (who he was talking to on the internet) about time slips. Also, it is interesting to note that the day on which this occurred, September 11, 2009, was six years to the day that I first met John Keel."

Tim is no stranger to time/space anomalies. Steve, an alien abductee in Pennsylvania, brought Tim a couple of such experiences into his life. "He actually showed me a hospital report, and in the report it says that he has metallic objects in his body," Tim told me. "One of the places where he claims to have been contacted is the George B. Stevenson Dam. It's a place out in the middle of nowhere and it's one of the places that he had encountered the aliens. He told us about it, and so every time that we go camping up there we go by the dam. We first visited the area in June of 2004 and we'd walk across the dam and there was a road for utility vehicles on the other side of the dam. It went a couple of hundred yards and then it dead ended at the base of a mountain. Me and my brother, we were there and followed the road to the base of the mountain. I said, 'That's weird. The road just dead ends at the base of the mountain. Why would they do that?' I also remember seeing it like this probably at least a half a dozen times."

"About a year later, we were at the dam with some friends of ours and we were hanging out watching for UFOs and watching the stars, and we were sitting on the other side of the dam where the gravel road starts. I had to take a leak, so I walked down to the end of the road to do my business and then came back. While I was gone, there was a vehicle that was driving down the road, and it was making some kind of real unearthly type noise, and one of our friends said, 'What is that noise?' John said, 'It's probably a car with squealing brakes' or something like that. I didn't hear it, but they heard it. Then I came back to where they were. The next day, we went back to the dam and our friend had John take some pictures of the area, to help document what they heard the previous night. Anyway, sometime during a future visit to the dam, I walked down to the end of the road that supposedly dead ends at the base of the mountain and I noticed that the road wrapped around and went down to the lake front and I said, 'Cool. They finally did something with the road so that it doesn't dead end at the base of the mountain anymore.'"

"Later I went and talked to one of the park rangers and I asked,

'When was the road put in at George B. Stevenson Dam that goes down to the lake front?' This was probably a couple of months later and I fully expected the park ranger to tell me that it was put in over the winter, or over the last couple of months, and the person told me that the road was put in when the dam was first built back in the 1950s.

"I have a clear recollection of the road not being there, and I also remember that I had made a comment to my brother about the road dead ending at the base of the mountain, and had posed the question, 'Why don't they do something with it?' I recall saying these actual words, and while my brother doesn't remember the details of the landscape, he does remember me making this statement. Also I mentioned that one of our friends had my brother take some pictures of the area. Well, one of the pictures he took shows the gravel road stretching into the distance, and if you look closely, you can see the road curve at the end. This was not there the previous night. I think the car with the squealing brakes, while not directly responsible for the time slip, was a part of the phenomena. Also, it's scary to think that if I had tarried at the end of the road, I might not have made it back to the reality I was supposed to be in, or worse yet, without knowing it, I could have switched places with a version of me from a different reality like something from an episode of *The Twilight Zone,* and the other 'me' could have taken my place in this reality."

"It's like I said about the guitar neck stretching into infinity. Our reality is one of those strings and all the other strings are other realities, with there being minute differences from reality to reality."

Tim remembered another odd experience he had in connection with Steve. "Back in 2008, he didn't have a phone and he doesn't have the Internet," he explained. "At the time, the only way to contact the guy was through writing letters through the mail. So he had written me a letter to set up a time that we could go camping, and he wanted to go camping on the 15th of August. When I wrote him back, I had the letter written a week before I had sent it, and me and my brother were going out of town and I was thinking, 'Should I mail the letter now, or should I wait and mail it when I return?' And I thought, 'What the heck. I'll just hold on to it and mail it when I get back.' And so we went out of town over the weekend. On Monday, August 4th, I went and mailed the letter at the post office, and in the letter I told Steve that the 15th wasn't good for me, how about the 22nd, and the very next day in the mail I got a letter from Steve wherein he specifically told me that August 22nd doesn't work for him, and that he was hoping I could make it on the 15th. The thing is, I had just mailed my letter to him the previous day and I got the reply on the very next day. The letter didn't have a postmark on it at all; it was stamped, but no postmark, and I had previously gotten letters from Steve that were postmarked three days prior to when I received them, so when he sends me a letter, it takes about three days to reach me. He lives somewhere in Pennsylvania and so, naturally, it's safe to assume that when I mail him something, it takes him three days to get it. He wrote me a seven-page letter (both sides), and on page two he told me that August 22nd wouldn't work for him. Then he went on to write another five pages. I mailed him the letter on Monday and I got his reply the very next day."

"I was totally blown away. I thought, 'How is this possible?' Then I thought, 'Say, wait a minute. This is the guy who claims to be an alien abductee. He experiences all kinds of weird stuff. This just adds validity to his claims.' I think what had happened was this. Remember I said that I had written the letter a week in advance and I was wondering if I should mail it, or just hold onto it and mail it when I got back? I think what happened was that in another reality I had mailed it a week in advance. In that reality, Steve had gotten the letter, wrote a reply, and mailed it back to me, and I had crossed over into that other reality. This explanation, as strange as it sounds, would give Steve time to write the seven-page letter and send it to me."

Time slips and other high-strangeness and weirdness aside, Tim also has had his own sightings of curious things airborne that have occasionally made him stop and ponder their meaning in the ultimate scheme of these things. "The very first time we went to Point Pleasant, back on August 18, 2002, me, my brother John, and our best friend Danny checked into the Blue Fountain motel [John Keel stayed there during his visits back in the 1960s] across the river in Ohio. It was around 11:30 at night," Tim recalled. "I said, 'Let's go to the TNT area. I've read all about it and I want to go and check it out.' Initially John was reluctant, as he had done most of the driving and was worn out, but Danny was for it, and pretty soon they both managed to talk him into it. "We were walking around and found one of the igloos," Tim said. "It was right around midnight. I was facing the igloo, and my brother John and our friend Danny had their backs to it. All of a sudden, I saw this object shooting across the sky. It looked like a meteor in the earth's atmosphere. It had a white head with flames shooting out of the back of it. I measured it out with my fingers and my thumb and it was like four inches long at arm's length. It was flying from right to left, which was north to south, parallel with the Ohio River."

"For a couple of years, I thought that was a meteor I had seen. Then I remembered that John Keel, in one of his books, said that sometimes UFOs will disguise themselves as planes or meteors. So I was thinking, 'Wow, I wonder if that could have been a UFO I saw?' Now I tend to think that it was. Keel also believed that UFOs would often travel along rivers and I thought it was a bit strange that I would see something spectacular the very first time I visited the TNT area."

"Now flash forward on to September 2007. It was a week after the Mothman Festival. I was contacted by the Biography Channel and they wanted our help with their documentary. So my brother and I drove to Point Pleasant from where we live in Cumberland, Maryland. It was the night of the 20th. After the day's shooting was over, and we were hanging out with friends at the TNT area; a friend named Brian and I were walking along igloo road #1. It was around 1:15 a.m. We were near the end of the road. I saw something shining from behind the tree cover. The first thing I thought was, 'Wow, is this a shooting star?' I took a couple of steps backwards and I saw this object, and from the best of my estimation the thing was like an inch and a half long at arm's length. It was rectangular, with very sharply defined edges on the front, and it had a huge tail behind it. We watched this thing for probably 10-12 seconds as it flew over our heads. It was in the earth's atmosphere but there was no way to gauge how close the thing was. It was totally silent."

"While the rectangular part of it was like an inch and a half long at arm's length, including the tail it was like four feet long at arm's length. By the time we saw this object, it was probably around 1:25 or close to 1:30 in the morning. It was moving south to north, angling toward the northwest. We ran back but my brother and our other friend with him didn't see it. It was kind of surprising because we thought that if we had seen it then they would have too, but they didn't. By the way, I was on the exact same road that I was on when I saw the 'meteor' back in 2002."

Tim also believes that he may have witnessed the legendary thunderbird on more than one occasion. "I had two (possibly three) thunderbird sightings," Tim stated. "Thunderbirds are large eagle-like creatures with wingspans anywhere from 10 to 25 feet. My thunderbird sightings all took place in 2004. Two in the summer and one in the fall.

"My first sighting took place on June 2, and happened in the afternoon, right outside my house. I was out cutting the grass when I looked up and saw a flying creature that appeared to have bat wings about 50 to 60 feet away from me. When I saw it, I figured whatever it was had a wingspan of at least 10 feet. Unfortunately, I only saw it for about two seconds before it disappeared behind some trees. Because I only saw it for a few seconds and wasn't able to observe it longer, I am skeptical of what I think I saw."

"The second sighting took place on July 18, near Linn Run State Park in Rector, Pennsylvania. My brother John and I had just left the park around 4:30, and within minutes of leaving the park, that's when we saw it. We were approaching an overpass (the top of the overpass was about 30 feet high), and about thirty feet above the overpass, we saw a bird that had a wingspan of four and a half inches at arm's length. I clearly remember holding my arm out and taking measurements by holding my thumb and fingers apart. This bird was big, and I'd say its wingspan would have to have been anywhere from 10 to 15 feet across. Also, Linn Run State Park is located near the edge of the Black Forest region of Pennsylvania, and the Black Forest is well-known for being inhabited by thunderbirds."

"My last sighting took place on October 6 in the late afternoon around 3:00 or 3:30 on Interstate 77 near Mineral Wells, West Virginia. I was in the passenger seat and was looking at something on my lap when my brother John (who was driving) said, 'A large bird just flew over the van!' I then quickly turned around and looked out the back window, and back in the road, about 120 feet away, I saw a huge bird soaring over the freeway, with its wings stretching from one side of the road to the other. Interstate 77 is a two-lane road and is about 22 feet wide. Also, the area where we saw this thunderbird was the same area where Woodrow Derenberger claimed to have seen a space ship come down, and Indrid Cold exit the craft. John Keel talks about this encounter in *The Mothman Prophecies* book."

"I would like to point out that in one of Pennsylvania researcher Stan Gordon's reports, someone driving on a two-lane road outside the town of Clendenin, West Virginia claimed to have had a close, visual sighting of a giant bird whose wingspan took up the whole road, which was about 21 feet. It is interesting to note that Clendenin is the town where the grave diggers saw the Mothman, about a week before it was seen by the Scarberrys and the Mallettes on November 15, 1966. Clendenin is about an hour and a half drive from where I had my sighting near Mineral Wells back in 2004, and according to Stan's report, the sighting took place in either late September or early October of 2007. I think this section of West Virginia, and possibly parts of Illinois, Ohio and Pennsylvania are parts of these bird's migratory route in the fall. After all, two individuals (myself and the person in Stan's report) saw them during the same time of year, near the same area. Also, my brother John and I were good friends with the late Carolyn Harris, who owned and ran the Harris Steak House (and who was also one of the main organizers of the Mothman Festival, along with Jeff Wamsley) in Point Pleasant, West Virginia. She told us that she'd heard reports from different truck drivers who claimed to have seen large birds fly over their rigs on Interstate 77, and I was on this roadway when I had one of my thunderbird sightings."

ELEVEN
ODD LIGHTNING, GEOMAGNETISM, AND SHAMANS

Andrew B. Colvin's *The Mothman's Photographer II* features a transcript of a rare lecture delivered by John Keel in 1994. Here is an interesting excerpt:

"I would always ask the police my usual list of peculiar questions. I still do this, and they always act astonished. One of my questions was, 'Has anyone been killed by lightning here lately?' This doesn't happen very often. It happens [only] 800 times a year worldwide. But whenever I asked this to police where they were having a lot of UFO sightings, their mouths would drop and they'd say, 'My God, how'd you know? Just last week somebody got killed by a lightning bolt.' It's a very unusual occurrence. In one town in Ohio, I arrived at the police station just as they were bringing in a body that had been killed by a lightning bolt. This was an odd link. There was something electrical going on in these towns."

As early as 1970, Keel had been interested in lightning deaths at UFO flap sites he visited. In his newsletter *Anomaly* (No. 4, July 1970), provided free to fellow investigators and researchers, he included of a case for which I had provided him details. His report, in part, was as follows:

"We continue to receive reports of strange coincidences involving our funny lightning bolts... The latest comes from researcher Brent Raynes... On the afternoon of Wednesday, June 3, 1970, Mr. Earl Whitney was found dead on the grounds of the Augusta, Maine Country Club, apparently the victim of a stray lightning bolt during a thunderstorm that day. According to the *Daily Kennebec Journal* (Augusta, Maine), 'said Whitney suffered a cardiac arrest at the time he was hit by lightning.' His body was found near a clump of trees off the ninth green around 3 p.m."

Whitney was 52, a World War II veteran and a deputy sheriff. He reported seeing UFOs on a number of occasions in the past. My friend Jim Carey and I had questioned Whitney about his encounters. One involved Whitney and a woman near an airport in Waterville, Maine, in 1945. Around 11-11:30 p.m., they observed the landing of a craft that resembled two aluminum pie plates attached lip to lip, with a dark band around the center. The craft had two bright spots lights on the underside. It landed on four landing legs and remained on the ground for 5-10 minutes. Afterward he found impressions on the ground left by the four legs. Years later, in 1965, Whitney was with two others at a Maine fish hatchery, where they observed a bright white disc-shaped object with a small blue dome-like structure on top, with lights rotating around the center, take off from a field. It was silent and moved off and out of sight toward the north. The sighting, which happened around 4-4:30 p.m., lasted an estimated 30 minutes.

Keel thought it was "quite significant" that Whitney had died on a Wednesday, as he had done a statistical study that showed that UFO activity, for some unknown reason, peaks on Wednesdays.

"The Force Field In The Sky"

I once asked Keel about the status of Florida's "Key West Incident," a high-strangeness event wherein a teenaged couple were struck by a powerful and mysterious beam of light that resulted in significant psychological and physiological effects and aftereffects, some similar to kundalini, including dramatic upswings in intelligence. In a letter to me dated May 27, 1970, Keel replied: "There has been no additional information on the Key West Incident. The investigator, Joseph Ule, had a narrow escape last spring when a bolt of lightning destroyed his study as he was typing a report to me. I haven't heard from him since." I later learned that Ule suddenly had an overwhelming compulsion to leave his study while he was typing. As soon as he went out the door, lightning struck, demolishing his study and the report, his notes and documentation.

Ule recreated his report in an article, "The Force Field In The Sky," in *Caper News,* published by my dear late friend, Ramona Clark Hibner, and reprinted in *Saucer Scoop* magazine (Vol. 4, #3, June 1969).

The incident happened on the night of Wednesday, January 1, 1969. The couple, sitting in the front seats of a station wagon behind a supermarket, were "suddenly startled by a hollow, deep, penetrating sound from topside, as though it came through a vast, long tunnel. ...This caused them to look up....[there] came down a rain of apparently concentrated hail, slow-moving, small needle-like pieces, which hit a compact area of the windshield, and front portion of the roof of the car....They both started to feel a sense of sudden warmth and the sensation of complete weightlessness as they felt an uncontrollable force tug at their solar plexus and travel upwards through their chests and into their heads to the top of their brains. They could not move. Tingling warm electric shudders and waves coursed throughout their whole bodies and an enormous sense of complete blankness came over them as their eyes were guided upwards without any apparent volition of their own – and riveted upon a brilliant, silver hued object, way out in the immensity of space."

"They at once clasped hands and felt a 'deep freeze' chill, like dry ice, and the inability to let go, just as intensely cold objects will glue to the skin and resist all efforts toward removal without tearing the skin. When this condition vanished, they bolted out of the car, looked all around but neither saw or heard anything." The male teenager, named Manuel Lopex, claimed that when they first heard the "deep hollow sound," that he had tried unsuccessfully to start the car, but it refused to go. "An inspection of the station wagon showed small pitting on the windshield and the front portion of the roof caused by the 'hail,'" Ule wrote. "Both Manuel's hands and Kay's hands showed the effects of their attempt to unclasp their hands. On Manuel's right thumb tip and Kay's left thumb, were cuts that bled."

An editor's note read: "We wish to express our appreciation to Pat Parks of the *Key West Citizen* for her help and cooperation in obtaining this report from Mr. Joseph Ule. The first publication of this unusual happening was written by Pat in her column for the *Key West Citizen*. Mr. Ule reports to us that on three occasions his neighbors witnessed UFOs over his house. He was asleep at the time."

A middle-aged couple came forward and revealed: "We were on Fleming Key at the precise time the paper said this thing occurred. [about 2 ½ miles north of the Food Fair store] We were very startled to see the hazy beam out of space directed to the area where this supermarket is located. The beam was hazy and the source of it was brilliant and it seemed to broaden slightly as it rayed earthwards. Also there were two civilian employees of the Navy with us; they were very perturbed when they saw what we saw and wanted to leave immediately. They did not like this and some of the other things they had observed at night on this lonely and uninhabited big Key. They said they were going to ask the Navy officials to transfer them to another job."

Ule intended to follow up and interview this couple, but it is not known if he did before the lightning episode, which may have terminated his interest in pursuing this investigation.

On May 3, Ule revisited Manuel. "He did not appear too willing to talk and he had a sort of knowing and far away look in his eyes," Ule noted in a report to John Keel. "He was very restless, and something seemed to be crowding him. Upon casually questioning him I discovered that he had done much, much better in school and was especially interested in electronics and math. In fact, his mother had already told me that he had been recommended for a scholarship. He told me he was highly elated about Kay. She had never been more than an E and F student and that now she was receiving A's and B's."

This is another area of inquiry that intrigued Keel: highly gifted children who had undergone strange experiences.

Keel, who had been on the lookout for "funny lightning" incidents, would no doubt have enjoyed this odd little tidbit I just found posted on a lightning site online (www.sky-fire.tv/index/cgi/lightning.html/#florida), where questions about lightning were answered.

Do we understand everything about atmospheric electricity? Based on the following story from the site's so-called truly weird department, apparently not. In 1991, two young girls near Bristol, England were playing frisbee. Suddenly the disk was hurled back at one of the girls by some unseen force. Then both were enveloped in some sort of "yellow bubble." They received slight electric shocks, were thrown to the ground, and had problems breathing. Eventually they freed themselves from their capture and ran home, quite terrified by their experience. The website attributed this experience to lightning, though you've got to wonder exactly what did indeed happen.

It is unknown if the girls underwent any significant psychological or physiological changes. It would have been interesting if there had been some follow-up reported.

British science writer Antony Milne, in his book *Fireballs, Skyquakes and Hums* (2011), stated that some people struck by lightning have reported experiences that sound like alien encounters. "Many victims feel as if they have lost time and find themselves recovering from the blackout a small distance from where they were," he said. "They seemed to have no awareness of what had happened. Dave Kezerle, in August 1977 while walking through woodland in Illinois, said he had a fisheye vision of being in a cylinder that was glowing with a 'beautiful aquamarine.' Then he felt he was being sucked up, and 'little sparks began to pop around me.' Another nearby witness who had to be hospitalized told how the intense flash had enveloped him 'like a flourescent light bulb, shimmering all over.'"

Interestingly, a number of people have reported acquiring psychic ability after being shocked by lightning. For example, noted American psychics Dannian Brinkley and Greta Alexander and Australian Brian Skinner. Holger Kalweit, a German ethnologist and psychologist stated: "The Greeks believed a person struck by lightning was in possession of magical powers and in tribal cultures throughout the world lightning shamans are often venerated and feared as the mightiest of shamans."

Keel had described how UFO activity was concentrated often in the same areas, which he called "windows," and how those areas often had magnetic deviations. He recommended ufologists acquire maps showing those magnetic faults from the U.S. Geological Survey, explaining how back in the 1950s they had flown specially equipped airplanes over most of the United States mapping such deviations.

Dr. Hynek: "John Keel may have been right about this whole thing."

In the 1980s, the Hudson Valley area of New York State was the scene of a wave of UFO activity, including sightings of black triangular craft. Acclaimed astronomer Dr. J. Allen Hynek, who had been a consultant to the U.S. Air Force's Project Blue Book, became involved. Hynek began his investigations as a skeptic, but eventually the evidence caused him to change his mind. During the Hudson Valley flap, he reportedly told one investigator, "You know, John Keel may have been right about this whole thing."

Many of the Hudson Valley UFOs were described as gigantic, football-field-sized, low-flying craft. They appeared at night over major highways. Hynek remarked, "When we're talking about an object that people are reporting that's larger than a football field, where do you put it during the day if it just comes out at night? How do you hide something that big?" Hynek was forced to ponder Keel's ideas – which had sounded rather wild years earlier -- about a "parallel world," objects from another time-space continuum.

I visited Hynek at his home in Evanston, Illinois, in September 1972. Hynek admitted to me then that he found some of Keel's ideas interesting, and he described a major "window" located on an Indian reservation in Yakima, Washington, where numerous UFO and Bigfoot sightings were being reported.

Jacques Vallee was contacted in 1978 by a man named Floyd Dillon, who shared details of an encounter he had had on an unpaved country road some 10 miles west of Yakima, around 4 in the afternoon, either in late April or early May of 1928! Seventeen at the time, he was driving a Model T Ford. As he reached the top of a slight rise in the road, he came upon an unusual silent craft about 75 feet in the air. It was a metallic hexagon-shaped object with a domed top, olive drab in color, and approximately 22 feet wide and seven feet high. It had a small window through which he could see the head and upper torso of a "man" wearing a dark blue uniform, who "would pass for an Italian in this world." The "man" was looking down intently at the witness. The craft moved slowly, then rotated and flew away at "terrific speed."

It sounds like the area of Yakima and the surrounding region have a compelling history of anomalous events.

"I pray on mounds..."

In 1976 and 1977, I twice visited a Native American shaman of Susquehannock ancestry at his home in Pennsylvania. He kept me spellbound for hours with personal tales of both "spirit" and ufonaut visitations. To him UFOs were not only interplanetary space craft ridden by space beings, they were associated with spirits, powers, forces and beings who materialize "to whom they will." Keel had long ago written of UFOs appearing in areas of Indian Mounds. This shaman constructed "prayer mounds," which he said elders had instructed him in their building since age four. Inside many mounds they placed crystals. "The primary purpose of the crystals in some mounds and other places are beacons to guide in the outer space craft," he explained. "Secondarily, the crystals have healing qualities."

"I pray on mounds and commune with the Great Spirit and the Spirit of Mother Earth," the shaman added. "We can communicate with powers, forces, spirits and elementals. Often they manifest to us in physical form. Sometimes only a voice."

Madeline Teagle of Cuyahoga Falls, Ohio, a UFO contactee with Iroquois ancestry, witnessed spirit manifestations in the Pennsylvania shaman's presence. Once she watched him perform a successful rain dance ceremony during a local dry spell. A cloud in the sky split in half and four beings appeared in the sky. She said one being looked "almost like a half bird, half human." Madeline had a prayer mound constructed on her property at a spot where, years earlier, she had had one of her first alien encounters in the form of a basketball-sized, lemon-colored ball of light. She explained that the sphere produced a clear voice that communicated how it was originating from a "craft" miles away.

The late Dr. John Mack, the Harvard psychiatrist who took a serious look at UFO abduction cases, featured a number of experiencers he had investigated in his book, *Abduction: Human Encounters with Aliens* (1994). One of his subjects, identified as Dave, a 38-year-old health care worker from south central Pennsylvania, whom he met in 1992, described a life-long series of apparent alien encounters going back to early childhood. Many took place around Pemsit Mountain, a site sacred to Native Americans, and associated with UFOs. At age 19, Dave and others had seen a UFO near the mountain, a story that made it into the local paper. He believed he had seen the dark eyes of a being looking down from the craft. From then on, Dave began to read all he could on UFOs and the unknown.

In addition to the Yakima Reservation, other Indian Reservations like Utah's Ute Indian Reservation have had concentrated UFO sightings. In 1970, Hopi Indians in Arizona were reporting a lot of UFOs and some Hopi traditionalists saw the activity as a sign connected with ancient Hopi prophecies. "This is all part of our religion," an elderly Chief Dan Katchongva told the media. A Hopi named Titus Lamson described a low-flying domed saucer-shaped craft over Hotevilla one night. The object's surface became transparent, and inside he could see a man with long blond hair who was dressed in a gray "ski-jump outfit." Many people were seeing UFOs in the area at the time.

In *Seed of Knowledge, Stone of Plenty* (2005), the late John Burke, an inventor with a university background in physics from SUNY Stony Brook, described using sensitive electronic instruments at such ancient sites. Burke found something quite amazing when he studied the standing stones at Avebury, England, especially the double row of large stones known as West Kennet Avenue. The huge stone slabs, which were brought from another location nearby called Marlborough Downs, contain black magnetite. Burke and his colleagues found that these slabs were aligned so that the south pole of each stone faced the next stone continuing toward a circle of stones. In the circular arrangement, they found the south poles were aligned with the next stone in a clockwise direction, except at the two intact entranceways where the magnetic poles align with the avenue stones.

Burke and his team duplicated the Avebury arrangement in their lab and found that airborne ions were channeled in one direction. He noted that this same principle was applied by modern physicists in Chicago's Fermi Lab, a powerful circular atomic accelerator -- although in 2,500 BC the prehistoric people of Avebury, Burke felt reasonably certain, had a motive and purpose that was decidedly different (i.e., altering consciousness instead of doing atomic energy research).

Tennessee psychologist and author Dr. Greg Little has an intense interest in ancient standing stones and earthworks. "The area around Silbury Hill and nearby Avebury is a hotbed of strange reports: UFOs, crop circles, humanoids, strange lights, and apparitional phenomena are frequently reported," he said. "Around 2006, my wife and I stayed with Andrew Collins for a week at Avebury exploring Silbury, the Avebury circle, and nearby sites. We spent several nights walking the standing stone grassy avenues leading for miles in various directions to different sites. Oddly, each night we observed small orbs of blue/green/white lights emanating from the hills running alongside the avenues."

Burke noted that elsewhere in England, Scotland, and at Carnac in Brittany, France, similar arrangements of huge stone rows lead to stone circles; the rows connected the stone circles to areas with water, where the air would have been easily ionized.

However, Burke had another idea as to what ancient mankind might have been using these alignments for: agricultural purposes.

"We realized that the geology below both Silbury Hill and Avebury Henge was special in another way," Burke told me. "Both were placed atop 'conductivity discontinuities,' something that sounds far more technical than it is. A conductivity discontinuity is simply the intersection of two zones of land, one of which conducts natural electrical ground current relatively well and the other less well. At such sites the normal daily fluctuations of the earth's geomagnetic field are magnified several hundred percent, and with them the telluric currents that flow through the ground."

"The way in which Silbury Hill and Avebury were designed and built further amplified this energy. Once we started looking at other places and other countries, we found out that this was the rule rather than the exception. Overwhelmingly, the ancient megalithic architects all over the world chose to build on conductivity discontinuities, and then designed and built these enormous structures in such a way as to further concentrate the natural electromagnetic energies present at those sites."

"We wondered how an ancient people without our fluxgate magnetometer, electrostatic voltmeter, and ground electrodes could have discovered such energies. But then we stumbled into a spot in the Black Hills of South Dakota that was both a geomagnetic anomaly and a vision quest site, dating from the days of Crazy Horse [19th century] and his visions. That's when we found that many sensitives, such as shamans, can sense these energies as well as our instruments can."

"Furthermore, we began examining the chronology at megalithic sites around the world, whether pyramid, henge, or mound and found that they overwhelmingly were built during a time of food crisis, and that after their construction the crisis seemed to have vanished. Now, at the time I was working for a company that enhanced agricultural seeds with an artificial version of such energies and obtained advanced yields as a result. I asked myself if the same thing might have been true for the ancient builders. So we began bringing seeds to the sites and the results were startling."

"We have used our instruments to examine henges, mounds, pyramids, and stone chambers in England, Guatemala, and across the U.S. While we did not get to France, and the oldest megalithic structures (circa 4,800 B.C.), a Belgian engineer named Pierre Mereaux spent 30 years surveying the region with the same types of instruments we used and came up with findings that precisely matched the pattern we found. For example, stone chambers we have examined in New England, starting just one hour north of

New York City, are structurally and electromagnetically identical to ones built from Ireland to India over a 6,000 year period. You cannot argue they were a cultural phenomenon because there was no one culture across that time span and geographic range. But they are functional. They are always sited on conductivity discontinuities, have a negative magnetic anomaly right at the entrance, and electrically charged air inside."

"Working at the New York chambers, we brought in samples of the same primitive varieties of corn used by Native American farmers from 700 A.D. onwards, about the same time period as the chambers were built. We would get statistically significant improvements in the growth rate and germination percentage of these seeds as compared to seeds left 100 feet outside the chambers and in the lab back home. The climax of this investigation came when we put nine samples of 100 seeds each inside several chambers and had them grown out to harvest organically by the same Harvard-trained ethno-botanist who had supplied the seed. The samples left in the chambers yielded double to triple the amount of corn vs. the samples placed outside. When you combine these results with the fact that most megalithic structures seem to have been erected at a time of food crisis, it becomes compelling evidence that there was a functional purpose to these things that would explain how you could mobilize a population to invest such vast resources in building them."

Burke learned in his investigations in Guatemala that the limestone Mayan pyramids were referred to as "maize mountains," and were often located near a cave. Even today Mayan farmers place bean and corn seeds atop these ancient pyramids, and then will later take them home.

What did Burke think was happening with the seeds? "At the time I was working for a company that enhanced agricultural seeds with an artificial version of such energies and obtained advanced yields as a result," he said.

Burke pointed out that neuroscientist Dr. Michael Persinger, in his pioneering work at Canada's Laurentian University had "confirmed that the magnitude of magnetic changes we have found at these sites conforms to those he has found capable of creating visions in volunteers in his lab."

The largest conductivity discontinuity that Burke had ever studied in the U.S. was at the Petroglyph National Monument near Albuquerque, New Mexico. "It contains thousands of rock carvings which are considered by anthropologists today to have been made by shamans illustrating their trance hallucinations," he told me. "I measured very powerful and extremely odd surges of electric current in the ground there. When the ranger at the Visitor Center heard what I was finding, she said to me, 'You know, periodically I get these 'New Age types' coming in here and telling me they just love to go sit up in the rocks and feel the energy. I thought they were a bunch of flakes, but you're telling me there might be something to this.'"

Here's my wife Joan admiring one of the large stones with ancient petroglyphs on it at the New Mexico site.

Thousands of ancient petroglyphs are scattered across a 17-mile long mesa that is composed of volcanic rock produced from eruptions an estimated 150,000 years ago. During a visit to the Petroglyph National Monument in 2008, I watched the needle of my handheld compass be deflected slightly by the tiny crystals of magnetite in the lava rocks. Of course, with a simple compass I was not equipped to detect the kind of electromagnetic fluctuations that Burke had. We walked part of the site with a shamanic practitioner of Apache and Spanish ancestry, who said she received an electric shock as we were walking up part of the mesa. Later she took us to a town in southern Colorado where there was an extinct volcano and where UFO and paranormal activity had been reported throughout the years. I wondered what Burke's instruments would have detected there. I suspected I had a pretty good idea already.

Keel found that there were noteworthy and enigmatic cycles and patterns that frequently reoccur with reported activity. "In our pilot study of 730 low-level UFO reports in 1966 we noted that the highest percentage of sightings seemed to take place on Wednesdays," he noted. (*Anomaly,* No. 5, Oct. 1970). "Recently, the American Flying Saucer Investigating Committee in Columbus, Ohio, completed an independent study of 929 UFO reports from the year 1968. They found that the highest number, 152, took place on Wednesdays."

Keel also referenced author Damon Knight, who had revisited the works of Charles Fort on wide-range of strange events. "In the course of his research Mr. Knight methodically indexed all of the major anomalies described in Fort's four books, some 1,200 in all," Keel said. "He then prepared involved charts and graphs, analyzing the material by years and types of events. Finally, he turned the whole mess over to C. L. Mallows of the Bell Telephone Laboratories who fed the data into a computer."

Keel said Fort's data analyzed in this way revealed "a number of clear-cut patterns." Knight reported, "I made a chart of all the data by years. I made charts of storms, charts of falls, of things seen in space and things seen in the sky. When I compared these charts, something interesting began to emerge. During the period 1877-1892, the correlations among the four charts are obvious – note in particular the peaks at 1877, 1883, 1889, and 1892."

Keel further quoted Knight: "The conclusion is inescapable that these cycles of activity which pass through our world like radio waves of enormous length, must have a common cause. The cause of the cycles, the controlling force that keeps them in synchrony, must lie outside the earth."

"All of this quickly leads Knight to the well-known Parallel Universe theory," Keel explained, "and, inevitably from PU (pronounced 'phew!') to theology."

A relationship between the pineal gland in the brain and psychic and religious manifestations has been known for centuries in mysticism and is studied today by some scientists. Keel saw the connection too and said the UFO contact experience was interconnected with the whole UFO/psychic/religious ball of wax. In Whitley Strieber's *Communion* (1987), the author expressed concern that his alien experiences might be related to temporal lobe epilepsy (TLE). A small number of researchers have been pursuing the possible TLE relationship to such experiences.

Keel had noted symptoms characteristic of epilepsy in his studies of experiencers. He cited a case in Forest Hills, New York where a 12-year-old girl experienced what he described as "hallucinosis followed by mental blackouts and many of the common symptoms of Jacksonian seizures." [which are described as simple partial seizures where electrical activity in the brain disrupts a small area and the person is aware during the seizure] He wrote, "She underwent extensive medical and psychiatric examinations and the attending doctors discovered she often blacked out when in the presence of flourescent lighting. Their rather far-out conclusion was that the girl's brain was 'tuned' to the same wavelength as such lights and their radiation directly interfered with her mental processes. The girl frequently saw and conversed with, beings whom she described as resembling Indians. She saw these apparitions in the family kitchen and in school. Fluorescent lighting was used in both places. Interestingly enough, her mother also saw these apparitions on a number of occasions but claimed they were diminutive. The girl said they were of normal size and form. The family has now moved, convinced that their own home was 'haunted.' The girl's seizures have diminished since she now avoids rooms with fluorescent illumination."

Keel speculated that UFO experiencers were being radiated by "electro-magnetic waves," resulting in a "pseudo-epileptic effect."

"It is probable that the same 'source' or electro-magnetic influence which generates some psychic-type apparitions also produces most of the UFO contactee experiences," he wrote. "Images, sounds, and other sensory impressions could conceivably be introduced into the brain by an electro-magnetic wave which bypasses the normal channels."

Keel was concerned that such possible EM influences could have detrimental effects over a period of time on a good number of experiencers, resulting in a "deterioration of personality." He noted that such a person "may develop obsessive-compulsive characteristics and become completely preoccupied with the contact experience. Such individuals devote a large part of their time to spreading the 'message' of the UFO occupants even though this may lead to the loss of their jobs and the eventual disintegration of their family life. They become 'space age messiahs' and willingly endure ridicule and hardship in order to advance the 'cause.'"

The 3 AM Wow!

"There's a phenomenon known to psychologists as 'the 3 AM Wow,' which is that time when you wake up in the middle of the night, you don't know why, but suddenly a solution pops into your mind to some problem that you've been struggling with," John Burke explained in an interview. "I find it interesting that that's the same time frame during the course of a day in which these energy fluctuations that I'm talking about are maximized."

Keel discussed this same phenomenon in his *Fate* magazine column *Beyond The Known* (October 1994). "If you have ever slept in a real jungle in Africa, Asia, or South America, you already know about the strange hour of silence that settles over the bush country just before dawn," Keel wrote. "Every morning, an hour or so before the sun comes up over the horizon, the atmosphere is filled with weird electrical noises – whistles, beeps, pops, hums, and hisses very low in the electromagnetic spectrum." NASA calls it "the dawn chorus." Keel noticed that many people specifically identified 3:20 a.m. as the "magical hour." Once he constructed a simple magnetic UFO detector with a loud bell attached, that he mounted in Ivan Sanderson's attic in New Jersey. There had been frequent UFO sightings in that area. After just a few weeks, Sanderson disconnected it, explaining to Keel that it annoyingly kept going off around 3 a.m.

According to Jacques Vallee, statistical UFO studies reflected that EM cases, physical trace reports, and occupant cases had a major peak around 9 p.m., with a secondary peak around 3 a.m. In addition, there's a sharp dip in body temperature at 3 a.m., and the pineal gland's melatonin levels reach their highest point at that time.

We often seem to be rediscovering bits and pieces of information that ancient mankind was already aware of. Hopefully, we can make good use of such recovered knowledge and information.

In the mid-1980s, my friend and colleague Dr. Greg Little was working in private practice at a mental health clinic in Memphis, Tennessee. He would occasionally use the clinic's Grahman

Potentializer for meditative sessions. "You lie on it and it focuses a magnetic field around your body," he said. "It also gently rotates in a circular fashion to mimic the flow of tidal waves." Greg had an out-of-body experience while using it. "I came to the edge of what I would call a hole into outer space. I could see countless stars. It was very impressive."

Then one day Greg introduced Lou White Eagle, a Cheyenne Arrow Priest, to the magnetic bed. Greg let the medicine man lie down on it and experience it while he went into another room to do some paperwork. "He suddenly appeared at my door and slowly walked in and sat down. He was in a sort of daze. There were several windows in the room and he said there were these 'little blue people' looking in at him through the windows. Then they came into the room through the walls and windows by just passing through them. Then the little people started poking around on his body. The experience shook him up."

Dr. Michael Persinger, the neuropsychologist with Laurentian University in Sudbury, Ontario, Canada, who for several decades conducted laboratory experiments on brain stimulation with volunteers (often college students), certainly did a lot of relevant sounding work. A volunteer enters an acoustic chamber and dons a helmet that produces electromagnetic impulses to stimulate brain sites that are sensitive to such energies, such as the hippocampus and amygdala, to try to duplicate the effects that might occur to a subject within the natural environment from plasma energy sources to geomagnetic fields. His volunteers frequently described visions of ghost like figures, faces, alien beings, angels, demonic beings, a feeling of the presence of God, and out-of-body type experiences.

Keel's groundbreaking work connecting locations with manifestations of UFO and paranormal activity paved the way for other authors. Paul Devereux, in his book *Shamanism and the Mystery Lines* (1993), described how mysterious lights have in some cultures been perceived as shamans in astral flight. In India and China temples had been built on sites frequented by such mysterious lights.

Shamanic astral flight

In fact, the concept of shamanic astral flight is widespread. Devereux cited a study by Dean Shiels of 67 indigenous societies, located on every continent in the world, which have had traditions of out-of-body travel. Devereux further explained that today there exist three variations of this experience: the near-death experience; out of body projection (Devereux included lucid dreaming in this category); and our modern alien abduction experiences. As an example of the third category, he cited a UFO case on the Yakima Indian reservation in Washington State in 1967. Five people were stranded on an isolated road when the car they were in broke down. During that UFO sighting five suffered a period of partial amnesia. However, one of them had a peculiar recall of being outside of his body, seeing himself and the others unable to move and looking up into the sky.

I don't believe such accounts are that uncommon. As an example, a man described how he was a passenger in his girlfriend's car as she was driving along a motorway near London, England. Suddenly a ball of light roughly the size of a grapefruit materialized between himself and the dashboard. Within moments he felt himself "rising up out of the top of the car. As I rose up I saw that the car had no roof then, I was just immersed in white light. I had no body; there was nothing to see. It was all just loving comfortable warm light. ...something was communicating with me telepathically." He said he had his "whole life recalled," which sounds very similar to the life review of near-death experiencers. In addition, he received, he said, a message on spiritual arrogance. Then he was suddenly back inside the car again; his girlfriend unaware that anything strange had just occurred.

In his book *Our Haunted Planet* (1971), Keel speculated that some UFOs might be "astral travelers" who are visible to certain psychically gifted persons as blobs of faint light in the night sky.

Other prominent UFO researchers such as Ann Druffel and Raymond Fowler have also speculated that the out-of-body experience could factor into some UFO encounters. Druffel first became aware of this during a hypnosis session she conducted with a woman abductee. "We were discussing what was happening to her and she said, 'I'm going now through the window with these entities,'" Druffel recalled. "'They are taking me through the window, and I looked back on my bed and there's my body lying there.' And she said, 'I'm not in my body. I am in an astral state.' If she hadn't looked back, she probably would have perceived it as a physically real experience."

While Keel was best known for his parallel world, anti "nuts and bolts" ET explanations for UFOs, in a 1976 *Saga* magazine article he did ponder the possibility of "time travel," and astral ETs. Considering the parapsychological evidence for out-of-body travel Keel felt it was "quite possible that intelligent beings in some distant star system may have the same ability to a very advanced degree."

Is such speculation over the top, or is it right on the mark?

In *Merging Dimensions: The Opening Portals of Sedona* (1995), authors Tom Dongo and Linda Bradshaw described some amazing personal experiences in the popular UFO-plagued Sedona area of Arizona. Mrs. Bradshaw's son, Victor, was asleep on the sofa one evening and awakened to see a tall, luminous humanoid being with a long blue robe floating through the house. The being soon floated right through a solid wall. The son got up and looked out a window and saw the tall being, along with a shorter being, crouched near his mother's truck. The creature looked at him, telepathically conveying that Victor should follow him, then lifted one knee, wrapped his arms around the uplifted knee, ducked his head, and became a ball of light, which disappeared. "Perhaps these are the balls of light we see so often," Bradshaw wrote, "and if they are, this would explain why we experience such peace when they are near."

When it comes to UFOs, Idaho businessman Kenneth Arnold was the person who became known as "the man who started it all" on account of his highly publicized sighting of nine crescent-shaped UFOs on June 24, 1947, flying near Mount Rainer in Washington State.

In an interview with Mike Clelland of the Eyewitness Radio Network, Arnold's daughter, Kim Arnold, revealed that shortly after that historic sighting a mysterious "ball of light" appeared inside their home. "That was shortly after he [Kenneth] had seen the flying saucers and it first appeared in my older sister's bedroom," Kim Said. "Then I guess it went down the hall and then it appeared in my mother and dad's bedroom, and my dad was so frightened he fell to his knees and started reciting the Lord's Prayer."

Kenneth Arnold also detected the presence of 'invisible visitors' in his home by noting deformations of his armchairs cushions, according to Kim.

"Toward the end of my dad's life he did an interview in 1982," Kim added. "He actually believed it was possible that the flying saucers were the connection between the living and the dead. He believed that possibly at the time of our death, that maybe this is just a different way we travel.".

"A New York psychiatrist once asked me if I'd ever heard of deceased people appearing in flying saucers," Keel wrote in *Saga* magazine's March 1976 edition. "He told me how a young patient, a teenaged boy, claimed to have witnessed a UFO landing and was astonished to see his late father emerge from the object. The psychiatrist knew nothing of UFOs and assumed the whole thing was nothing but a childish fantasy. Actually, however, there have been hundreds of similar reports although they are usually ignored by the hardcore believers in extraterrestrial spaceships."

I interviewed a woman, Shirley Fickett of Portland, Maine, who had a series of out-of-body experiences in 1969. She felt that some intelligence was "training" her in "astral projection." One time while she was partially out of her body, she thought she glimpsed her trainer – a non-human being about four feet tall, with a coconut-shaped head, two slits for eyes, a tiny slit where the nose should be, and no visible mouth. In another instance, she was transported down the road from her home to another house, where she perceived her father embracing a young boy. Then she was transported back to her house and into her body, whereupon the boy's astral form appeared to her.

"I held my physical hand out in acceptance to receive him, or let him know I did," Fickett said. "He then vanished." Not long afterward, she had a conversation with a stranger who told her his son was having psychic experiences. She became convinced that it was the same boy she had met astrally. She felt her late father's presence was connected with this young man, perhaps by reincarnation.

Then something happened that caused her to speculate about UFOs. One morning around 5:30 in late November 1972, this boy [name withheld but on file] was understandably alarmed when a beam of light came through a wall in his bedroom and pinned him to his bed. The hands on his electric clock spun wildly around, and a high frequency noise filled the air. The boy stated, "I felt like it was robbers but they [a voice] kept saying it was from Christ." Not long afterward, Fickett read the story of Israeli psychic Uri Geller's alleged childhood experience of being struck by a beam of light from a UFO, and when she added his similar childhood story to this boy's and the strange entity she had seen in the OBE, she felt there was a connection.

In an interview with ufologist Greg Long for the MUFON *UFO Journal,* November 1981, Kenneth Arnold said when he was a young boy of seven, he and others had seen a globe of light in the same room where the body of his great-grandmother lay in state. When he became a pilot and took part in search and rescue missions, Arnold claimed that he had seen similar mysterious lights at airplane crash sites where there had been fatalities. He described one case in which a family at a ranch in California had sighted two basketball sized balls of light soon after a nearby fatal small plane crash claimed the lives of two young men who had been on board.

Ufology has many such neglected accounts. For example, one of the most famous alien abduction stories involved a married couple, Betty and Barney Hill, whose encounter with alien beings occurred in September 1961 in the White Mountains of New Hampshire. From July 12-16, 1976) I was Betty Hill's guest at her mother's home in Kingston, New Hampshire. I heard a variety of stories of UFO activity that had happened in the area in the past. I visited the nearby home of Betty's sister, Janet Miller, and learned that Janet believed her home was haunted. Years later, prominent ufologist and abduction researcher Kathleen Marden, the niece of Betty Hill and the daughter of Janet Miller, shared with me an "orb" experience that happened at her mother's house in Kingston in 1983. One night Kathleen slept in her childhood bedroom and her five-year-old son slept in her brother's old room. Kathleen recalled: "I was awoken by a ruckus coming from his room, so I went next door to check on him. I was shocked by what I saw. He was romping around the room attempting to bat a light orb out of the air. I quickly picked him up and took him to my bedroom for the remainder of the night."

Raymond Fowler's *The Watchers* (1990) tells the story of contactee Betty Andreasson Luca and her family. In 1978, she and her husband Bob once found themselves in an out-of-body state at their home in Meriden, Connecticut. A mysterious dull whirring sound originating from above the roof over their upstairs bedroom had proceeded this. Later under hypnosis, more details were revealed. They recalled coming together and embracing, at which point they both found their OBE selves (which reportedly resembled their physical selves) rising into the air through the ceiling into a misty realm. As they were rising they were pulled apart. Betty found herself becoming ghostlike in appearance and then becoming a golden human outline of light, all other features disappearing. Then she noticed other "human forms" composed of light that moved into a huge round golden room with a domed roof. The light beings lay back against sloped portions of a huge revolving wheel moving in a counterclockwise direction, as though they were on a recliner.

"Those beings just seem to roll into a ball of bright light..." Betty said. Then, after a moment, the balls of light "changed back into those beings." The light beings, once again, were just human outlines of light, with no facial features or any other details. Then they went into a sidewise squat with arms out from their bodies, bent at the elbows with palms facing upwards. The beings had in their open palms bright lights of different colors and different shapes.

The first light being Betty described had a tiny sphere in one hand and a tiny pyramid in the other, while another was observed to have a curlicue shaped object in one hand and a diamond-type object in the other. Then the beings began leaping into the air, flinging these different shaped lights into the air as they did so. One of the light beings had a pole-like object that emitted a bright white light. One by one, the small lighted objects that had been flung into the air and were bouncing around were drawn toward the pole and stuck to it.

Betty had the impression that the light beings were enjoying themselves and it seemed as though they were playing some sort of strange game. As the hypnotic process unfolded it became apparent that Betty herself had been one of those light forms!

Madeline Teagle, a UFO contactee in Cuyahoga Falls, Ohio, described to me a handsome humanoid named Amana from her encounters. "When he appears, however, there is generally a brilliant white tube of light first," she said. "Then he just seems to form within it. When I have touched him in the process of deforming something like a sharp electrical shock runs through the area of my own body that is touching him. And I feel sort of as though the cells of my body at that place are separated, that they are apart and loose. Can see that this is not so, but it feels as though whatever part of me is touching him is not very well tried together."

I later found similar experiences reported by others. "Sometimes people feel as if they are coming apart in these UFO beams," Kathleen Marden, who had co-authored *The Alien Abduction Files* (2013) with Denise Stoner, told me.

Kathleen Marden, UFO author, researcher, and hypnotist

From time to time, from some of the most solid seeming "nuts and bolts" UFO cases, anomalous "paranormal" components enter the picture, as well as indications of interest in such components by members of the intelligence community too.

On the night of October 18, 1973, at approximately 10:30, the crew of a U.S. Army Reserve helicopter, a Bell Huey jet, left Port Columbus, Ohio for their home base at Cleveland Hopkins Airport, 96 nautical miles to the north-northeast. In command of the flight was Captain Lawrence J. Coyne, age 36, with 19 years of flying experience, with First Lieutenant Arrigo Jezzi, 26, at the controls, Sergeant John Healey, 35, the flight medic, and Sergeant Robert Yanacsek, 23, a computer technician. They were cruising at about 2,500 feet above sea level. They were a few miles south of Mansfield, and about 50 miles south of the Cleveland airport when a red light was spotted. Captain Coyne was not overly concerned, ordering Yanacsek to "keep an eye on it." Then perhaps 30 seconds later, Yanacsek reported that the light was moving towards them. At about 11:10 PM Coyne took the controls from Jezzi, putting the helicopter into a dive at approximately 500 feet per minute in order to avoid a possible midair collision. Coyne also initiated radio contact with the Mansfield control tower, suspecting that an Air National Guard F-100 fighter jet from there might have closed in on them. However, radio contact failed and even UHF and VHF frequencies suddenly didn't work. Later it was learned that all F-100 aircraft from there were on the ground at that time.

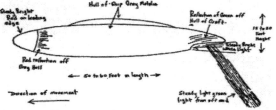

Dr. J. Allen Hynek sent Jennie Zeidman to investigate the case. Zeidman was a highly trusted former technical assistant he had worked with during the Air Force's Project Blue Book. In a summary of this incident, Zeidman described what happened next:

"The red light continued its radial bearing and increased greatly in intensity. Coyne increased his rate of descent to 2,000 feet per minute and his airspeed to 100 knots. The last altitude he noted was 1,700 feet. Just as a collision appeared imminent, the unknown light halted in its westward course and assumed a hovering relationship above and in front of the helicopter. 'It wasn't cruising, it was stopped. For maybe 10 to 12 seconds - just stopped,' Yanacsek reported. Coyne, Healey, and Yanacsek agree that a cigar-shaped, slightly domed object subtended an angle of nearly the width of the front windshield. A featureless, gray, metallic-looking structure was precisely delineated against the background stars. Yanacsek reported 'a suggestion of windows' along the top dome section. The red light emanated from the bow, a white light became visible at a slightly indented stern, and then, from aft/below, a green 'pyramid shaped' beam equated to a directional spotlight became visible. The green beam passed upward over the helicopter nose, swung up through the windshield, continued upward and entered the tinted upper window panels. At that point (and not before), the cockpit was enveloped in green light. Jezzi reported only a bright white light, comparable to the leading light of a small aircraft, visible through the top 'greenhouse' panels of the windshield. After the estimated ten seconds of 'hovering,' the object began to accelerate off to the west, now with only the white 'tail' light visible. The white light maintained its intensity even as its distance appeared to increase, and finally (according to Coyne and Healey), it appeared to execute a decisive 45 degree turn to the right, head out toward Lake Erie, and then 'snap out' over the horizon. Healey reported that he watched the object moving westward 'for a couple of minutes.' Jezzi said it moved faster than the 250-knot limit for aircraft below 10,000 feet, but not as fast as the 600-knot approach speed reported by the others. There was no noise from the object or turbulence during the encounter, except for one 'bump' as the object moved away to the west. After the object had broken off its hovering relationship, Jezzi and Coyne noted that the magnetic compass disk was rotating approximately four times per minute and that the altimeter read approximately 3,500 feet; a 1,000 foot-per-minute climb was in progress. Coyne insists that the collective was still bottomed from his evasive descent. Since the collective could not be lowered further, he had no alternative but to lift it, whatever the results, and after a few seconds of gingerly maneuvering controls (during which the helicopter reached nearly 3,800 feet), positive control was achieved. By that time the white light had already moved into the Mansfield area. Coyne had been subliminally aware of the climb; the others not at all, yet they had all been acutely aware of the g-forces of the dive. The helicopter was brought back to the flight plan altitude of 2,500 feet, radio contact was achieved with Canton/Akron, the night proceeded uneventfully to Cleveland." [nuforc.org/Coyne.html]

It was also reported that five witnesses on the ground had also reported the UFO.

According to Raymond Fowler, Zeidman learned from Coyne that about three weeks after the UFO encounter a man identifying himself as a staff member of the Surgeon General's office of the Department of the Army had reached Coyne by telephone. The man wanted to know if Coyne or any of his fellow crew members had had any unusual dreams since the UFO incident. Coyne responded that he had had two, in fact. The first one, which he said happened two or three days after the incident, occurred after he got up out of bed, where he had been sleeping peacefully moments before. He walked into a nearby hallway and happened to turn around and then saw himself still sleeping in bed! Frightened, he decided to return to bed and then laid back down. He felt a strange kind of "sinking into something" sensation. Then he woke up again, but this time everything was the way it should be.

The second "dream" about two days later was very vivid, he said. A voice clearly told him, "The answer is in the circle." He saw in his hand a clear, bluish-white sphere.

Sergeant John Healey acknowledged that he had dreamed of body separation. He dreamed that he was floating above what he perceived as his dead body lying on the bed below him. The only thing that upset him about it was wondering what would become of his two sons. For a while, Healey said, the Pentagon periodically called Coyne with new questions and asked him to circulate them among his crew. He mailed whatever information he collected to the Pentagon.

To Fowler, these Pentagon inquiries indicated that someone there possessed a detailed knowledge of the characteristics of the alien abduction experience. Betty Luca's experiences contained very similar elements, such as the out-of-body experience and the small sphere. In 1968, Fowler learned about a joint Air Force and NASA study of PK (psychokinetic) subjects. An Air Force employee working with the project allegedly told one of these PK subjects that their good information was sent on to the CIA in Washington, D.C., and that the CIA suspected a connection between people with psychic abilities and their encounters with UFO occupants.

Dr. Melvin Morse, a former pediatrician from Washington State, wrote a book entitled *Transformed by The Light* (1992), co-authored with Paul Perry, which explored the near-death experience. He explained that at the point of death an organism's cells emit an intense level of electromagnetic energy more than a thousand times greater than occurs when an organism is in a normal resting state. Is this biological evidence for an energetic upload to somewhere else beyond the physical body? Numerous spiritual and metaphysical traditions and beliefs associate spirit with light. I discussed this with Barbara Mango, Ph.D., an author and researcher who has collaborated with more than 20 other authors on a book entitled *The Transformative Power of Near-Death Experiences*. A few weeks before her father's transition, he told Mango he and a "glowing being" had hovered together above the foot of his bed and he looked down at himself on the bed. He had encounters with multiple beings of white/golden illumination, shimmery in appearance. "He kept saying they were waiting for him," Mango said. "He was so comforted by this and had such a look of peace and love." She described some dramatic effects, in particular his unexpected, sudden change from being an atheist to a believer.

With her father in hospice in Florida, Barbara was sad to have to return to her home in Connecticut, but before she did something quite interesting happened. "Before her shift was over, the night nurse grabbed my arm," Barbara stated. "In the middle of the night my father awoke and insisted that she play a particularly beautiful hymn, one that she had never before heard. She found the song on her cell phone and played it for my father. He rarely sings and as far as I know, doesn't know the words to any hymn nor religious song. Yet, he placed his weak and trembling hands in a prayer position, and while looking intently towards the ceiling, sang every word clearly and correctly. Immediately afterwards he said that he saw his name 'written' above him and was at utter and complete peace. The 'beings' were waiting for him! The nurse said, 'I knew there was a purpose why I was chosen to come to this house tonight. It was the most peaceful, beautiful evening I've ever had in my 35 years of hospice work. The energy in the room was so serene it was palpable.'"

In some instances, Dr. Morse said bystanders have witnessed light emanating from, or in the vicinity, of a person who is dying. He called such an event a "light shout."

In April 1977, while in Somerville, New Jersey interviewing Bigfoot witnesses, I was introduced to a gentleman who described something strange that he had seen while visiting a home years ago in High Bridge, where, sadly, a 12-year-old boy was dying of a brain tumor. The boy had a convulsive seizure, and a nurse stepped out to call a doctor. My informant and another man stayed and watched over the boy. As they stood by with concern, a luminous bar of light appeared over the child's bed. "It started as a minor light blue light, became brighter blue, and then turned white," he told me. "Throughout all of this time, even with the white light, it didn't show any brilliance on the wall. It then diminished and went out again, and by that time he had relaxed."

The boy's father was well-known UFO contactee Howard Menger! The boy passed away the following week.

In Russellville, Alabama, I met a woman, Loren Capsopoulos, who had experienced a dramatic "light shout" event in connection with the passing of her 14-year-old daughter, Catherine, on May 28, 2004. "She had myelodysplastic syndrome (MDS) up until May 25 when it turned into acute myeloid leukemia," she told me. "We were scheduled for bone marrow transplant the next week. Her condition was the first that St. Jude has seen in children because it was complicated by what is called Monosomy 7 -- part of the seventh chromosome was missing." Her illness had first been diagnosed only a short time before, on March 1.

"At the moment of her death, with 10 doctors around her, we witnessed a luminous glow which surrounded her," she added. "There was an enormous feeling of total love and everyone in that room felt it. Although the room was well lit, there was a strange 'glow' around everything immediately after they stopped resuscitation attempts and shut off the machines. And this had an effect on every person in that room. I've never had such a beautiful experience, even though that may sound weird to most people. It was like she was released at that moment and her essence flooded the room because that's what everyone could feel, this intense amount of love, because I found myself responding to people very calmly and saying things that she would have said to them. It was like she was talking through me."

"Afterward, I requested time with her and lay down on the bed and cuddled for about four hours. I remember I would periodically get this 'shock' (that would) go through me, like it was coming from her body. I was also making weird noises like she would do when she slept during the last week of her life. I thought that was strange but had no control over it."

Following Catherine's death, a number of peculiar happenings transpired at Loren's home: "ringing bells, an appearance of the largest rabbit I've ever seen, electronic glitches, shadows, and smells."

"One day my sister-in-law called our house and instead of the answering machine, she swore my daughter answered the phone and told her I was not at home," Loren recalled. "When she tried to question further, the phone cut off. I've also had experiences of someone touching me, footsteps coming down the hall, and visions. I woke up one night to a light coming from the hall near her room. It was very, very bright and a voice said, 'Be not afraid.'"

When Loren was 17, she experienced a mysterious light that reminded her of the light just described, as well as the light experience at the hospital. "I have always been a light sleeper, but wasn't that night," Loren said. "I recall being in a very deep slumber when I woke up suddenly, realized I was above the bed, became very frightened, noticed the bright light at the same time coming from the window. It was like I was bathed in this light."

Loren fell back onto the mattress and the light disappeared. She believes that this was an "actual levitation."

Accounts of levitation are always intriguing. How can it possibly happen? Yet many people have described it as an actual event.

Jon Thunder, a professional Apache artist, witnessed a gravity-defying event "around 1983 at a place called the Cut in the Grand Canyon."

"I happened to be at a circle, at a gathering of nations, and I met some people there that could show me another side of spiritualism," he told me. "If you've heard of the legends of the shape-shifters, people who can separate their physical body from a spiritual body and go to different places, and a person who really explains it well is Carlos Castaneda. He writes about don Juan Matus, a Yaqui Indian. So if you kind of know about that setting then we can jump into the setting that we're talking about. It's the same type of persona. The same legends, the same beliefs."

"So roughly in the gathering of about, I would say, almost maybe a hundred people...I witnessed a man walk a good 30-40 feet off the lip of the canyon out into the air. It wasn't levitation because levitation is rising from a platform. He just stepped off and it was like there was an invisible glass bridge. He stood out there and turned around and he spoke to us. I did not understand the words that he was saying because I'm Apache and this man was of Navajo origin. He was speaking old, old Navajo, and I could make out some words, but even if I could understand the words, I wouldn't repeat them anyway. But I did understand what I was seeing."

"There was no ingesting of peyote or any type of plant. Was it mass hypnosis? Was it the power of suggestion? I didn't go there as a believer. I didn't even go there as a skeptic. I just went there as someone who was interested."

In 2008 I did a phone interview with Native American author Dr. A.C. Ross, who was given the Dakota name Ehanamani (Walks Among) in a traditional ceremony. Ehanamani was the name of his patrilineal great, great grandfather, a Santee spiritual leader. It was an honor to talk with him in person as my wife Joan and I had both read his book *Mitakuye Oyasin "We are all related"* (1989). To hear him describe various parts of his spiritual journey that we had read about in his book was a wonderful experience. One story that I particularly liked happened in 1967 when he was on a Hopi Indian reservation, and he witnessed a Hopi woman dressed as Mother Kachina climb up out of a kiva...and continue to go up into the air. "The ladder comes out of the kiva and it only sticks up four or five feet," he said. "She levitated just a couple feet above that and I was gone. I was out of there."

Indeed, that must have been a startling experience!

TWELVE
ELEMENTALS ARE EVERYWHERE

"No matter where you live on this planet, someone within two hundred miles of your home has had a direct confrontation with a frightening apparition or inexplicable 'monster' within the last generation," Keel wrote in chapter one of *Strange Creatures from Time and Space* (1970). Nearly a half century ago that may have sounded startling. But these days we're working with a much larger pool of data and I can tell you that right from my own home here in the quiet and very rural Bible Belt of Wayne County, Tennessee, a good deal has happened much closer than that.

For example, in the 1980s I interviewed a family about eight miles east of where I live who claimed they were seeing a glowing white beachball-sized object moving about two feet off the ground, and luminous white human-shaped figures at different times approaching the house. They would disappear at about the same spot too. The family, which was quite religious, felt that they were quite possibly angels.

A paranormal investigator from the Nashville area named Marge described encountering an elemental type of being at Stones River Battlefield about 106 miles east-northeast of me. She told me how it happened on the anniversary of the Battle there, on January 1. "Three team members and their families joined us to 'investigate' the Slaughter Pen area," she said. "Within this area is a Walking Trail. I started walking this trail and about half a mile in, on my right, I felt multiple spirit presences. I walked off the path into a wooded area approximately 100 feet from the walking path. I stopped and sat down to see if any of the spirits would talk with me. I always talk to the earth when I'm out in the woods. Respect and connection to these energies help me to communicate at times. While sitting quietly, I saw a whitish blue light, no larger than a ping pong ball. My feeling was it wasn't a spirit orb. When the orb was approximately 15-20 feet away, it looked as though it burst. When the burst happened, a little, very thin woman appeared. Although looking human, I knew it wasn't human nor spirit. She was about two feet tall, white skinned and wearing a greenish brown gossamer 'dress.' Seeing her was like picking out a person in camouflage amongst the wooded background."

"Her eyes were dark colored. From the distance between us, I couldn't tell you the actual color. She just smiled at me, touched a cedar tree and disappeared."

The need for interdisciplinary studies and research becomes increasingly evident the more one delves into these strange reports. They fall into so many different categories, like folklore, the paranormal, the occult, cryptozoology, ufology, demonology, or the one that most psychologists and psychiatrists would prefer, hallucinations. While we are going to have different points of view, serious researchers need to agree to disagree and move forward as constructively and objectively as possible and engage in the critical task of comparing notes and engaging in meaningful dialogue.

One night in the 1930s, some 10 miles north of here, a young man was walking home after visiting with his girlfriend when he had a terrifying encounter with 'little men'! They had reddish complexions, long noses and wrinkled skin, and some had beards. He had nightmares about the experience for years and feared that it was some sort of "omen."

Weird creatures, winged or bipedal humanoids, are seemingly everywhere. Keel repeatedly noted they shared much in common with the mysterious supernatural beings occultists long ago called "elementals."

Keel was certainly engaged in the critical task of comparative analysis and struggled to engage in meaningful dialogue with other researchers, but too often they were too deeply entrenched within the limited focus of understanding and belief of their particular discipline and thus were often unable to think outside of that box, so to speak.

In 1975, I visited the home of author and researcher Don Worley of Connersville, Indiana. Worley is well-known for his investigative work and studies in eyewitness accounts of everything from cryptozoological phenomena like Bigfoot to ghosts to alien beings abducting people. He was a field investigator for APRO (Aerial Phenomena Research Organization) and a field reporter, he said, for the Psychical Research Foundation out of Durham, North Carolina. Soon he shared with me a report he had made of what some have come to call the "Vietnam Mothwoman," though Worley simply called it the "winged lady in black."

Back in 1971, Worley interviewed a 21-year-old military man about a bizarre encounter that he had had near Da Nang, Vietnam, in 1969. Worley had known this young man all his life. In fact, he was a step-nephew of his and he considered him a "reliable observer." He added, "He has no unusual interests or knowledge of the paranormal and had never heard of such a thing as this before in his life."

The remarkable incident happened before the monsoons in either July or August 1969, around 1 or 1:30 a.m. The witness described to Worley how he and two other men noticed something in the sky, that had some sort of glow to it, headed in their direction. It seemed to be moving very slowly. "All of a sudden we saw what looked like wings, like a bat, only it was gigantic compared to what a regular bat would be. After it got close enough, so we could see what it was, it looked like a woman. A naked woman."

"Her body was black. The wings were black. Everything was black. But it glowed. It glowed in the night, with kind of a greenish cast to it. There was a glow on her and around her."

It wasn't until the winged woman was approximately 10 feet from them that they could hear the sound of the wings flapping. She had arms, the witness stated, that resembled human arms, with hands and fingers, that were attached to the wings, but the way the arms moved with the flapping of the wings didn't look to the men like they had bones in them. The speed was comparable to a person walking, and while this being was flying over them it looked down at them briefly and then returned its gaze straight ahead to see where it was going. It looked as though, at its closest, that it was approximately 6 to 7 feet up and at one point it reportedly blotted out the moon for an estimated 10 seconds or so.

"We couldn't do anything," Worley was told. "We didn't know what to do. We just froze. We just watched what was going over because we couldn't believe our eyes."

The sighting lasted an estimated 3 to 4 minutes. The soldier said she was of medium build and that if she had been standing up he believed she would have been a little over 5 foot tall. When asked if they had reported their sighting the witness replied, "Of course, we did, to our lieutenant and junior executives, and they kind of just looked at us and then walked off. Like we had been on dope or something. That night, after it happened, we called the next post down the perimeter and asked them if they had seen anything in the sky and when they said no, what are you guys talking about, we shut up and didn't say anymore."

In 2014, I did an interview for *Alternate Perceptions* magazine with Cuban born ufologist Albert S. Rosales, today a resident of Miami, Florida. As a young man living in Cuba, he witnessed a metallic egg-shaped object with a beam of light that was being projected down toward the ground. Over the years, he has had a variety of UFO and paranormal experiences that have only further fueled his deep interest in the UFO phenomenon and in particular, reports dealing with entities who are associated with these encounters. He has collected and translated more than 17,000 cases from all over the globe, and approximately 95 percent involve humanoid beings.

I discussed with Mr. Rosales how Keel as early as 1969 was lumping these so-called "ufonauts" in with the elementals of occult literature. "Yes, a lot of these experiences I don't feel have anything to do with extraterrestrials," he said. "I do think that there is an extraterrestrial presence on earth. There appear to be either elemental forces or interdimensional beings or creatures that we see worldwide, in many instances, which a lot of people confuse with extraterrestrials, which I don't think they are."

"There are a myriad of dimensions and other realms perhaps around us, that at times co-exist together with ours and at times inhabitants of that realm visit us."

Rosales shared with me a number of unusual winged creature reports from his former homeland of Cuba, which of course brings to mind Keel's Mothman investigations too. For example, around midnight in February 1996, a man stepped out on his balcony in La Habana, to do some yoga when he reportedly observed a winged man-like figure with shiny eyes silently gliding overhead.

On the evening of December 21, 1993, at Caibarien, in the province of Las Villas, several local anglers were fishing at one of the offshore keys when they allegedly observed a hovering disc-shaped craft with several "winged humanoids" moving about nearby.

On the afternoon of September 14, 1952, near Remedios, in Santa Clara, a farm worker named Caridad Martinez claimed he encountered a winged yellow skinned, round faced being over seven feet tall that carried a luminous object in each hand. As he watched in disbelief, the winged figure rose up into the air and soon disappeared from sight in the distance.

One of Rosales' earliest Cuban accounts goes back to one evening in March 1933, in the area of Escambray, where a young girl, Onelia Fernandez, age 12, was reportedly picking mangos near a river when she was attacked by a tall, black figure with huge wings and large claws that was dragging the young girl, who was unconscious at that point, down toward the river. Family members armed with sticks and knives went into action and rushed the dark creature which released the girl as it fled the scene making loud screeching noises.

Keel seemed fond of the expression "the game is afoot," and the winged humanoids certainly set their feet down on ground all over the world. What are they, what is their true nature and reality, and where do they originate from? These are the kinds of questions Keel struggled to answer and which today researchers continue to seek the proverbial truth about. As Mr. Rosales noted, "I think that we are not alone." Well, it's either that or as one researcher once remarked, Carl Jung's archetypes of the collective unconscious have run amok! And, one might add, more than just a little bit!

THIRTEEN
THE ENIGMATIC MIB

In my early correspondence with John Keel back in 1970, he mentioned how numerous "pre-1947 MIB cases" existed within other frames of reference or disciplines that went back centuries and bore striking and noteworthy similarities to those of the ufological literature. For instance, he pointed out how noted ufologist Allen Greenfield had compiled "a list of references from books on witchcraft and the like, all describing rather typical MIB cases." He assured me that "the MIB stuff is not confined to UFOs at all."

"In earlier times, the manifestations were blamed on black-magic practitioners, witches, alchemists, the Fairy Commonwealth, the Rosicrucians, the Gypsies," Keel wrote in *Fate* magazine (Sept. 2007). "Now we know that whoever is behind it all has the ability to use advanced techniques of hypnosis and brainwashing."

Keel even pointed out to me and others how he suspected that some people were in a kind of mind controlled "possessed" type state, and surprisingly he was especially interested in Gypsies, explaining that he felt that they were rather vulnerable "as part of the possessed type of phenomenon." Keel has written that the

Gypsy religion is a mixture of witchcraft, black magic, and elementalism, and that Gypsies often drive black Cadillacs (a typical mode of transportation associated with the MIB) and how they have often turned up in active "window" areas during UFO flaps.

"A majority of our MIB seem to be three-dimensional apparitions," Keel noted. "While possessed persons can be made to play an MIB role, the 3-D apparitions are not biochemical entities. They are projections of a most sophisticated sort."

Keel felt that people with certain religious and racial backgrounds were more prone to the contactee experience than others. He felt that this was a selective process on the part of the intelligence behind these occurrences.

"The majority of our contactees have either Native American or Gypsy blood," Keel stated back in 1969. "If you are Jewish, your chances of being contacted are almost zero. We have very few Jewish contactees for some reason. On the other hand, we have a great many ex-Catholic contactees. So, the religious factor seems to be of some significance."

"But the Native American factor is the most important of all. If you live near an Indian reservation, and if you have the tact and ability to win the confidence of the Indians, they will tell you a great deal about the UFO phenomenon. They know all about it. A great many of them have been contactees for years and years. But you will have to go onto the reservation. You will have to spend some time there and win their confidence. You couldn't do it in an afternoon."

"Also, if you should encounter real Gypsies, and if you should be able to win their confidence, you would learn a great deal from them. They, too, know all about the UFO phenomenon. It is no mystery or secret to them at all. They know the whole story."

Keel seemed quite convinced that some very sinister, even deadly events were happening to people. In *Operation Trojan Horse*, he wrote of how a young man who was involved in investigating a wave of UFO activity in Ithaca, New York in 1967, one evening the fall of that year had gotten into his car to leave for a meeting, but then for some reason, that he couldn't explain, he got out of his vehicle and returned inside his home, performing a number of senseless tasks, like moving a book on the table up on a shelf. Eventually he found himself thinking, 'Okay, it's time,' at which point he remembers leaving the house for his car. The next thing he knew he was in a hospital bed. He found out that he had driven about four miles to a railroad crossing just in the nick of time to meet an oncoming train. "His car was demolished, but he escaped rather miraculously with only a few minor injuries," Keel wrote. "If he had not gone back into the house and carried out those meaningless, time-killing chores, he would have avoided the train altogether."

Keel encouraged me and others to research Gypsies. He cited a newspaper clipping that stated how Fred Lee Crisman had been "working with Gypsies." Crisman was a controversial UFO figure who played a prominent role in the famous Maury Island Incident in Washington State. Allegedly on June 21, 1947, around 2 p.m., a salvage boat piloted by a Harold Dahl, with his son and two other crewmen onboard, were in Puget Sound off the coast of Tacoma, off the east shore of Maury Island, when they reportedly observed six huge doughnut shaped craft that appeared overhead and hovered an estimated 2,000 feet above the sea. One of the craft seemed to develop mechanical trouble and descended to about 500 feet altitude. Dahl decided to head for shore when suddenly the craft discharged large quantities of silvery material and hot slag that damaged the boat, allegedly killing a dog onboard and striking and burning one of Dahl's son's arms.

Two Army Air Force intelligence officers from Hamilton Field near San Francisco flew in, interviewed witnesses and collected samples of the slag and then took off from McChord Air Force Base in their B-25 Bomber to return to their base, but sadly crashed near Kelso, Washington. Both officers perished in the crash, and the investigation after that became something of a tangled and controversial saga. Military intelligence and the FBI soon dismissed it as a hoax. An FBI teletype dated August 5, 1947 stated: "Analysis of the fragments shows them to be from a Tacoma slag mill." Jacques Vallee never found any data describing the composition of the slag. Kenneth Arnold, who looked into the story, stated that he saw the silvery material and it appeared to be "aluminum foil."

Vallee was very interesting in these UFO/slag cases – he had investigated what he felt were some reliable reports - and Keel was interested too. In fact, Keel even pointed out how a century earlier, slag inexplicably fell from out of the sky over Darmstadt, Germany, on June 7, 1846!

Curiously, Crisman had written Ray Palmer, editor of the science fiction magazine *Amazing Stories,* about a run-in he and another airman allegedly had in Burma with a possible robot they encountered in a cave that shot mysterious rays at them. The story ran in the June 1946 issue of *Amazing Stories*.

As if Crisman had not been controversial enough, years later he was subpoenaed by New Orleans District Attorney Jim Garrison in November 1968, as he had been identified as one of the three "mystery tramps" in Dallas on the day of President John Kennedy's assassination. Garrison implied that Crisman had been part of an "undercover" operation, possibly connected with the CIA, and that his cover was often that of a preacher.

Garrison had called an evangelist named Thomas Beckham from Omaha, Nebraska, to also give testimony. The year before, interestingly enough, Beckham and Crisman reportedly helped to put together a UFO convention in Omaha on August 12, 1967, with contactee and evangelical types like "Rev." Frank Stranges, Wayne Aho, and Milton Northdurft. In 1985, I wrote to Northdurft who explained to me that he had been a Methodist minister for 41 years and a long-time "metaphysical student" as well. He confirmed details of the convention and I learned how in his "35 years of UFO research" he had met many well-known figures including Brad Steiger, George Adamski, George Hunt Williamson, Mark Prophet, Kenneth Arnold, Richard Shaver, and Ray Palmer, who upon his death he was asked to conduct a funeral service for up in Amherst, Wisconsin, which he did.

While many today dismiss the Maury Island case as having been a probable hoax, there were those who weren't so sure. Beckham told Northdurft that Crisman was an outstanding individual who held a Ph.D. in psychology, a point Crisman confirmed (or someone claiming to have been him anyway) in a letter to ufologist Gary Lesley in 1967 when he described himself as an "industrial psychologist."

"I have never been any man of 'mystery' as so many of these old books and the newer authors attempt to describe," this "Crisman" wrote. "Such public attention is NOT good for my business relations. I have no secret facts, beyond the truths that were suppressed in Project Blue Book."

Harold Dahl described how early the next morning he was approached by a stranger in a black suit who drove a black 1947 Buick sedan. Dahl at first thought it was someone interested in perhaps buying some salvage lumber from him, which was not an uncommon occurrence. However, the stranger soon made it clear that he knew much about Dahl, made some not so veiled threats about the continued happiness and well-being of his family, and knew the full details of his UFO experience! He later told Kenneth Arnold, "I did think it was rather fantastic how this gentleman happened to know what I had seen and I was quite sure that he hadn't talked to any of my crew, and I know he hadn't talked to me before. In fact, I had never seen him before." In the annals of modern Ufology, this appears to have been the first alleged encounter with an MIB! However, as Keel had already pointed out, within other frames of reference or disciplines this type of occurrence was not unheard of. For example, during an intense religious revival in Wales in the winter of 1904-05, there were all sorts of bewildering UFO-type light displays, many observed by seemingly very credible witnesses, including skeptical journalists, and in one instance, during a visit to Brynerug, a person described as a professional and another as a farmer of good standing noticed one of the mysterious sinister appearing black figures (often associated by the locals at that time with the devil) put in an appearance nearby. One of the men uttered a prayer, when suddenly a light in the sky appeared overhead from which a white beam shot down striking the figure, which immediately vanished into thin air.

Now You See Him, Now You Don't!

I wrote to Allen Greenfield to get his views on the MIB phenomenon. He replied (07/05/13): "Here's the deal. There is a myth that MIB cases have diminished. They have not. What has happened is that the core people who investigated this type of case have, unfortunately, died off, some under mysterious circumstances (Ron Bonds of IllumiNet Press and Jim Keith, the author aka Jay Katz). Others, as with Keel, just got old and passed on, as far as I know. Those of us who keep tabs on the broad range of strange phenomena find MIB cases about as often in 2013 as they did in 1953 or 1968-69, or as Keel alludes, throughout history under only slightly different guises. Taken as a whole though, there are a few hoaxes and a number of government investigators taken to be men in black, but for the most part they appear to be a quasi-physical phenomenon attempting, with some success, to 'seem human,' apparently with difficulty, and only briefly. They may require some 'material basis' as is the case with certain Workings known for centuries in the occult world."

Greenfield had his own MIB experience years ago: "It was in Charleston, West Virginia, on or about June 25, 1969, at the National UFO Conference that year. This was, be it noted, in 'Mothman Country' during the Mothman/UFO/MIB wave in that area. I noticed this atypical guy hanging around the convention but not directly involved. He fit the MIB description. When he followed us the last day of the convention across the street from the hotel and hovered behind us when a number of delegates were dining, I decided to take matters into my hands, so I jumped up without warning, knocking over my chair in the process, and he slowly walked to the door of the restaurant and outside, but not before I got in front of him. He paused – his movements seemed 'artificial' and I took a sunlit photo of him with my 35 mm camera. On Sunday in downtown Charleston, be it noted, it was truly quiet and dead. He rounded a corner and I followed, not more than two seconds behind him or it, or whatever, and he was - gone. I have no opinion other than others have apparently seen the photo years later and say it's the same young, pasty-faced MIB I saw, no sign of aging."

Keel let it be known that he wanted to catch the physical MIB and question them. He felt that he had a better chance of doing that than catching the elusive flying saucers and their occupants. He had near misses where he arrived at homes just minutes after the MIB had allegedly been there. In one instance on Long Island, Keel claimed that he had received an anonymous phone call that directed him to a location where he encountered a black Cadillac with MIB-type occupants inside. He pursued them down a dead-end road where they impossibly disappeared.

Besides Gypsy MIBs, Keel was also interested in Laplanders. "Because Scandinavia is now so thinly populated (in the north) and vast areas are so isolated, it is highly probable that someone – a terrestrial someone – has been using that part of the country," Keel wrote to Hakan Blomqvist in 1984. "Whenever I talk to MIB witnesses I slyly show them photos of Laplanders and they always exclaim, 'That's them! That's just what they looked like!'"

Cadillacs with strange illuminated dashboards

Keel suspected some MIB victims were placed into a hypnotic trance state. One of his best-known cases of this kind is featured in *The Mothman Prophecies*. The incident happened on June 21, 1967, on Long Island, to a contactee named Jaye P. Paro. It was around 8 p.m., while Paro was out walking and a black Cadillac pulled up alongside her. A man in the back seat spoke the name of a friend of hers and ordered her inside. She assumed it was okay to get in. It turned out to be a big mistake. "There was a funny smell inside," a traumatized Paro told Keel later. "Antiseptic...like a hospital. And there were flashing lights on the dashboard. I couldn't take my eyes off them. I felt like they were hypnotizing me."

They arrived at a crossroads in the area of Mount Misery, a location known for strange and spooky happenings, where a man stood holding what resembled a doctor's bag. The car pulled over and the man got in and was soon waving something like a bottle of smelling salts in her face. At that point her will power was gone. Then the men asked her questions that made no sense to her. No mention of what any of those questions were in the narrative. Then afterward she was dropped back off where she had been picked up at.

Keel described a similar incident where a man on Long Island claimed he was taken to a secret underground UFO base in a "black Cadillac with a dashboard festooned with flashing colored lights."

Another interesting MIB account comes from long-time ufologist Steve Ward, a fellow student of Keelian mysteries. In 2014 Ward attended a Michigan MUFON gathering. He was at a table discussing the MIB subject with others, and a woman, "Mrs. Findley" (a pseudonym given her by Ward) asked him if he'd like to hear her personal MIB story. Naturally, he said he would. She said it happened around the mid-1960s. She had just gotten married and she and her husband were out in the Las Vegas area. They were hitchhiking when a large black car stopped and picked them up. It had two occupants.

"The men were dressed in classic Man in Black attire, complete with black suits and black fedoras," Ward said. "Otherwise, they looked quite 'normal.'"

"One thing that was different about the vehicle they were riding in was that the dashboard was very unconventional and had all kinds of lights on it," Ward continued. "Some of the lights were continually flashing. Mrs. Findley had never seen anything like it before." Ward asked her questions to assess her knowledge on the MIB subject, which seemed quite limited. She even seemed unaware of Gray Barker and John Keel's writings.

"The strangers took them to their destination and when they stopped the car the driver recommended that they not leave right away, but that they should wait a while. Mrs. Findley said that they both found themselves falling asleep in their seats. When they woke up, they didn't know for how long they had been unconscious. They departed and thanked their strange hosts for the ride and walked off to find a motel. They eventually found accommodations and went to check in. The proprietor standing behind the counter looked at them with a shocked expression on his face. He explained that the police had just arrested two people who had robbed a convenience store nearby. The perpetrators looked like them. If they had shown up earlier, they could well have been mistaken for the thieves and may have been arrested."

"Mrs. Findley told me her story in a straight-forward manner with no embellishments. She certainly didn't appear to be the type to spin a tale just for the fun of it and, as I mentioned before, her knowledge of reports of alleged MIB experiences seemed to be limited. It was a MIB story with a twist."

"We have all heard stories about people who have said that they have had encounters with angels. Someone will have been in great danger and suddenly a stranger shows up and intervenes in the situation. The mysterious individual then vanishes, leaving no trace, and is assumed to be an angel. Mrs. Findley's experience fits the 'angelic intervention' category like a glove – except central casting seems to have issued her two benefactors the wrong costumes. The Men in Black performing good deeds? Those guys might get their charter revoked."

Puerto Rican ufologist Jorge Martin knew of only three possible MIB incidents in his UFO-infested country, but the one he shared with me was most intriguing. "The most MIB-like event occurred in the 1940s, in the town of Lajas, in the southwest," he said. "One morning a father and his son were walking in a cane field and a large flying saucer shaped craft suspended itself over them, engulfing them in a beam of light that issued from the craft's underside. Immediately, both father and son felt a great heat and a burning sensation on their skin. The father threw his son to the ground next to some bushes, trying to get some cover, and covered his son with his own body, to protect him from the searing heat."

"Moments later, the light from the saucer vanished. The craft flew away very fast vertically and disappeared from sight. They went home at once and the father ordered his son to take a bath, to calm the burning sensation, but he did not do it until later. Once the boy bathed, the burning sensation ceased."

"However, the father became ill and died weeks later."

"Even though the doctors could not say what it was that was affecting him, the symptoms were similar to what would be described today as strong radiation poisoning. Sometime later the son was walking on a road and was contacted by several strange men " in black suits and ties, with black hats, who were traveling in a big black Cadillac-like car. They asked him if he was Francisco Vargas (his name) and asked him to enter the car and accompany them, which he did. According to Vargas, they asked him if he was the young boy who had observed the saucer, and whose father had died. He replied he was, and they asked him many questions about what they had seen that day."

"After that, they opened the car's door and asked him to get out, which he did. He began to walk, feeling somewhat dazed. Moments later, he looked back and the car was not there. It disappeared."

"Mr. Vargas told me that the car looked normal, but once inside he saw that on the front panel there were many buttons and lights, something he had not seen before in any car. He described the men as human-looking, but of an oriental type, with slanted eyes, and a somewhat pale appearance."

Some MIB-types are very Human – Some are not?

On the night of July 29, 1977, Joseph Randle Murphy, who had been working for the Canadian Pacific Railway, was headed south on a remote stretch of Highway 95 between Golden and Radium in British Columbia, Canada. An early model black Cadillac, in pristine appearance, unexpectedly shot across the highway in front of him going east to west. He slammed on his brakes, missing a collision with the Cadillac by mere inches. With high beams on, he could see three men inside the vehicle, all dressed in black overcoats, hats and, oddly enough, sunglasses. The driver of the Cadillac was staring straight ahead, his face illuminated by a dull purple glow from the dashboard. The front passenger and another in the back seat were looking out at him, their faces pasty white, intense and expressionless.

After stepping out of his Pontiac station wagon to investigate, he was puzzled to discover that where the Cadillac had crossed the road, there was no road to be seen that intersected with the highway, nor any tire tracks, no damage to vegetation, or any other evidence. The Cadillac had originated straight across from the side of the highway where there was a dense forest that rose up a mountain side, while it departed on the opposite west side down into a valley. There was simply no road there! The befuddled motorist switched off his motor and aimed his car's headlights down toward the valley but could see and hear nothing more except for a temporary mist in the air where the phantom vehicle had departed.

Dr. Peter Rojcewicz described in a report for the *MUFON UFO Journal* (Mar. 1990, #263) a case that took place near Philadelphia, Pennsylvania in 1983 wherein an MIB character unexpectedly appeared, as if out of thin air, in a bookstore. After police arrived, he vanished. The main witness, Robert Yates, complained of suddenly becoming nauseated, light-headed and weak for no apparent reason. A store clerk, he had been transcribing several audiotapes of MIB narratives for a local ufologist. He felt that his MIB was in fact an "earthly military man in a possession state."

Yates was disturbed as to how the man could inexplicably appear and disappear from the store. The mystery man reportedly left behind various papers that indicated that he held a governmental intelligence and security background. Rojcewicz noted that unlike "other MIB narratives," he had reliable information on this so-called MIB's name, occupation, phone number, and post office box.

Interestingly, Rojcewicz, had his own MIB encounter in 1980, before he became a noted professor of humanities and folklore at New York's Juilliard School. He was in the University of Pennsylvania library minding his own business and quietly reading a UFO book recommended by a professor when he suddenly noticed a pale, gaunt man standing before him, dressed in a loose black suit with bláck tie and a bright white shirt. The man plopped down in a chair across from Rojcewicz, all in one peculiar single movement, folded his hands on top of a stack of books before him, and asked Rojcewicz what he was doing. Rojcewicz replied that he was reading about flying saucers, to which the odd stranger asked if he'd ever seen one. Rojcewicz answered that he didn't know that much about the subject and wasn't that sure he was interested. "Flying saucers are the most important fact of the century and you are not interested!?" the stranger screamed. He stood up, again in a single odd movement, placed a hand on Rojcewicz's shoulder and stated: "Go well on your purpose." Then he left.

"I had a sense that this man was out of the ordinary and that idea frightened me," Rojcewicz later recalled. "I got up and walked around the stacks toward where the reference librarians usually are. The librarians weren't there. There were no guards there – there was nobody else in the library...I was utterly alone and terrified." Rojcewicz returned to his seat to pull himself together. "It took me about an hour," he stated. "Then I got up and everything was back to normal; the people were all there."

I ran into an interesting situation myself, also near Philadelphia, in April 1972. There were a couple of unusual and charismatic "MIBish" individuals involved who were active in the local metaphysical community. Two ufologists in the area, who I had come to know rather well, became my best informants on them. I was told that the two men had "much in common" with MIBs, although they were "much more socially acceptable." They seemed to be "awakening latent awareness in humans," but at the same time they were "often charming liars." One of them, in fact, used to send along secret messages and warnings to John Keel in the mail through one of the ufologists. He wanted to talk with Keel before it was "too late" (whatever that meant).

One of the ufologists, who had a background in psychiatric social work, recalled: "My son had MIB dreams at a period when I was deeply involved in the physical investigation of UFOs. ...(he) would wake up sweating and glassy eyed, crying that 'they' had come for him...sometimes he would come downstairs and stare out of the window, shaking and resisting efforts to move him. On one occasion, a large black car parked outside the house, without lights. ...Only when it drove off did (he) calm down. He had no memory of any of this. We also had weird phone calls, a real MIB visiting the house and talking to my daughter, bad smells and TV interference...all the classic manifestations."

Her family's problems with MIB manifestations were resolved thanks to the two MIBish gentlemen she called "genies." "I do not say that they gave us all the answers or all true answers because lying (or creative truth as they prefer to call it) and confusion all seem to be part of this 'game with humans,'" she said they explained.

The other ufologist awakened one night to a strange paralysis. He explained that he felt as though he had had a psychic awakening that he associated with "what advanced yogis call the 'awakening of the kundalini nerve.'" Following this experience, he found his mind was "able to soar to heights of abstract thought" that were "quite advanced." Later he approached one of the two men and got involved in a heavy metaphysics discussion and was surprised that he could keep up with it (as previously he had not). "The fact that I was able to keep up with him so well on most points startled me," the ufologist explained. "It's a strange feeling to have your mind dive deep into the ultimate."

One of the MIBish men, who had been described once as looking the most like a classic MIB, right down to a monotone voice, supposedly possessed much knowledge on the subject of the MIB and metaphysics and was presumed to be quite psychic. He had ties with local practitioners of witchcraft and fringe metaphysical movements. I met some of these people and heard some strange stories, including a woman who claimed that she had met him on the astral plane where he appeared as a dark hooded figure.

I briefly met this character on the evening of April 17, 1972. We both happened to be at the same place at the same time – an area metaphysical study group. I was invited to sit in his car and chat awhile (one of those ufologist friends/informants of mine had kindly put in a good word for me when he spotted him, and told him I had traveled all the way from Maine and had a lot of interest in such things as the paranormal and UFOs). Honestly, I wasn't quite sure at the time who it was I was suddenly being thrust headlong into an interview with. Naturally my first question was who he was, to which he replied that it didn't matter and to "call me anything you like." Then he added that I would need to ask a lot of direct questions in order to get anything meaningful from our conversation. I took a stab at it, beginning with something like whether he had ever had an out-of-body experience, to which he simply replied "yes." I asked what it was like and he said it was a pure energy state. He began to talk about medical explanations, secondary personalities and such, while I was attempting to direct his focus more onto the paranormal/spiritual areas. Then he said he realized what I was trying to do and that if I would allow him to take the lead with the questions then we could move on. I agreed, and soon we went into a variety of interesting and odd areas of discussion.

He said my absolute goal was not to document cases of UFOs, astral projection, and all sorts of other mysterious events, but that I was looking for something deeper and buried below the surface. He said I could continue to delve deeply into the investigation and documentation of case after case and still get nowhere. He told me I had to be careful not to waste my valuable time as so many other potentially "beautiful souls" are doing. He explored my interest in UFOs and got me to talking about my studies of contactees and MIB. He seemed particularly interested in the MIB aspect (imagine that) and displayed obvious knowledge as to how it was supposed to work, saying it was a psychological game (which was Keel's belief).

Whether he was doing a good "cold reading" or a genuine psychic reading, he did tell me things about myself that were accurate, but I can't honestly say that he acquired such psychically. Regarding the psychological game playing, he also said that he could be, at that very moment, diverting my attention from some other area (where something significant might be going on). I thought that was interesting as we had planned to spend the night inside the home used for these metaphysical gatherings because it was reportedly haunted. But we hadn't gotten around to getting permission, as my unexpected interview with him had distracted us from doing so, and the place was now closed.

Then things turned rather weird. It was a nice temperature outside, a star-studded night, but suddenly this man decided to put the top up on his convertible, roll up the automatic windows, and turn on the heater. I was forced to roll my window down while he continued to talk in a monotone voice, sounding as calm and cool as a cucumber, so to speak. Then he got into a silly mood, quite a departure from our conversation just moments before. We were talking about the possibility of robot-mechanical MIBs and he began to talk about how fun it would be to torture an MIB and cut one of its fingers off to see if it had blood, at which point he laughed.

In 1973, in Jacksonville Beach, Florida, I tracked down an odd fellow that a Navy friend of mine (I was in the US Navy at this time) had met earlier at a bus station. This man, who would go out dressed in a black suit coat, black pants and shoes, with a white turtleneck, had, from an early age, practiced witchcraft. He claimed that he was a walk-in for two space aliens, a male and a female. He would chatter on for hours about these beings and their reality. He said two Adamski-type scout ships had come to his home and the entities came to him in their "true astral form," resembling glowing white bowling pins! His mother told me how she had once seen two "ferris wheel" looking objects, large and "quite lit up," sort of "rolling across the sky," witnessed also by a neighbor. Were these what this young contactee was describing as Adamski-type scout ships?

I questioned him about his alleged dual identity, and he said he was an MIB himself. He described how one time he felt that the space beings tried to contact him through his black and white television. An insect like head with housefly type eyes appeared at the top of the TV screen and a mother ship with smaller UFOs surrounded it.

The following year, I was investigating the claims of a nearby Jacksonville man who was fishing alone on the St. Johns River in the early morning hours in January 1972 when a domed disk hovered directly over his small boat. Later the tide went out and he was stuck. He walked along the beach on Blount Island and came upon "the darnest looking humanoid creature one could ever imagine," whereupon he was struck by a "brilliant white light" that caused him to collapse. His arms and legs went numb. "For the first hour I was sure I would die," he stated. "But I prayed and prayed, and then the numbness began going away. About day break I was able to get on my knees and crawl."

Soon after he began to have strange "dreams" of an underground UFO base and of being on another planet. He predicted that on Mars we would discover statues, pyramids, and mounds similar to those on earth. I learned that this wasn't the first time he had seen the humanoid. He had seen three such creatures in 1947 while exploring a cave in Georgia. It shook him up badly and he thought that he had quite literally encountered demons from hell!

He admitted that he had dabbled in black magick for years. He described techniques he had used to magically influence humans and dogs. He told me that human females are "very curious animals" and love to gossip. To demonstrate and experiment with this aspect he said he had dressed himself in a black outfit (suitcoat, pants, tie, shoes) and drove into a certain section of Jacksonville and acted peculiar "to stir up gossip and then watch it develop." I remember thinking to myself, "What normal person does this?'"

Not far from this man's harrowing encounter on the St. Johns River, at Mayport, a UFO friend and colleague named Ramona

Hibner had a close encounter with a domed, disc-shaped object in July 1967, followed by poltergeist activity and 3 a.m. episodes of paralysis like the fisherman, and an "evil" humanoid entity with a cat-like face that appeared to her in her bedroom. For Ramona, prayer was a crucial defense mechanism against those frightening nocturnal occurrences.

I met Ramona Hibner in 1973; she was the wife of a Navy man whose ship was stationed at Mayport. Hers was quite a story. She, her husband, and their teenage son had a close encounter with a domed, disc-shaped object about 40-45 feet in diameter on July 29, 1967, around 9 p.m., near the base. They were about to turn onto Route A1A from a dirt road in an area known as the Little Jetties, when they and other motorists on A1A first spotted the object. It initially appeared to be a plane with landing lights coming in over the water near a U.S. Coast Guard Station. On the other side of the A1A was the airfield for the Mayport Naval Station. Everyone stopped their cars and waited, presumably to let what they thought was a plane pass in front of them as it made a low descent into that airfield. Instead it unexpectedly stopped and hovered about 15-20 feet in the air at the edge of the water. Suddenly, there appeared bluish lights that seemed to drop down from the object onto the edge of the road. "They looked like welding arcs," Ramona told me. "If you've ever seen anybody weld, the sparks that fly off of it will hit and kind of bounce. This is what was happening. They were coming out toward the cars and I thought, 'My goodness, they're taking pictures.' I don't know why I thought that. But these lights would bounce around on the edge of the road by the cars."

By this time, the motorists in front of the Clark's (Ramona was a Clark at this time) realized that this was not conventional aircraft activity and took off. "I mean burning rubber getting out of there!" Ramona exclaimed. "It's amazing how fast they disappeared." In moments, it was just Ramona and her family and a dark disk, making a rocking type motion, low in front of their car moving slowly ahead of them as they drove at about 30 miles an hour. At one point, it stopped and hovered at a small bridge for about a minute, and then it continued on to an intersection with Wonderwood Road where Indian burial mounds and a cemetery had been located nearby. [When I checked the area myself in 1973, I found that the Indian mounds had been destroyed] There it hovered again, over trees on the right side of the road, as though waiting to see which way they were going to go next. They turned slowly left, and as they did the UFO slowly moved across the road and low above them. The object had been a dark form as it moved down the road, but now they could see amber and green lights underneath it, as well as a red one that Ramona felt may have been on an antenna. "You could see right in the center of it what looked like a great big black hole," Ramona noted. She added that her husband and son both said that they had heard a low humming sound like a generator. The son, who had been in the back seat behind his father, who was driving, was suddenly hanging out the back window to get a better look at the UFO. "I said, 'Get your head back in the car,' because you know it could be dangerous," Ramona recalled. "Our headlights just seemed to kind of draw back into the car. It was real strange. They didn't just go out – they just seemed to come backwards and went out completely." During this time, the headlights, as they were retracting, had turned a yellowish color, and then after the UFO got 100 or more feet away the lights came back on and were normal again.

The disk was now headed over a marsh back towards the Naval Station, so the Clark family turned their 1962 Ford around and stopped on the side of the road up near the Jetties again. They could see a bright red light hanging over the Coast Guard Station. Next they could hear someone talking over a loudspeaker (weren't able to tell what was being said) and searchlights were scanning around the river. "Suddenly, this thing began to glow and get bigger. It just spread out and reminded me of looking at a coal on fire," Ramona told me. "You could see it sort of change colors and brighten up." It slowly moved eastward toward the ocean, continuing to get "bigger and bigger." Then two jet fighters came in flying low and fast from the direction of the Naval Air Station's Cecil Field in Jacksonville. The jets split up and one went up higher while the other continued on a straight path. She thought they were trying to maneuver it into an intercept position, but by this time the UFO had accelerated at a speed faster than the jets. All three disappeared over the Atlantic Ocean.

Within about four days of the UFO sighting, the Clark home began to experience poltergeist activity. It began with mysterious "voices" -- a loud male voice on her left side would call her first name and make breathing sounds "just behind the left ear," she noted. "I'd turn around to look and there was nobody there." It would happen at different locations, such as inside the house or outside while she worked in her flower garden. Interestingly, others in paranormal situations have reported hearing "voices" on their left side as well. British "direct voice" medium Leslie Flint described "voices" that manifested to him above his head and off to the left side, at what seemed like a distance of about two feet. Arigo, the famed Brazilian psychic healer, was allegedly guided by a spirit "doctor" who reportedly spoke into his left ear. A man named Colin Parsons in his book entitled Encounters With The Unknown, wrote how for some 30 years a voice whispered messages into his left ear. It was able to tell him things that it was humanly impossible for him to have known.

Ramona reported too that there were unexplained footsteps and knocking sounds. In the weeks and months that followed, the paranormal activity escalated. Ramona would awaken around 3 a.m., immobilized in a state of tingling paralysis, while she observed a frightening humanoid figure. "I noticed the open shirt collar on the entity very clearly," Ramona told me. "It 'stood out' more so than the face. The face, in fact, seemed distorted or fuzzy." At times, the face would remind Ramona of her first husband, who died tragically early in the marriage, and then "it faded...to be replaced by a cat-like face." The second face seemed "evil."

Ramona's teenaged son would come into her bedroom late at night upset with similar stories. She hadn't told him what had been happening to her. "He would have these akinesia [paralysis] spells and say there were people pulling at his arms and legs, and men in black were telling him that they were going to kidnap his mother and take her away," Ramona stated. "(He) had no knowledge of the men in black. None whatsoever. He never had any knowledge of what was happening to me because I never had told anyone about it."

Small glowing balls of bluish or golden lights appeared in her bedroom as well. "When the blue ones were around nothing bad went on but when the little gold ones were around then something bad would go on," Ramona said. Years later, Ramona's husband (she was remarried at this point) watched in amazement as a small glowing ball of light came into the bedroom through an open window, hovered briefly in front of her sleeping face, and then flew back out the window. "I had these experiences for six or eight months before I had read anything about it," Ramona noted. John Keel's writings had proven particularly relevant for her.

The humanoid with the cat like face that zapped the frightened fisherman on Blount Island was followed by 21 nights of visions that would begin right at the threshold of sleep. He said that he "almost went crazy" from it all. In these visions, the Blount Island alien appeared to him again, and together they went aboard the *S.S. Constitution,* a cruise liner that was docked nearby. The alien showed him a globe of the earth and drew upon it a five-pointed star that went through Georgia's ancient Eagle Mound as well as distant locations like the Cheops Pyramid and Easter Island. For several weeks following the visions, the fisherman would suddenly wake up at exactly 3 a.m. He thought it all very strange.

I found it interesting that we had the alien with the cat-like face, the paralysis, and the 3 a.m. time of occurrence described by two different experiencers in the same general area, and that neither knew one another.

I came to suspect that the St. Johns River was also a part of one of Keel's "window" locations where all sorts of weird anomalies may appear, including perhaps even sea monsters

"I don't know what it was," Brenda Langley of Jacksonville,

Florida told me. "It was early in the morning about 9:30 and there was a storm coming up. The water was real calm and it was real black, the sky was, and this thing came up two times and then it come up by the boat. ...It was about three or four feet out of the water and about the color, a pinkish color, like boiled shrimp. It had a real ugly looking face on it. It was pitiful looking, and it had snail like horns, and it had this little jagged thing, scales or little horns going down its back, like a dinosaur."

Another witness, Mrs. Dorothy Abram, also saw the creature, which had a head about the size of that of a human's head. "We saw it had a neck about three feet long," she told me. "It had two little horns on top of the head like a snail." The location was the Saint Johns River, near Jacksonville. The date of the sighting was May 10, 1975. The witnesses (five total) were in a fishing boat together. "All five of us saw it," Mrs. Langley added. "It sure frightened us all, whatever it was."

I kept running into reports of strange cryptids, apparitions, spectral intrusions – whatever the heck was behind such unusual perceptions.

In 1973, I joined military buddies at a home outside Mayport for a Thanksgiving meal. I learned that the young military family (Mike and Elaine) had been disturbed by unexplained knocking sounds, "creepy feelings," and a door opening on occasion by itself. Within weeks the activity escalated and soon the wife was seeing a three-foot tall, blurry figure with glowing non-blinking white or golden eyes, floating over the floor of their trailer home. It appeared day and night, most often behind the wife and on her left side. She even saw it while walking along the Mayport Road. At first it was dark and shaped like a tree stump. Then it took on a more human-like form with glowing red eyes. She sometimes felt as though she was being watched and would turn around and see it.

The couple had a baby and she became concerned for its safety. Elaine woke up one morning unable to move, hearing her baby crying, and at the same time noticing the strange dark little figure moving around inside the trailer. One day, a neighbor named Betty heard a knock at her back door. When she asked who it was, she heard a voice say, "It's me, Mike." It sounded just like him, but Mike and I had returned to our ship at the Mayport base.

Early one morning, Mike and his dog were both awakened by the movement of the bed. A brown hunting dog had its paws on the bed and was looking down at them. "Beautiful animal," Mike remarked. Then it dropped to the floor and disappeared into thin air.

On two nights in a row, October 9 and 10, 1973, at about 9:30, a disc-shaped object about 25 feet in diameter that produced a "whistling" sound was reported appearing at treetop level just down the road from the main entrance to the Jacksonville Naval Air Station. The object had a series of white lights along its outer edge that pulsated in unison. In May 1974 there were a series of security alerts on the base when strange lights and forms were reported on the runways and at other locations on the base on several different nights. Mike, assigned to the base at that time, was present at one of these occurrences when, he saw something resembling a peculiar cone-shaped object off the end of a runway around 3 a.m. It was about 10 feet in front of a blast wall. The mysterious "cone" was about five to six feet tall and two feet across at the bottom and was pointed at the top. It was surrounded by a luminous aura with a well-defined edge that was an estimated 15 feet across. The object was visible for perhaps five to 10 minutes and then faded away.

This manifestation had happened before, and Mike was ready with a Polaroid camera. Oddly, the developed print was not what he had seen. The cone shaped anomaly appeared in the print as a "big thing of reflecting metal with sun reflecting off of it," he said, with the surrounding area lit up like daylight, including the river and about a half mile across it a tree line on the other side. What he had seen visually was more like shining car headlights into a fluorescent road sign at night. Not that bright.

Mike showed the picture that night to a lieutenant junior grade officer who he worked under. The next day he was placed in a room with two men in green khaki uniforms. They were a standard security investigating team and questioned him about the incident. They also obtained the picture from him saying that it would be returned to him later. It was not and he was told not to talk about the incident.

Ramona was working at the Shrimp Coop in Mayport, where the fishing boats would routinely drop off a fresh boat load of shrimp, when two odd strangers dressed in black showed up. This was right after the UFO sighting. "You know yourself how remote Mayport is," Ramona told me. "That's a long walk from anywhere and the only other way in is across the river on the ferry." They ordered Coca-Colas. "One of them drank part of his and I don't think that the other one touched his," Ramona said. "They didn't know how much a Coca-Cola cost and the man didn't know how to count money. He was very confused, and he just laid money on the counter and let me pick out what they owed."

"They wanted to catch a plane at a certain time, or so they said," Ramona continued. "I said, 'You'll never make it.'" The airport was 30 miles away. Their flight was supposed to take off in about 35 minutes and they were on foot.

"I told them that they wouldn't be able to catch their plane and they kept sitting there!" Ramona exclaimed. Eventually, they got up and left on foot. "They went toward Atlantic Village, walking on a very hot day with winter suits on. It was very unusual."

A few years later, Ramona was reading *Stranger at the Pentagon* by Dr. Frank Stranges, which had photographs of an alleged alien, who appeared human, identified as Valiant Thor. Another man (allegedly one "V. Cmdr. Donn") was pictured with him. She was surprised to see the pictures because the men looked identical to the two men she had seen at the Shrimp Coop. The photos had been taken by ufologist August Roberts at High Bridge, New Jersey, sometime in 1958, at the home of the famous contactee Howard Menger.

The contactee world introduced other odd characters into Ramona's already strange life. She became acquainted with Madeleine Rodeffer, a follower of the best-known contactee of all, George Adamski. A motion picture film allegedly taken by Rodeffer on February 26, 1965, while George Adamski was visiting her and her husband at their home in Silver Springs, Maryland, portrays one of the Adamski scout ships. The footage allegedly was shot by Adamski.

According to Ramona, a man named Johnson, who lived in Florida and who claimed he was with the government, was visited at his home by Rodeffer, who lived in Washington, DC. "This man was a very close associate of hers," Ramona told me. "When she would show the film, she would always look at this man when she was talking, as if to say, 'Am I doing all right?' He would nod his head and she would go on. It was a strange sort of relationship they had." Her activities eventually cost Rodeffer her marriage.

Ramona recalled a time when there was some sort of UFO meeting in Jacksonville and she had stepped outside to get a breath of fresh air as the crowded room was filled with cigarette smoke. "He (Johnson) followed me out and was telling me if I was ever invited aboard a saucer not to accept, not to ever go near a saucer, that it was dangerous," Ramona recalled he said. "I could be physically assaulted by these people, even be raped, and so on. I stood there and listened to him kind of shocked. Why did he pick me out to tell me these things? He told me definitely never to go with anyone who seemed to think anything about saucers unless I had a male companion with me that I could trust."

As if that weren't strange enough, the would-be good Samaritan began to keep an eye on her home. Was it a protective eye? "My neighbors saw him driving up and down in front of my house when I wasn't home, and he would always be in a different car every time, usually old beat up automobiles that were falling apart."

"Apparently outer space is filled with all kinds of creepy

characters," I recall Keel began in a recorded 1967 lecture I listened to as a teenager. I don't remember hearing anyone in the audience laugh at all. Keel sounded nervous to me. Little doubt he was well aware that some of the high strangeness he was about to share might not set too well with many sitting before him.

Humor was a large part of Keel's professional stock and trade. In 1966, he wrote a spy and superhero spoof novel entitled "The Fickle Finger of Fate," that sold over 800,000 copies and helped to finance his full-time UFO field work and research operation for about three years. He had been a head writer for such TV celebrity giants as Merv Griffin and Gene Rayburn, and humor was a good part of what worked for him in the entertainment arena. But the UFO audiences were often a tough crowd!

I feel pretty sure he saw some of those "creepy characters" among the "UFO buffs" he described being annoyed with. Of course, when it came to "creepy characters" Keel was far more interested and concerned with the MIB types.

Here's a case that I was told Keel nearly became involved with that allegedly involved an unusual man with psychic abilities who was even suspected of perhaps being an alien.

Lee Walsh was a columnist/writer for a newsstand magazine called *UFO Update* in the 1970s and early 1980s. "On March 11, 1975, I left Fabens, Texas, for the small town of Maybrook, New York," Walsh told me. "I was directed to move there by a friend who has a yoga center in LA. I was told that I would have an alien contact if I moved. I was born and spent most of my life in upstate New York, but I do not like it and didn't want to return. Every instinct told me not to go. In fact, many physical things were hindering my getting ready for the move and I cancelled plane reservations three times before finally leaving."

After several weeks in New York she began to worry that she had made a big mistake, as there seemed no interest in UFOs and no UFO activity reported in the area. "I felt I was victim of an expensive hoax," Lee confessed.

Then suddenly all that changed. "It came as a surprise then that an interesting story was reported to the news media," she said. "Two police officers, in the nearby town of Walden, had reported a 'strange man' they had encountered while stopped for a traffic light. They stated that the man was crossing the street on the red light and when he passed by their patrol car all power stopped for a moment, and the officers reported they 'could feel the hair of their body stand on end'! The traffic light went out, their patrol car stalled, and their radio went dead. As if this wasn't unnerving enough, they also reported that the man seemed to 'vanish right before their eyes.' A waitress, in a nearby delicatessen, reported some odd behavior by this man, noting in particular his odd eyes."

Lee had begun contributing articles to a local paper, the *Citizen Herald,* and had appeared as a guest several times on local cable TV. In the months that followed, many UFO sightings were reported. "Residents were having experiences they had never before thought were possible. I made a plea on cable TV for this man to contact me. He did. The policemen warned me to stay away from him, feeling he was dangerous." Lee found the officers reluctant to discuss any further their encounter with the strange man. She went to the home of one of the officers. "His wife, surrounded by several of their children, answered the door," Lee recalled. "She was very cordial and sympathetic, but I was not invited in. However, she did confirm the story as it had been related, and the fact that they (the officers) had felt they had done the wrong thing by reporting the incident."

In time Lee and the strange man, R., became close and even talked of marriage. She had written author Gray Barker about what was happening, and he forwarded her letter to John Keel. "Mr. Keel was coming to see me but circumstances in New York became so unbearable that I decided to return to Fabens, which I did. Several months later the 'man,' or someone I believed to be him, came to Fabens. He left me a note in some sort of code saying that it would be deciphered by someone else, in time. I must tell you here that for many reasons I do not believe that the man who came here was the same man I knew in New York. Although they did look alike there were some distinct differences that wouldn't be noticed unless someone was close to him.

"There were rumors and more rumors about him," Lee added. "One odd thing was that a particular friend in New York, with a close association to him (the three of us were together constantly in New York, and he called her Venus) swore she saw him in New York when I knew he was still in Fabens."

Lee and her three young daughters had strange paranormal episodes with this man. Two were twins who were around 10-11 years of age. The other daughter is one year older. R. would take the girls to a drugstore in a few blocks away for ice cream sodas.

"My German girlfriend, who knew R. and didn't like him, was working part-time in the drugstore. She came one night and asked me why I let the girls stay so long with R. downtown. They even went over to the Catholic church and played the organ. This is the one thing that R. did several times in Fabens that the R. did in Maybrook too. The only difference was that the R. in Maybrook would promptly go at two every afternoon and play this odd melody on the church organ. I mean promptly. He didn't have a watch, but whether in the middle of a conversation or not, he would get up and go to the church. I always believed it was some sort of communication, for I am a strong believer in the harmonics of the ancients and that way to communicate messages. In any case, I wasn't aware of a time difference. It seemed to me they were gone a short while."

"One day after R. left, the twins started telling me about the walks R. used to take them on in Fabens -- l-o-n-g walks, way out into the desert. I said they were crazy, there would not have been time. They said they moved very swiftly and seemed to glide. They really couldn't explain it. Frankly, so many odd, worse than odd, things happened in those two years that I just shrugged off."

"One Sunday my friend who works at the post office suggested we take a ride out the back roads around Fabens. We had been in the car for about half an hour when the twins said, 'Oh, up around the next corner is where we walked with R. There is a little old building with a stream next to it and a few trees. We rested and it was cool. Only we came this way.' And they pointed to the desert at the left, indicating they had cut through the desert. Around the corner, on the left, was what used to be some sort of small adobe building. It was crumbling away. Next to it was a small irrigation ditch with water and there were trees around. My friend and I were dumbfounded to say the least."

One of the twins acquired an apparitional double, a ghostly doppelganger. "She (the double) seems to fade away, perhaps going into another dimension," Lee wrote me in November 1977. "She is fair skinned, has shoulder length blond hair, and wears a knee-length light blue nightgown. She is the exact image of one of my twin daughters who is 13. That is why I thought it was her walking through the hallway. The image was that clear as to appear as a solid figure. However, when I checked, the twins were both sleeping soundly as was my other daughter J. in the next bedroom. Several days later, J. was combing her hair in the bathroom. The mirror faces the hallway. She saw the double in the mirror. I have seen her twice in the past week. First a shadow catches my eye and then I see her. This morning at 4:30 J. called to me. She was sitting up in bed. Something had tried to pull the blanket from her bed (this is not a new experience) and she was clutching it. She said she told 'her' to let go and immediately 'she' started smoothing out the blanket."

I eventually met Lee Walsh in person after she had moved to Maine. Before meeting her I visited the office of her publisher in New York City, and met with Harry Belil, the editor of *UFO Update* and *Beyond Reality*, and one of his assistants. Allegedly a janitor in the building reported seeing some men in "black suits" wearing "dark glasses" hanging around the office door, after which a lot of material turned up missing in Belil's office. Some of it was important material from NASA that he was going to use.

Are there indeed people who walk among us, who have highly developed psychic abilities and are able to influence our thoughts and perceptions, who are mysteriously connected to, and perhaps even controlled by the forces and intelligences that interface with the UFO phenomenon? We know that many experiencers claim they strongly affect electrical/electronic equipment; just "know" things in a paranormal way; and have elevated precognitive and telepathic awareness and impressions about people and things around them. I talked with an experiencer who had seen mysterious humanoid entities, and had missing time, UFO encounters, and a variety of alien type memories. He met a woman who could enter his and his mother's dream worlds and told him things about himself and his dreams that she, a total stranger, could not possibly have known. She seemed inexplicably tied into his alien experiences, but he could not figure out how or why.

Alien Lefties?

In December 2009, I interviewed a Tennessee man who, along with his wife, had seen a disc-shaped object with yellow-white lights around its rim silently and slowly flying low over their neighborhood. Around December 1991 he had an encounter while he was out hunting alone in a wooded area of Cherry Creek, New York. He spotted a deer with antlers at an estimated 50 yards distance. Oddly, he had no urge to shoot it. After watching it for perhaps 30 seconds he was suddenly seeing not the deer but a person wearing a tight-fitting suit covering its body. The clothing glistened in the sunlight with a mother of pearl quality. "It's funny though that I can remember those details but can't see the face of the person," he added.

This "person" raised his left arm and there in his left hand was a shiny silver metallic ball with a chrome looking finish. "I watched this silver ball rise up out of his hand and then it was almost instantaneously in my face," he said. It was about the size of a golf ball, was at eye level, and a mere six to eight inches away!

"That's all I can remember," he noted. "Then I woke up." He had been in the middle of a very high-strangeness encounter, which had his full undivided attention, and then he found himself coming back into conscious aware, as if he had briefly for a time fallen asleep in the midst of such a bewildering event and was now waking up.

This wouldn't be the only time that the perception of a deer might have been a so-called "screen memory" in an alien encounter. Apparent "screen memories" are reported in many alien abduction and contact cases where the memory of an encounter experience is replaced with the sighting of seeing an owl, a wolf, a deer, or something else of a more acceptable conscious context than say an alien humanoid. Such a memory is seen as either a psychological self-defense mechanism to protect the psyche of the experiencer from the trauma of the episode, or else the alien non-human presence has somehow implanted the substitute memory to mislead the percipient. Whitley Strieber wrote in *Communion* (1987) of his apparent "screen memories" of a wolf and an owl.

This hunter in the Cherry Creek incident had a twin brother who still lived in New York. Like many twins, they have shared a psychic bond that goes back to childhood. They both have many strange memories of a psychic nature and incidents with entities – some ghostly and others perhaps related to UFO encounters. His twin was once an avid hunter who loved bow hunting, but he lost his desire to hunt after an incident wherein the deer suffered greatly in its death, its final vocalizations "reaching into my soul," he said. During that same hunt he heard for about five minutes a mysterious "low resonating hum" like a didgeridoo coming at him from every direction. "I sold my bow, gave my tree stands away, and asked the spirits for forgiveness."

The Tennessean has a psychic gift. Sometimes while he's talking with someone, a deceased relative will come through. He will develop a light-headedness and see a strange haze around the person, and then clear images will come to him. "The image then begins to tell me things or show me pictures in my head. I then relay this information back to the person I'm talking to." His wife's deceased father came to him before they were married. "She was crying," he recalled. "She wanted to know how I knew such intimate details of her life with him."

He said that this happens to him many times but that he seldom mentions it to the person he's with. "My left hand shakes for some unknown reason when I have had those experiences," he added. "It also gets hard to breathe, like I'm trying to catch my breath."

He is right-handed, while his twin in New York is left-handed.

What intrigued me is that I uncovered similar cases of left-handed aliens manipulating mysterious spherical objects! In 2009 I interviewed Johnny Sands, a country singer, entertainer and stuntman in Nashville who had seen a UFO in Nevada in 1976 and had a close encounter with a humanoid being that produced a grapefruit-sized, silver-colored sphere out of his left hand, which grew to the size of a basketball. "Then he let go of it and it began to rotate," Sands told me. "As it did he would put his fingers over the top of it and like firecrackers would go off on top of this ball."

Next Sands was given a message: "You see, nuclear explosions are causing a problem in the solar system. These things that you're setting off on this earth are causing troubles not only for you but for us and we cannot have this kind of thing to continue because it is going to upset the balance of everything that we intend for the future."

Another case took place on June 14, 1968, at Villa Carlos Paz near Cordola, Argentina, at the Motel La Cuesta. Shortly after 1 a.m., Maria Elodia Pretzel, 19, had just let two guests out a side door into the parking lot and had turned off some of the lights on the ground floor. She left three fluorescent lights on in the dining room and had headed toward the back door to lock it. The young woman noticed a light blue glow emanating from the dining room. Returning to it, she encountered a humanoid figure dressed in a shiny light blue, tight-fitting one-piece suit. It stood slightly over two meters tall. "In his left hand he was holding a glassy-looking sphere which irradiated a coherent beam of light – light of a faintly pale blue color, almost white," noted investigator and lawyer Dr. Oscar A. Galindez (Vol. 26, No. 5, January 1981, *Flying Saucer Review,* England). "The sphere was constantly moving forward and backward and lighting up the whole dining room quite independently of the fluorescent tubes. The entity was smiling the whole time."

Another remarkable case, also investigated by Dr. Galindez (Vol. 21, No. 5, 1975, *FSR*), took place in Argentina and involved a 52-year-old truck driver, Luftolde Rodriquez. On September 28, 1972 at around 3:40 a.m., Rodriguez was making a delivery to a plant in Santa Isabel when he had a strange humanoid encounter. Dr. Galindez wrote: "In his left hand he displayed something that looked like a billiard-ball, which was permanently emitting a very white light. The right arm was drawn back somewhat. He was wearing a wide, silvery belt, with a little box or casket of the same color on the right-hand side."

On January 7, 1970, at Imjarvi, Finland, two skiers came upon a small humanoid figure standing in a beam of light beneath a domed disc-shaped object. Afterward, both men had more UFO-related encounters. One of them, Aarno Heinonen, said that on May 5, 1972, he met a strange woman with a high-pitched voice with shoulder length yellow hair who wore a close-fitting dress that glittered when she moved, and silvery shoes with red rosettes. He added: "In her left hand she held something that looked like a ball, silver in color and connected to a rod which she held in her hand. On the ball were three antennae, each about 30 centimeters long, and each of which pointed towards me."

They talked for about five minutes. The woman was beautiful, her face and hands fair skinned, and her large eyes were blue. She said she came from the other side of the galaxy. He met her again, around the same time of the day, on June 18, 1972. She carried with her the same silvery sphere. Their meeting lasted about the same length of time. Heinonen asked her how she had arrived, and she told him he would see their beautiful vehicle on his way home. He did indeed, and that it was a silvery disc-shaped object about five to seven meters across. He added, "Her method of departure was very odd: she seemed to 'float' away and disappear. Her gait was stiff, and her knees did not bend."

Is it a mere coincidence that we have here five separate cases, from Cherry Creek, New York, and Las Vegas, Nevada, all the way to Santa Isabel and Villa Carlos Paz, Argentina, to Imjarvi, Finland, involving peculiar humanoid beings manipulating in their *left hands mysterious spherical objects* which in three instances produced light displays (even a coherent light beam in one), levitated in the air in two instances, and perhaps even caused one witness to lapse into unconsciousness? In the Finnish case, ufologists speculated that the object was some kind of "language" device, perhaps for language translations.

In May 2018, I caught a glimpse on TV of the final last few minutes of Ancient Aliens. Two photos were shown that immediately caught my eye. One was a Salvator Mundi painting of Christ, attributed to the Italian Renaissance artist Leonardo da Vinci (1513 A.D.), and the other was a painting of a Buddha from the 14th century, and in both these paintings these religious figures were holding a sphere in their *left* hand. Author and mythologist William Henry, a frequent guest on this program, was talking about them. I contacted him by email to see if I could learn more. He told me he'd keep an eye out for more images of these "orb holders," as he called them. He identified them with the Tibetan symbol of the Chintamani (pronounced chinta-mun-eye), described as the stone of heaven. The "orb handler" would purportedly possess the powers of the universe.

Could there be a connection?

While left-handed people are a minority, Keel claimed that he had found in his investigations that he was dealing with "more left-handed contactees than right-handed ones." Keel was very interested in any possible psychological, medical, and genetic characteristics or factors that might distinguish the UFO "contactee" from the regular populace.

Hemispheric brain shifts?

"The left-handedness seems to indicate the increased participation of the right lobe of the brain in mediumistic states," the late Dr. Nandor Fodor, a New York psychoanalyst, said in his exhaustive volume *An Encyclopedia of Psychic Science* (1966). In reviewing the literature of the investigations and reports of individuals with mediumistic abilities Fodor noted that in quite a number of instances during reported mediumistic entrancements the mediums would switch from being right-handed to left-handed, with other symptoms that reflected hemispheric shifts of consciousness as well.

A California contactee named Brian Scott was described being in a strange trance state while doing something like automatic writing (November 5, 1975) reported by someone identified as one Lou Savage, who said: "He looked strange: facial features were taut, like a semi-solid rock. His eyes had a fixed stare. Not on the paper, but on the wall in front of his desk, and his facial color was a dull gray; nothing even resembling skin tone as I know it. All the while Brian's eyes were fixed on the wall his left hand continued writing. *Brian is not left handed...*"

It was downright scandalous in Keel's view that the only full-scale psychological study of a contactee had been conducted back in the 1890s by Swiss psychologist Theodor Flournoy of the University of Geneva. His subject was a popular medium known as Helene Smith, who produced a complex "Martian" language. When in a trance state, Smith would often look for her pocket on the left side instead of the right, and if one of her fingers was pinched or pricked behind a screen, the corresponding finger on the opposite hand would be agitated.

Alien MIBs?

Sometimes the MIB encounters are of such high-strangeness that you can't help but wonder if they're the ever elusive non-human alien beings themselves! William Kent Senter of Burlington, North Carolina, who I interviewed for *Alternate Perceptions* back in 2017, had two spectacular, close range UFO sightings around ages nine and 14. He had another UFO sighting in the mid-1980s in adulthood and decided to get involved in UFO investigative work. He reached out for help to a well-known and respected ufologist, George Fawcett, who was also living in North Carolina.

Here is Senter's account:

"As a state section director and field investigator for MUFON [Mutual UFO Network], I received a call by MUFON HQ to the State Director to respond to the Alamance Co. Sheriff's Dept. request for possible help. I was to investigate a sighting and a cattle mutilation and abduction of an elderly farmer's prized cow. I met three deputy sheriffs and the farmer, who was highly upset, at his farm. Two days later, I got a visit from three MIB."

"I operated a mobile home community as well as an apartment community out of a mobile home/office that was my residence. I was familiar with having police come out occasionally to check on certain occupants. When the three MIBs were approaching the door, which was open to a glass storm door, my peripheral vision of them led me to think that the police were coming in again. I immediately swiveled around in my office chair to unlock the occupant files to my right, before turning to look at them as they entered. I am attaching a diagram of the office, so this will make sense to you."

"As I turned left to look at them, the first MIB came in and went to the corner chair (blue star). I immediately felt physically stunned as if I was being paralyzed with a strong sensation like an electric current running through my stomach. I was confused like being hit unexpectedly but extremely alert and conscious that something wasn't right. The first MIB was not normal in appearance as he must have been close to 7'- 8' tall and with the typical Sinatra/Fedora hat, had to bend his head down to come in the door. His body and face shocked me as it was abnormal in the fact that his face was extremely thin and skin that looked "milky white and almost translucent." Very tall and lanky. Then the red star MIB that I will call "Shorty" came in and asked, "Are you William Senter?" Then he was followed by the third MIB, who took all of my attention at once as he was "identical" to the first, and I cannot express enough how alarmingly identical they were! I immediately knew something strange was happening as I couldn't move. Sitting, I looked up to the tall MIB at the door. When he entered, he turned toward me with his back facing the opened door, almost like a robot and standing at attention. As they all had dark sunglasses on, I wanted to see their eyes as I knew they were not normal. I was shocked as the millisecond that I thought I wanted to see his eyes from under his glasses (as I was sitting and he was standing) he immediately dropped his head toward the floor so I could not look under his lenses and see them. I felt and I 'knew' that he was reading my thoughts. I kept saying over and over in my head, 'I know you hear me and I want to see your eyes.'"

"Over and over and over again. I could not take my eyes off of him for what seemed like minutes, then I could hear 'Shorty,' as he had been talking, but I did not hear anything but background mumbling, as I was focused on the MIB at the door. I couldn't even speak! It seemed like my focus broke as I turned to Shorty who was screaming at me by now, and saying, 'You are not to go back out there! Do you understand?' As I turned my head to him, peripherally I could see the first MIB was now crouched to my left right behind me. I could not move or turn around but noticed his hands were cupped over as if you were trying to touch your wrist with your fingers. He was also next to my left shoulder now. As my eyes looked up at Shorty, it was if he was also reading my thoughts as he angrily ripped off his glasses, as if to honor my thoughts, exposing the bluest and strangest eyes I have ever personally seen. They were bigger than silver dollars and *perfectly* round with almost all of the eye the brightest blue and hardly any white surrounding, and with a large black pupil. I will also attach my attempt to show you his eyes. Another strange point is that none of them had any facial hair including Shorty who did not even have eyebrows. No hair around their hats, etc. Shorty was also the only one who talked and he was short and stocky, not too much taller than me sitting in my chair. At this point they just left as I was turned facing the front wall, which I do not remember doing. I remember that I thought to get up and see the license plates on their car, but I couldn't move. I was able to get up as they drove away and it was a older model sedan with G/S government plates, but I could not see the numbers as they turned to leave. With what seemed like five minutes had passed, I noticed that it was 25 minutes later and when I went to the VHS camera that was in the kitchen, the tape door was opened and the tape was gone. I immediately sat down knowing that they were not normal and that I just had a physical encounter."

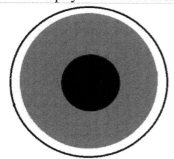

"Another strange thing is that my wife bought me a copy of Nick Redfern's book, *The Real Men in Black*, in 2012, and Shorty looks like the MIB pictured on page 65, except shorter. Keep in mind that I had this encounter at the end of May 1993 and told my wife in 2002. This event caused me to back off investigations for years. I never noticed their hands except the cuffed over one who was crouching by my left shoulder, and it seemed Shorty pulled his glasses off with his left hand. The electric stunning sensation lasted until they were out the door. If I saw these beings in the middle of Times Square on New Year's Eve, I would know them instantly. Their appearance is permanently etched in my memory. Another strange item is that I just introduced myself to the deputies as Kent with MUFON. I just gave them my middle name and no first or last name and no address when I contacted them by phone. The MIB's showed up at my home/work office and asked me if I was William Senter."

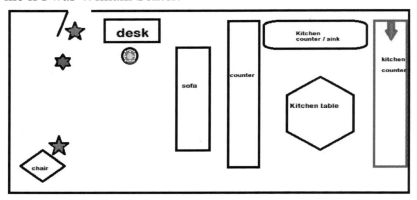

"George Fawcett once told me about an MIB encounter he had in the 60's while speaking in Chicago. They threatened him to stop talking about UFOs and when he arrived back in North Carolina, he found out they had shown up at his daughter's college harassing her. He was shocked that they knew where he was in Chicago and also where his daughter went to college out of state."

I was at a meeting of the New England UFO Study Group in Braintree, Massachusetts on Oct. 16, 1977, where George Fawcett was a speaker. He told an MIB story that happened in Columbia, South Carolina. George had done a slide presentation. Afterward, a stranger told him that he wished to speak to him privately. He was about five feet 10 inches tall, about 180 pounds, and had a rounded face. He looked "Arabic." The man gave his name, which George later could not recall, and showed George an identification card that had four letters on it.

George followed the man outside to a new black-colored car. The man told George that his associate had committed suicide earlier that week. He asked George a series of psychological questions. The test took about 20 minutes. The man told George he passed the test and tried to get him to sign some sort of paper. George refused, which seemed to upset the man. The man even offered to pay George a large sum of money, showing him about $10,000 in cash. The MIB told George he could take him out to meet the UFO beings if he liked. "I'll make you a wealthy man," the stranger told him. George said it was tempting, as he was semi-employed at the time, but he still refused. The stranger then gave him $200 and told him to take his family out to eat. At first George refused, but the man insisted. George later used that money to take his 10-year-old son, a Civil War buff, to Virginia on a historic site tour.

The late Dr. P.M.H. Edwards, a former Professor of Linguistics at the University of Victoria, British Columbia, investigated a high-strangeness MIB situation. Dr. Edwards was an extremely thorough and objective investigator and was a former contributor to England's *Flying Saucer Review,* and even my own *Alternate Perceptions* magazine. There were two witnesses to the MIB incident, both of whom lived in North Victoria a few miles from where Dr. Edwards lived. One witness, Grant Breiland, a 16-year-old high school student, was of above average intelligence and a keen observer who had created his own part-time business inspecting the homes of absent people. He had even helped in the arrest of a man who was trying to break into a parked car. He handcuffed the man and the police took him to the station. He carried a CB walkie-talkie radio around with him and had a two-way desk radio at his home office, from which he ran his business. "I have also noticed that he is meticulous about keeping important items always under lock and key; and he has proved himself reliable in several ways, besides," Dr. Edwards noted. "These are some of the reasons why I felt inclined to believe his story implicitly."

Dr. Edwards was alerted to this case on Sunday morning, October 4, 1981, when an acquaintance notified him that the Sunday morning edition of the *Victoria Times-Colonist* carried a story about a 16-year-old boy who had photographed an apparent UFO on Friday, October 2, 1981, around 9:30 p.m. The sky had just turned clear, as most clouds had moved westward. Young Grant was standing outside when he noticed an unusually large and bright "star" high in the sky. He tried to point it out to his sister and mother, who were nearby, but they could not see it for some reason. Many stars were visible in the sky.

Convinced that one particular "star" stood out as distinctly unusual from the rest, Grant got on his walkie-talkie and asked if anyone listening was up on Mount Tolmie, a location some three miles from him that provided a clear view of the sky. A 19-year-old referred to simply as N.B. in Edwards's report (anonymity requested), said he could see it, and checked it out with binoculars.

Grant went inside his house and retrieved his camera and a tripod, which he quickly brought outside and set up. He had a Ricoh KR 5, a 35mm Pentax; a tripod VELBON VGB 3; and color film ASA 100. Grant attached to the camera a Telsor Super-zoom Lens, 2 x 22 converter to 400mm, which he pointed up at a 45-degree angle. What he saw next convinced him that it was no ordinary star.

Edwards wrote: "It looked like an inverted object, because the dome was underneath. In the center of the UFO, there was a small diamond-shaped red light, that kept moving back and forth along the width of the object, and then down to the bottom of the dome and around, up the invisible side of the craft, and finally up over the top edge, and down again in front, in continual circular motion. Each time this little red light reached the center of the object, it halted for a brief instant, before resuming its gyrations."

"At the 12 o'clock, 3 o'clock, 6 o'clock and 9 o'clock positions around the object, and at some distance from it, Grant saw four fairly large white lights, a good deal bigger than the little red light, but smaller than the main object. These remained at a constant distance from the craft; when the latter moved, they moved with it, as though attached to it by an invisible link. On these four white lights that Grant described as circular, he thought he saw many dark dots, which he took to be – possibly – windows; these are shown, arranged in a pattern, on the accompanying diagram of the UFO. It will also be noticed that the central portions of these four lights displayed no dots; the latter were clustered at both 'ends' of each circular light, rather than in the middle. From the Mother-craft there were many yellow beams of light aimed towards each of these four lights; nowhere else were such yellow beams in evidence. Grant then took a picture, but it has not yet been developed."

"The craft then started to move slowly sideways to the left and to the right; then slowly upwards and downwards – just like the hand motions of a priest making the sign of the Cross. The four large white lights kept at the same distance from the central object, the small red light continuing its regular movement left and right, and then down, over, up, and down again, all around the large craft. However, at one point, the small red light stopped for two seconds in the center and beamed a red light directly at Grant's eyes; then it resumed its movements. At 9:59 p.m., he looked at his wrist watch, then back to the UFO, and, at precisely 10 p.m. everything was switched off, like an electric light bulb being extinguished."

Grant's impression of the red light being beamed at him is interesting, as earlier the other witness, N.D., stated: "All I can see now, is one big red light – and it's pointing right at me."

A few days later, the real high-strangeness began. On Monday afternoon, October 5, around 3:15, Grant headed to a Radio Shack to acquire a part for a radio that he had ordered. However, the part had not arrived, so he wandered the K-Mart shopping mall, where the Radio Shack was located, in hopes of finding a friend of his who he expected to meet up with there. After a while he called his friend's house on a pay phone to see if he was at home instead. He reached his friend's sister, who informed Grant that her brother had just broken his arm and would not be coming to the mall. After Grant hung up he turned around and immediately noticed two odd looking men nearby who were looking at him. Initially, he thought they were with the police, but then he dismissed that because they looked so odd, and this caused him to become frightened. Edwards noted: "Another thing that caused him fear, was the – at that moment – total absence of people passing through the vestibule while he was with those 'men.' Yet he distinctly remembered having seen many people walking about inside the store and along the outside sidewalk, since all the doors are transparent."

Grant said the two "men" were motionless and stood as though "at attention." They wore extremely dark blue clothing and shoes. They appeared suntanned, as though they had just had a "holiday in Hawaii." Their lips were not reddish but were exactly the same color as their skin. Their faces were devoid of expression and they didn't blink. Their eyes were dark and did not reflect any light. They had no eyebrows, but did appear to have eyelashes. Their hair was black (they wore no hats). He noticed that their earlobes looked oddly "squarish." They both had perfect looking teeth, but when they spoke their lips did not move at all, and they spoke in a monotonous, robot-type of voice. One of them asked him, "What is your name?" "I'm not going to tell you," Grant replied. Then the other said, "Where do you live?" Grant replied, "I'm not going to tell you that." Then he heard, from the one who had just asked where he lived, "What is your number?" He wasn't sure if they wanted his phone number or what was meant by that question, but he decided to not speak to them anymore. For about five seconds they just stood there staring at him.

"Then, as one man, they mechanically turned on their heels, and left by the main doors on to the sidewalk," Dr. Edwards wrote. "This they crossed, went stiffly down the short slope to the roadway (this slope is an aid for customers in wheel-chairs), and then turned stiffly, in complete synchronization, to the left as in military drill, and walked along the roadway parallel to the side-walk, towards the northern end of the car-parking area. At the edge of a ploughed-up field, they stopped for a short while in the heavy rain."

"Grant had followed them very closely at a distance of about two feet, and reports that they did not speak, neither did they turn round to look at him again. The strange thing, now, was that whereas in the vestibule Grant had distinctly seen very many people walking up and down the sidewalk outside, and many cars driving past, yet when he went out through the main doors to follow the 'men' there was no sign of life anywhere, and no moving cars; (he only noticed parked cars, some distance away). By now, Grant was getting quite drenched by the rain. He stopped by a line of decorative shrubs along the wall of the store and waited to see what the 'men' would do at the edge of the rough, ploughed up muddy field. (This field has since been bulldozed, preparatory to the erection of new buildings). On the farthest side of the field, some nine car lengths away, there is a stout wooden fence, and beyond that three white stucco houses. But, on October 5, the bulldozers had not yet begun their work, and the field was simply muddy, and full of small puddles, with practically no grass left."

"Suddenly, Grant thought he heard someone calling him by his first name from some 20 feet away behind him; he turned, but there was no one near him. He looked back at the MIB and saw that they were still standing at the edge of the rough field, in the heavy rain. I asked him whether he noticed if their hair and clothes were showing signs of becoming drenched; but he cannot remember this. Again, he looked back to make sure no one was calling him, but there was nobody there. He looked once more towards the MIB and saw that they had begun walking across the mud, in the direction of the wooden fence. He then again thought he heard his first name called out behind him from a little distance away, and he again turned around. No one was in sight. By that time, the MIB were three-quarters of the way across the field; then, they seemed to vanish into thin air."

"There are no trees or shrubs behind which they could have hidden in so short a time."

"Grant ran towards that spot, using exactly the same part of the field on which he had seen the MIB walking. His shoes quickly became very muddy, and he saw that the MIB had left absolutely no footprints anywhere. This thoroughly frightened him, so he turned back, ran to the bus-stop, and caught the Gordon He northwards so as to get home quickly..."

That same day, October 5, around noontime, about three to four hours prior to Grant's strange encounter, two slender "men" with white hair, pale skin, and dressed just like the two who had visited Grant later that day, also visited N.B. They showed up at the gas station where he worked, saying they needed gas for their car, which apparently was out of sight around some street corner. He located an empty can and asked them if they wanted leaded or unleaded gas. One of them replied, "I don't know," so he gave them unleaded. He asked for their names, so that he could get them to sign for the can of gas, but the same man who had spoken before said they couldn't give any name (the other never spoke). He asked how long they would be and was told 15 minutes. He then informed them that they owed him $2.65, and they gave him a bank note for 10 dollars. N.B. gave them their change and he noticed that the hand that was held out for the money had no fingernails (Grant didn't think that the "men" he had encountered had fingernails either). They examined the change as though they had never seen such objects before.

The "men" then turned around in a mechanical manner, walking stiffly, without bending their knees. He watched them walk away and turn into a side street. When they returned it had been exactly 15 minutes. They put the can down and looked at N.B. "Where do you live in this fine city?" he was asked. He told them, "At Gordon Head." They then turned around and walked away. After the "men" had left N.B. picked up the gas can which was still full of gas!

Making some kind of sense out of these high-strangeness MIB incidents is certainly a huge and challenging task. Some of them are certainly not ordinary narratives!

FOURTEEN
RELIGIOUS EVENTS, SHAPESHIFTERS, AND PHANTOM LANDSCAPES

The noted occultist Aleister Crowley claimed that he had established contact with a mysterious being named Lam. His drawing of Lam bears a haunting similarity to the alien greys of modern ufology. Crowley's being was small in stature, slender with a large head and eyes, and had grey skin. "Most magicians consider Lam and his ilk no different from the alien greys reported to be abducting people," wrote Michael Craft in *Alien Impact* (1996). "There are now active cults of Lam in Europe and North America, where people enact rituals for contacting these paraphysical aliens."

Turkish-born ufologist Farah Yurdozu further affirmed this connection in an article in *UFO Magazine* (Issue #157, October 2011). She wrote: "For some researchers, the modern UFO-ET era started with British occultist Aleister Crowley's ritual magick works. Between January and March 1918, Aleister Crowley conducted a magickal ritual in New York City. According to his account, he opened and activated a stargate, and a being he called Lam entered our physical dimension. The drawing of Lam made by Crowley has a remarkable resemblance with the typical gray aliens."

Psychologist and author Greg Little found in Chapter XLIV of the Book of Enoch (1928 translation) similar descriptions of what are called the "watchmen." "The Book of Enoch says that when evil people die the Watchers use a long tube to literally suck the soul up into them, and they contain it until they get to the gates of hell, which is also called Sheol," Greg explained. "Then they rotate it around and push the soul through the gates. The Book of Enoch went on to say that the creatures have the appearance of children, that *they're the size of small children, and that they're gray in color.*"

In 1896, Crowley was hiking in the Swiss Alps, at a location known as Arolla, near Zermatt, when he came upon two strange little men. He made a gesture to them but they failed to respond, and instead disappeared among the rocks. Jacques Vallee included this account in with many other early entity reports that go back years, and sometimes centuries, prior to the modern "flying saucer era," pondering their possible connection to the modern ufonaut stories in his thought-provoking book, *Passport to Magonia* (1969).

Many experiencers of close encounters with UFOs and their entities are "zapped" or temporarily paralyzed, perhaps to avoid confrontation and give the aliens -- or else give them an opportunity to take people aboard their "craft" for what many have described as a medical examination. "The 'fairies' of Ireland paralyzed the folk, and they distorted reality in all kinds of 'magical' ways," Keel noted. "Whole villages have been involved in celebrated, well-documented 'fairy' incidents. The 'trolls' of Scandinavia and the 'elves' of Germany's Black Forest may have been part of the same package, along with the 'Stick Indians' and the legendary 'Trickster' of the Southwest Pueblo culture."

The "little people" of the fairy legends and lore also could cause people to have mysterious lapses of time, which is hauntingly similar to our "missing time" episodes that repeatedly crop up in our hundreds of modern UFO alien contacts and so-called "alien abductions." Also, the reality distortions that Keel alluded to, like the term "Oz Effect" coined by British ufologist Jenny Randles, or the "screen memories" noted by UFO abduction researcher Budd Hopkins, all suggest further indications that the consciousness of the experiencer may have undergone some sort of altered state of awareness that may affect his perceptions and memories of what fully or actually occurred.

Unexplained landscapes

"Actually there are a great many cases in which the witnesses found they could not relocate the site of their experience," Keel noted in *The Mothman Prophecies* (1975). "Buildings and landmarks clearly seen at the time seem to vanish. Roads and highways disappear. This bewildering phenomenon is well-known in psychic lore also, probably because many psychic experiences are hallucinatory, too. There are innumerable stories about restaurants that seemed to dissolve after the witnesses stopped there. Tales of disappearing houses are common."

Keel wrote about such cases, including a brief mention of his own experience, in his column Beyond the Known in the December 1993 edition of *Fate* magazine. "I once visited a house in Ohio that wasn't there the next day," he wrote. "People in the area told me the house only appeared on dark and stormy nights. The weather was clear during my visit."

I know a retired college teacher and UFO contact experiencer who has many stories going all the way back to childhood. Once while on the Scottish island of Iona, he and a priest friend were hiking along the coastline that was rocky and had many ridges. They came upon a small flat ledge with a small stone building that had walls about eight feet tall, a moss-covered roof, and, oddly, had no doors or windows. Suddenly they saw nearby a small humanoid figure about a foot and half to two feet tall, "dressed in knickers et al and who looked like the traditional leprechaun." The being leaped off the ledge, and the men raced to it. When they looked down they saw only a large "jumble of boulders." Darkness was approaching so the two men moved on. Years later, my friend returned to the island. "I searched but could not find any area resembling our earlier climb, and, thus, no ledge and no windowless (or) doorless house and no little guy," he said.

British Nessie hunter F. W. Holiday wrote to Keel about a family in the south of England who had for years spent their weekends in search of a lake they had come upon some 15 years earlier. In the middle of the lake was a huge rock with a sword stuck in it. Intrigued they returned to research the matter further but could find no trace of the lake. There was nothing showing on any maps, and no one in the area had heard of it.

In 1976, I frequently visited Madeline Teagle of Cuyahoga Falls, Ohio, a woman who was a local contact person for anyone seeing UFOs, and who had also undergone the UFO contact experience herself years earlier. One evening a lady visited her and said she had just seen a ball of light four to five feet in diameter shoot straight up from the ground near a large oak tree by her home. Madeline, the woman and several others rushed to the location. It wasn't yet dark as they set out across a cornfield to get to where the woman had seen the strange light.

"All of a sudden I thought, 'That's odd,' because we had cut across a cornfield – but suddenly there wasn't any corn," Madeline recalled. "There was like a path but no trees on the other side of it and the path just seemed like it sort of disappeared into a grassy kind of meadow. I looked around and everybody else had this very funny expression on their faces. Immediately we got scared because we looked for the house and couldn't see the house. We figured we couldn't possibly be very far away. So we started to scream. We'd scream help and all kinds of stuff like that. We didn't hear anything at all. Then we decided that one person would touch the tree and we would like touch each other's arm and we would go out as far as we could, going in what we thought was the direction of the house and we would see if somebody could break through whatever it was we were in. At some point, one got in and said, 'Wow, we're in it -we're in a cornfield,' and the rest of us like went right straight through. Then we decided to turn around and go back in. It didn't happen that time."

"We got back to the house. They [the people who had remained at the house] were watching us the whole time. They could see us back there and they were wondering what in the world we were doing because they said we were running all over like chickens with our heads cut off. We said, 'Didn't you hear us screaming?' And they said, 'Yes, we heard you screaming, and we answered you and we kept answering you. But you never answered us.'"

Journalist Bob Teets investigated more than 150 eyewitness accounts for his book *West Virginia UFOs: Close Encounters in The Mountain State* (1995). One of my favorite UFO "hocus pocus" cases in the book involved a man named Gregg Knight, a deputy with the Harrison County Police Department. Gregg described an old man named Brian (pseudonym) who was quite a "mentally disturbed individual" who had "quit work because of events in his life and in his daughter's life in Louisiana because of contact with aliens."

One clear afternoon in 1990, Gregg and Brian were standing outside at a trailer park in Belmont, West Virginia, engaged in conversation. Brian was known to be very knowledgeable about Biblical matters and, in their conversation, Gregg said words to the effect, "If I ask my Dad a question, he answers. If I ask God the Father something, he won't answer, sometimes for years. Now why is that?"

Brian responded, "It depends on what you ask." Gregg came back with, "Like UFOs, what could they be? I want to see an alien craft not of this world." Brian said, "Look there," and Gregg looked to the west, and what he saw, he admitted, "took my breath away."

Bob's account of this story follows:

"It was a massive craft, so huge it "blocked out the sun, and yet it didn't cast a shadow." Gregg estimated it was more than 2,000 feet in length, with a finish like that of "a Chrysler 426 hemi-engine, that's it exactly." Its features resembled "a battleship turned upside

253

down. "I yelled for my wife as loud as I could, or at least I thought I did, but no one came out."

After it was gone, Gregg looked at Brian. "Did you see that!" he asked, incredulously. "Sure," Brian answered. "That ain't nothing, that's just a mother ship. You ought to see a colony ship. And then wait 'til you talk to 'em."

Brian's son, who was 20 miles away in Parkersburg, saw it too. From his perspective, it appeared to be about the size of a baseball on the horizon. Gregg became an active member of the Mutual UFO Network as a direct result of his dramatic encounter that strange afternoon in 1990.

This isn't the only UFO case where a small group of people observed something quite spectacular and massive in size that hundreds of others should have been quite startled by – something that should have resulted in a media sensation. Despite Gregg yelling to his wife at the top of his lungs, no one else ventured outside to observe the huge object. Indeed, often witnesses to UFO close encounters become somehow isolated from others. The neighborhood, the streets, the highways suddenly become eerily quiet and devoid of normal human activity or automobile traffic. As mentioned earlier, British ufologist Jenny Randles coined the term "The Oz Effect" for such situations. Have such witnesses become unknowingly and temporarily pulled into a parallel world that outwardly resembles our own on the surface? Or is this an experience similar to religious visionary phenomena, induced perhaps by an alien intelligence of some sort that floods our consciousness with powerful imagery through altered states?

When I was 19, I wrote Keel to gain some information and insight he might be willing to share on how I could investigate experiencers of the UFO contactee syndrome. "Essentially, the contactee experience is identical to religious apparition phenomenon and probably is caused by the same factors," he wrote. "It might be best to familiarize yourself with the medical and psychiatric studies of the religious cases before you tackle the UFO variation."

UFO-type Lights and Religious Revivals

In Ireland in 1859, a huge religious revival was underway. Many of the revival events were conducted outdoors, with as many as 600 to 1,000 persons in attendance. A dazzling "cloud of fire" would descend and hover over many of these revivals. Similarly, an intense religious revival broke out in Wales during the winter of 1904-05, and many observed mysterious lights in the sky. A 38-year-old Welsh woman named Mary Jones, described as an ordinary, happily married peasant woman who was deeply religious, became a central figure in this revival. Reporters from the *Liverpool Echo, Daily Mail, Daily Mirror,* and *London Daily News* travelled to these gatherings to see what was going on. The reporters wrote about seeing unexplained light phenomena. For example, Mary Jones was in a carriage with three women returning home one night after a meeting when their carriage was suddenly illuminated as though it were broad daylight. Quite a number of others witnessed it, as well as two skeptical reporters from London. Beriah G. Evans, a writer for the *London Daily News* (February 9, 1905) wrote: "'We cannot start yet,' she (Mary Jones) told me on the occasion of my visit, 'the lights have not yet come. I never go without them.' A few minutes later, on going out to see, she returned saying: 'Come. It is time to go. The lights have come!'"

On Tuesday, January 31, 1905 at about 6:15 PM, Evans, Jones, and three others witnessed a brilliant star-like object to the south emitting "diamond-like sparklets." "It took a sudden leap of considerable distance towards the mountains, then back again to its first position, and again rushing towards us," Evans reported. It disappeared from sight and then reappeared much closer to their position, and then it went out. "Following the disappearance of the star came immediately two brilliant and distinct flash-lights, illuminating the stone dykes and heather on the mountain side, the first flash two miles away, the second immediately following a mile higher up the valley, and in the direction we should have to travel. 'Come,' said Mrs. Jones, recognizing the omens, 'We shall have a glorious meeting!' And we did."

Up to that point, all five had seen the same things, but the next two anomalous displays were only witnessed by Jones and Evans, even though all five of them were still walking in the road together and all five should have seen what followed next. Evans wrote: "Three bars of clear white light crossing the road in front from right to left, climbing up the stone wall to the left, showing every interstice and bit of moss as clearly as though a searchlight had been turned upon it. There was no house, or human being other than our party, near, and no conceivable human agency could have produced this effect.'"

Subjective Encounters

Next a "blood-red light" appeared about a foot off the ground, in the middle of the roadway. Interestingly, Evans noted that it "did not illumine surrounding objects." He was surprised when he later learned that the others had not seen what he and Jones had seen and wrote that those others were equally astounded. "Mrs. Jones, without any suggestion from me, described there and then the appearances precisely as they had presented themselves to me."

Evans learned of a similar instance involving a London journalist who witnessed, along with a woman standing near him, a white light that swept along the ground near a chapel, stopping on a wall. Half a dozen other witnesses present said they didn't see it.

The late Swiss psychologist Dr. Carl G. Jung struggled to understand such anomalies. He wrote: "I was once at a spiritualistic séance where four of the five people present saw an object like a moon floating above the abdomen of the medium. They showed me, the fifth person present, exactly where it was, and it was absolutely incomprehensible to them that I could see nothing of the sort."

Jung knew of a few other cases like this and could not determine an explanation.

"A great number of UFO sightings are entirely subjective," Keel wrote in his privately circulated newsletter, *Anomaly* (No. 3,

December 1969). "RAF Air Marshall Sir Victor Goddard
[involved in the UK's Royal Air Force's UFO investigations in the
early 1950s] has suggested that such sightings are made by persons
with latent or active psychic abilities, but that when non-psychics
stand within the 'aura' of the psychic percipients they are also able
to see objects which would normally be invisible to them."

Victor Goddard, on a very personal level, little doubt had a much
deeper grasp of high-strangeness in these matters than most. In
1934, as a Royal Air Force pilot, flying a Hawker Hart biplane
fighter, he found himself caught in a dangerous thunderstorm over
Scotland. This was in a time before pilots had the electronics and
navigational aids they have today. He was guided largely by
intuition and his knowledge of the landscape. He cut back on his
power and glided downward, carefully avoiding the blackest
clouds ahead of him. He was hoping to locate an abandoned airport
known as Drem. He figured that if he could make it there then he
could hopefully make it to safety by landing on one of its old and
unused airstrips.

Gradually he descended through increasing turbulence, coming out
beneath a boiling cloud base, soon recognizing what appeared to
be familiar landmarks. If he was correct, then Drem was just
ahead. Then he saw it, dead ahead, when unexpectedly, at a
distance of about quarter of a mile, the dark and ominous clouds
separated and the landscape below was bathed in a dazzling golden
illumination.

Goddard decided to first fly over the airfield and ascertain the
condition of the runway before attempting to land his plane. When
he did so, he couldn't believe his eyes, because although it was
indeed Drem, it was no longer an abandoned airfield in ruins, but
rather a bustling airport with hundreds of people and rows of
airplanes! He had flown over at a height of only some 50 feet,
thinking it odd that no one looked up at him as he buzzed the
airport at such low altitude. He made a second pass, again ignoreby
people on the ground. He stared in disbelief at mechanics below in
blue coveralls who were working on rows of planes painted in

bright yellow. This threw him, since he knew that this had to be a training field, but the Royal Air Force trainers at that time were all painted silver. He didn't see a single silver-colored aircraft anywhere.

After the pilot's second pass the clouds lifted suddenly and he decided to return to the sky and continued on to his original destination. This story is said to be in the official registry of the Royal Air Force.

Martin Caidin, a professional pilot, veteran of World War II and a former FAA examiner, wrote in his book, *Ghosts of the Air*: "In 1938, with war with Germany fast becoming a reality, the Royal Air Force returned to Drem with a crash program to rebuild the airfield and transform it into a top-priority, top-quality training installation. Soon Drem was a major RAF training base, and when it opened for full operation, *the color scheme of all the RAF trainers was changed from silver to yellow.*"

In Keel's *Anomaly* newsletter, the second edition back in September 1969, he provided his readers an extended series of quotes from a very thought-provoking UFO talk that Sir Goddard gave on May 3, 1969, at Caxton Hall, in London, England. Keel pointed out that there was a publicized UFO flap going on in England at that time. Goddard described how UFOs could be "paraphysical" and "normally invisible" to us and even speculated how they might be composed of material of a "relatively aetheric" nature. "The astral world of illusion which (on psychical evidence) is greatly inhabited by illusion-prone spirits, is well-known," he further remarked.

Keel went on to speculate that when a person or persons with the appropriate psychic qualifications was at a site of elevated UFO activity "when specific electromagnetic conditions" were just right, then they might perceive things beyond the visible EM spectrum, or even "intercept a 'signal' which plants an image in his or her mind."

Again returning to the Welsh revival, divine signs and marvels were everywhere. Late one evening, Jones was getting a ride home after a revival meeting from a man described as "a respectable country tradesman," who harbored some personal doubts about the phenomena. During the drive he silently prayed to himself that if Jones was indeed a divine messenger of heaven, he be given a sign. Immediately a "misty star" ahead of them was transformed into a luminous cross composed of sparkling diamonds, and upon the cross was a draped human form with head bowed. Then, as mysteriously as it had appeared, the cross vanished, and, as the account reads, "he went on his way rejoicing."

Sinister Apparitions

Mary Jones described to Evans a remarkable personal experience that she had as she was returning home from a revival another night. The driver let her off near her home. She thought her brother was coming down the lane to meet her, as he often did. She walked toward him, but he turned and began walking just ahead of her. She called out to him and then the figure looked back over its shoulder, at which point she realized it wasn't her brother. She began softly singing a revival hymn. Her suspicion was confirmed when the human like figure transformed into an enormous black dog that began to run back and forth across the road before her. "And then," she told Evans, "I knew it was the Devil himself, angered at my assault upon his kingdom. I prayed for strength – and as I prayed he rushed growling into this very hillock," which Mrs. Jones pointed to on the side of the lane.

"In the neighborhood dwells an exceptionally intelligent young woman of the peasant class, whose bedroom has been visited three nights in succession at midnight by a man dressed in black, whose appearance corresponds with that of the person seen by Mrs. Jones," Evans wrote. "This figure has delivered a message to the girl, which, however, she is forbidden to relate."

Not far away, at Abergynolwyn, a center of mining, there was yet another report of "an apparition, appearing first as a man and then transforming itself into a large black dog."

There were a number of similar reports. One of Mrs. Jones's converts had been an aged Welsh man who, had it not been for the "temptations of the tavern and its accompaniments of cup and bottle," had the potential talent to have been a poet. Crossing some fields in broad daylight that December, he suddenly found himself in an unfamiliar place where "a number of ravening beasts," attacked him, Evans wrote. However, a man in white garments came to his aid, whereupon the "beasts" backed off. Then, once again, he was back on the path he had been on before. Afterward, confused by what had happened, he relapsed into drinking heavily for a couple of days. Then again, in the daylight, he was once more crossing a field when he found himself in a strange land. The man in the white garments appeared again, this time leading him to the banks of a great river. On the other side was a crowd of people in white happily singing songs. The stranger told him that that was where he should be and that he had work to do. "Thou must first conquer the beasts – and to do that I give thee my help." After this, the man gave up drinking and threw himself into "revivalist work."

The phrase "thou must first conquer the beasts" reminded me of an Ohio contactee case I looked into in 1975. A man claimed he was beamed up into an "enormous green translucent sphere" and taken in a short time to a strange new world out in space. On this other planet, robed humanoid beings with large heads and slanted eyebrows placed him in the middle of a large stone octagonal court with gates around the outer edge. He was given what appeared to be a spiritual test clothed in the language of symbology. The beings called it "the lion test," for lions emerged from gates that raised up. He was told to "stand it" and to "watch this force that contains the lion."

"They had a force that kept that lion from moving," he said. "I was led to understand that evolution can occur in different directions at this point. That is, the thought forms that constitute the spirit are not the same as the thought forms that constitute the appearance of the body. They were showing that this force contained these lions or held the balance of nature so that nature does not attack."

Meanwhile, black beasts that resemble large dogs have, down through the centuries, figured into many frightful religious accounts. One well-known one, which Keel pointed out was recorded in numerous historical documents, happened on Sunday, August 4, 1577, in England. It began when lightning struck a church in Bliborough, in Suffolk, killing two people and injuring several others. That same day, some parishioners reportedly died when "a thing like a black dog" materialized at a church in Bungay. Seven miles from there, at a church in Blythburgh, a creature resembling a giant dog allegedly attacked and killed two men and a boy, leaving deep claw marks in church masonry.

Such creatures are still afoot to this day. Michael Craft, in his book *Alien Impact* (1996), described a personal encounter in 1976. He and fellow graduating high school classmates were sorrowing over the suicide of one of their own. After attending the funeral, he and a group of friends headed to an abandoned house nearby in Towson, Maryland, where they had in the past often hung out with their friend. The location had a reputation for being haunted, and this night would validate that notion completely. The group of 14 teenagers eventually dwindled to five. While getting ready to leave, Craft and his four friends suddenly noticed a strange glowing "green fog" pouring out of an empty fireplace. The fog carried a pungent, chemical odor, and though there was no wind, it suddenly became quite cold. The teenagers were terrified. For Craft, it was his first experience of having his hair "standing on end."

"As we descended the front steps of the house, we glanced behind us and saw the shape of a huge, black dog with burning red eyes standing in the doorway we had just left!" Craft wrote. "Though there was little light except for the stars and we had no flashlight, the dog's brightly glowing eyes were clearly seen."

Cynthia Newby Luce, an American with a master's degrees in experimental psychology and anthropology, lived in Brazil for years and investigated UFO cases. One involved a family in Petropolis, a large city where a chupacabra outbreak was being reported in the local newspapers. At the same time, the family was seeing a low-level UFO flying around. The husband and his younger sister saw a "black, furry, dog-like creature with red-glowing eyes between two houses on several occasions. It seemed menacing."

Something Stinks, and it's not just in Denmark

"The most common trait of UFOs is their vanishing act," Lyn Halper, Ph.D., a New York transpersonal psychologist and a professor of psychology at Mercy College told me. Dr. Halper authored the book *Adventures of a Suburban Mystic* (2001), which recounts her personal experiences with kundalini. She worked for years with noted Polish born parapsychologist Dr. Alex Imich, who was a good friend of John Keel. "Yetis leave tracks that end abruptly as though they've disappeared into thin air," Dr. Halper said. "My friend and interviewee, Heshheru, a Jamaican shaman, tells me that Jamaica vibrates with paranormal phenomena. He describes a rolling calf with glowing red eyes seen for decades by islanders that is always accompanied by a noxious odor like burning chemicals or electrical wiring. This same phenomenon, the chemical-burn odor, is commonly reported around UFO close encounters."

Scorched earth and a strong smell of brimstone lingered where these phantom black dogs have appeared. "Mothman, like phantom kangaroos and the redoubtable Bigfoot, [belonged] to that class of beasties known to the ancient Greeks as Chimeras," Keel wrote. "The Greeks noted that such animals usually had fiery red eyes, were often surrounded by the smell of 'fire and brimstone' (hydrogen sulfide) and often disappeared as suddenly and mysteriously as they had come. In countless UFO cases we also find all of these characteristics. The UFO is surrounded by a terrible smell, like the smell of rotten eggs (hydrogen sulfide again), sometimes making the witnesses ill."

The Jamaican shaman also conducted seances for Dr. Imich, which produced some intriguing paranormal phenomena at times. Dr. Halper said Keel attended a couple of these sessions. She later read a number of Keel's books and found them quite thought-provoking and revealing.

The glowing red eyes are believed by many to indicate the presence of an evil or demonic spirit. Keel noted that controversial religious texts some two thousand years old described how Christ had ordered followers to stone a pitiful looking beggar. They were taken aback by this order, but nonetheless obeyed, and that once the stones began to strike the beggar he slowly changed into a hairy beast with fiery red eyes!

"Lightning often accompanies these manifestations," Keel noted, and provided additional examples in his book, *Strange Creatures from Time and Space* (1970). For example, in 856 A.D. at a church in Trier, Prussia, "a dog of immense size" appeared in the midst of a storm. The floor of the church opened up and a huge creature rose out and ran back and forth to the altar.

At Christmas Eve, 1171 A.D. at a church in Andover, Hunts, England, a "gigantic pig-like creature" allegedly dashed around the altar as the priest was struck and killed by lightning -- which appeared from within the church itself!

Keel was also intrigued by strange "monsters" that reportedly lurked in the Black River in the Adirondack Mountains of New York. He cited the case of a man named Wash Mellick who was fishing in that river in 1951when a 15-foot tall "monster" rose from the water near his boat. "It was dark brown in color and had a round, tapered body. It had fins like two hands, and its eyes stuck out like silver dollars. I threw stones at it, but it only stared at me."

The newspapers in the area noted that these occurrences seemed to always occur during electrical storms.

Lightning strikes accompanied by unusually large black dogs with glowing eyes and other assorted "monsters" aren't the only disturbing occurrences that have been reported. According to author Vincent Gaddis, in his book *Mysterious Fires and Lights* (1967), the Welsh revival quickly spread into Scotland and England, where it degenerated into mass hysteria. People stood outside football games and theaters trying to keep others from entering and some burst into police stations trying to convert the police. In Liverpool, there were riots where revivalists slugged Catholics and stoned their homes. One man, taking the Bible literally, cut off his right hand. Another man led a nightly procession, dragging a coffin behind him. Groups of women in Leeds stopped carriages and cars in the streets and tried to force their passengers to join them in street meetings. Men entered stores to return items that they had not even stolen. Suicides and mental breakdowns became commonplace. "Holy dancers" appeared on the streets of London. A Liverpool magistrate proclaimed, "When you see one of these processions, run from it as you would from a mad bull."

Spontaneous human combustion

"And it was in the midst of this excitement that there were instances of apparent spontaneous human combustion," Gaddis added. Five to be exact, from December 16, 1904, beginning with a widow, Mrs. Thomas Cochrane, of Rosehall, Falkirk, whose remains had been found in a chair in her bedroom "burned beyond recognition." The pillows and cushions surrounding her body had not been burned, and there had been no outcry and no fire in the grate. The last occurred on February 28, 1905 in Blyth with the death of 77-year-old Barbara Bell, whose body had been found "fearfully charred," lying on a sofa, looking as though the woman had been subjected for an extended period of time to "intense flames." Neighbors had noticed smoke issuing from the windows of the widow's cottage.

About a week after Mrs. Cochrane's death, an elderly Elizabeth Clark, who lived in Trinity Almshouse in Hull, was discovered with burns covering her body, but she was still alive. She died later, but while still alive was unable to explain her own injuries. Her bedclothing was not scorched and people in nearby rooms had heard no outcry. There had been "no fire nor light in the room."

Early in February 1905, a coroner in London was puzzled with the discovery of a fatally burned woman who had apparently fallen asleep in front of the fireplace. While the coroner conceded that a cinder might have ignited the woman's clothing, the burns were on her back and her body was found facing the fire. Around this same time, a coroner in Louth was puzzled by the body of Ashton Clodd, 75, who died of severe burns at the Louth Hospital, despite very little fire in his fireplace.

On September 13, 1967 an experienced fire officer in England, Jack Stacey, led a fire crew into a deserted building in Lambeth, London. They confronted a strange situation. In the building was a tramp named Bailey who was on fire. Curiously, a blue flame was coming out of a four-inch slit in his abdomen! The firemen placed a hose into his abdominal cavity. "Bailey was alive when he started burning and must have been in terrible pain," Stacy stated. "His teeth were sunk into the mahogany newel post of the staircase." They were unable to save him.

"Contrary to what was once believed, SHC [spontaneous human combustion] is not always fatal and the existence of survivors poses a profound challenge to the debunker," American author Larry E. Arnold, a SHC researcher who has done exhaustive research on this subject has been quoted saying.

In the *Transactions of the Medical Society of Tennessee* for 1835, the volume 17 edition of the *American Journal of Medical Science,* Dr. John Overton, M.D. described the puzzling partial spontaneous combustion of a 35-year-old mathematics professor in Nashville, Tennessee.

The subject, Mr. H., stated that the episode occurred on January 5, 1835. He had just walked about three-fourths of a mile from the university to his home. It was a chilling eight degrees above zero. Shortly upon arriving home Mr. H. stepped outside when he became aware of a pain in his left leg. The pain was steady and had the intensity of a hornet sting accompanied by a sensation of heat. Glancing down, Mr. H. perceived a bright flame several inches in length with a width of a dime. He slapped at it several times, but it kept burning. Then with his bare hands, he cupped his hands over it, figuring he could cut off the oxygen, and that extinguished the flame.

Gradually the pain lessened. Returning inside, H. removed his trousers and underwear and inspected his leg. He found a small abrasion-like burn, about three-fourths of an inch in width and three inches in length. The trousers were not burned at all, although a small hole had burned through his underwear. Although the burn was like any ordinary burn in appearance, it was deeper and did not heal as quickly as such burns normally do.

And, of course, there was the fundamental question of what caused Mr. H's flesh to ignite in the first place? He was outside in freezing weather and nowhere near any source of heat.

Science is at a loss to explain spontaneous human combustion. In these cases, the body can be reduced mostly to ashes. Consider that cremating a body requires hours at about 3,000 degrees Fahrenheit! Curiously, in cases of spontaneous combustion the feet, hands, and head are only partially burned.

Can something unknown about human chemistry account for these bizarre fires? Ivan T. Sanderson said spontaneous human combustion reminded him of atomic heat. Another explanation put forward is heat generated by kundalini.

The Mystic Fire – Kundalini?

Ancient eastern wisdom describes kundalini, also known as "mystic fire" and "liquid fire," as an energy that can flow from the base of the spine up the spinal column to the top of the head, opening energy centers called chakras along the way. Kundalini is a spiritualizing force associated with enlightenment, but if it is awakened forcefully can wreak havoc on the physical body as well as one's mental and emotional states. Tibetans and Hindus have meditation exercises to gradually and carefully guide one through the awakening process. Kundalini can awaken spontaneously through accident, trauma, emotional crisis and other triggers. Do victims of SHC experience a spontaneous rush of intense kundalini?

The Kung shamans of the Kalahari Desert utilize special ceremonial dance movements to generate a fiery psychic energy called the Num. The Num travels up the spinal column into the skull where it results in a transformative state they refer to as Kia. The Hopi Indians describe a force that moves up through the solar plexus, the heart, throat and forehead to the crown of the head, which are the same energy centers (chakras) recognized by the Tibetan and Hindu mystics of the East; they just have different names for them. Both the Hopi Indians and the Eastern Indians agree that the crown is the highest center, and it is where consciousness enters the body at birth and leaves the body at death.

Michigan researcher Dennis Morrison investigated the Chippewa tradition of the Mock-wa-mosa, also known as the Bearwalker. Practitioners shape-shift, and can appear as a bear, an owl, or a glowing orb. People claim to have actually encountered such manifestations. Chief Nahgahgwan told Morrison that he and another man had come upon one of these while walking on a wooded path near Mikado Reservation. It appeared first as an approaching "bright ball of light." "He told me that the one way to be able to render the Mock-wa-mosa powerless was to double back on it, where it had already come down a path, take a pinch of sand and put it in your cheek, and that renders them powerless," Morrison recalled. "I think he said that they were actually able to put their arms around it and the individual turned from the light back into the person that it was. It was a woman. He wouldn't tell me her name because she still lives up there, but later I interviewed, for an article that I did, a lady named Mrs. Beaver, and she was a very elderly lady. She couldn't tell me how old she was but her face was so deeply etched with wrinkles and I remember her talking about the power that she had. She wouldn't say the word Mock-wa-mosa but the power that she had that she could actually go in and steal people's souls when they were sleeping. It was an evil power and it was a power that a person had to use and it was a power that was bestowed upon them, that was not necessarily something that they wanted. But a relative who maybe was dying could bestow that power to them."

In Hawaii, a mysterious UFO-like ball of light is called an *akualele,* which means "flying god." According to Hawaiian born UFO researcher Kalani Hanohano, this light is also something dark. "The *akualele* are devices manufactured by kahuna sorcery whose main function is to harm or kill another human being," he told me, adding that it is a "supernaturally generated light phenomenon." As in other UFO encounters, a car engine may temporarily conk out while an *akualele* flies nearby.

From shapeshifters to mysterious lights generated by sorcery, some mediums reportedly can not only take on the different voice of a supposed spirit but also a completely different physical appearance. None of these bizarre manifestations would have particularly surprised Keel. He was quite familiar with the concept of a "tulpa," called such by ancient Vajrayana and Tibetan Buddhism. A "tulpa" is a thoughtform wherein energy can presumably be temporarily manipulated and even altered at the level of physical matter. He explained how we know that all solid matter is composed of energy and all energies are of an electromagnetic nature. He reasoned that within the electromagnetic spectrum there existed "an omnipotent intelligence" that usually remained hidden from our detection and that is capable of manipulating the energy of the EM spectrum in remarkable ways. "It can, quite literally, manipulate any kind of object into existence on our plane," Keel wrote. He explained that for centuries occultists and religionists had called this process transmutation and transmogrification.

Keel felt that this mysterious omnipotent intelligence resided in an energy field he called the superspectrum, which can occupy the same space that we do. "Two bodies cannot occupy the same space at the same time," he wrote in *The Eighth Tower* (1975). However, there was a catch. "Because the energy of the superspectrum is markedly different from the energy of the electromagnetic spectrum, the two can occupy a single space."

Could that other space be composed of what we today have been calling "dark matter" and "dark energy" I wonder? Keel speculated that in the "superspectrum" an intelligent energy existed that has a great deal of awareness about us while we're only vaguely aware of it. Furthermore, from its unique vantage point it could know about future events in our dimension. "The field is like a massive radio wave, and certain human brains have the ability to tune into it," Keel wrote. "Some of these brains are adjusted to the frequency of the bank of future data."

There is a popular account of a Belgian-French explorer and Buddhist scholar named Alexandra David-Neel who allegedly created her own tulpa during her travels in Tibet in the early 20th century. She claimed to have seen tulpas that others had created, and so one day she went about creating her own, out of curiosity and loneliness it seemed. She made it in the form of a fat and jolly Friar Tuck. "There is nothing strange in the fact that I may have created my own hallucination," she wrote. "The interesting point is that in these cases of materialization, others see the thoughtforms that have been created." Over time the friar tulpa lost weight and became rather sullen and David-Neel began to feel vaguely threatened and decided to be rid of him.

Dr. Kirby Surprise, who has a doctorate in counseling psychology, in his book *Synchronicity* (2012), described how he personally experimented with the tulpa phenomenon in his apartment in the San Francisco Bay Area. As his wife and he worked opposite shifts, he decided to create a tulpa to keep him company, as the apartment seemed a bit lonely and empty during her absence. So he visualized a transparent human figure about five foot tall. It had only the vague outline of a human form. When it was time to leave for work he "stopped the meditation." When he returned home 10 hours later he discovered that not only had it become real for him, but his wife as well. She had known nothing of his experiment, but while he was away she had gone to bed and had fallen to sleep. Until, that is, her husband's tulpa entered the bedroom and sat down on the bed next to her, waking her up. Knowing that he had been reading David-Neel's story of how she had created a tulpa, Dr. Surprise's wife angrily exclaimed, "Don't give me that innocent look, you made one of those things!" She ordered him to get rid of it, though later she decided he could continue with it so long as he kept it in his den area.

He agreed. Once after watching Jurassic Park he decided to create a fun raptor, one about three feet tall, with a lot of gold bling and diamonds set in his teeth, wearing a baseball cap. "He's a Veloci-rapper," Surprise wrote. "It's programmed to hang out in the den and greet people. Of course, nobody sees him. Almost nobody. Last year my daughter's friend Rose went into my den to look for something, and came out rattled and upset. She's a little high strung anyway. She said there was a giant lizard in my room. It jumped up and greeted her like a puppy dog. She said it was some kind of dinosaur. Some things are only funny if you have a sense of humor."

Such accounts certainly make you wonder what sort of mind created manifestations and possible interactions with Keel's "superspectrum" might be possible.

"The minister from London was on my right and the medium's wife was on my left, and we were all practically touching each other, just inches away," Frank C. Tribbe, a former U.S. Government attorney of 40 years, told me in an interview back in 2004. "This medium went into trance and the communicator from spirit turned out to be a Chinese person. Apparently it was one of the more common communicators who came through this particular medium and the minister from London had been to this medium before and he recognized the voice and spoke to him and welcomed him. The thing of it was here was this medium, only a foot or two from me, and his face was as typical a British face as you can imagine, but as soon as that communicator, who was supposedly a Chinese person from two or three centuries past, began speaking through the medium, that face changed into a round, Chinese yellowish face. For about 45 minutes, as this reading went on, it was like that face right in front of me there, of a Chinese. Then finally when the reading ended and the minister on my right told the communicator thank you and goodbye, the yellow round Chinese face vanished and the normal British face of the medium returned."

Tribbe said this phenomenon is not uncommon. "It's something that the British Society has done over the years," he explained. "I've got a huge library of several thousand books and I have books from the Society there in London where they have photographed these images, and very often there would be two clairvoyants. One was getting a message and the other was getting a face of the communicator. She died only two or three years ago, but I have her book that she published only 15 years ago, and she would sit there and see the same spirit that the clairvoyant that was giving the message was seeing, only the one was hearing the words and speaking to the recipient, whoever it was, and this other one was an artist, and she would be doing a sketch. Several of them are recorded in this book and typically when she got through doing her picture she would pull it off her easel and give it to the person in the audience whom the reading was for, and time after time the person would come back the next day, or the next week, and show them photographs of the deceased person that was communicating and which this artist was copying as the other one was speaking, and they were almost a perfect match."

Robbert van den Broeke of the Netherlands is described as a remarkable psychic who gets precognitive impressions of crop circles that later appear, and has encounters with UFOs, balls of light, alien beings and spirits. "People come to him for all kinds of help, and one of the things that they come to him for is if somebody died in their family and they're upset – he sees their dead relatives when the client is there," crop circle researcher Nancy Talbott told me. "He takes photographs of the dead relatives when the client is there. He takes photographs of the dead relative and gives them to the client. That's how he knows that they are the relatives. The clients will tell him."

"My brother Bill died very unexpectedly," Nancy added. "Robbert had never met Bill, but two months after Bill's death I was in Holland and Robbert took 60+ photos of him." Nancy has made several trips to study Robbert's abilities and is convinced that he's the real deal. Various scientists have also been involved in studying the inexplicable things he can do. "He has an ability to access realities that we can't," she explained. "Now whether that means other dimensions or other worlds, I don't know."

Dan Drasin, the professional documentary filmmaker who had been a close friend of Keel's, visited Robbert van den Broeke where he lives near the small village of Hoeven, in February 2014. Drasin conducted a photo session with him that had controls designed to safeguard against fraud. A small video camera was mounted nearby on a tripod and the main video camera was attached to Drasin's upper torso by a body brace. Van den Broeke was positioned standing in front of a dark blue curtain. The two video cameras monitored Drasin and van den Broeke's interactions. Drasin also introduced a digital camera for taking still shots. The camera had no internal memory. Drasin used memory cards that had not been manufactured for at least five years, so it's not likely something that the vast majority could likely pull a smooth sleight-of-hand replacement with, and each card had been numbered in advance. Broeke handled the camera and snapped shots, trying for paranormal images. When he was finished, he handed the camera to Drasin, who moved to a nearby coffee table and unloaded each memory card into a password protected laptop computer. The computer, memory cards, and the still camera were in Drasin's view at all times. In one image a human looking hand appeared, and then there were two clear facial images that Drasin immediately recognized as appearing to be that of the late Friedrich Jurgenson, a well-known pioneer in EVP research.

While I was working on this chapter, I read an online post by Scott Gunn entitled "Angels: setting the record straight," in which he explained that our Hallmark versions of angels and cherubs as strikingly handsome and beautiful humans and cute little cupid baby forms isn't quite correct. They can often be strange and frightening in appearance Gunn said, pointing out that nearly every time angels appear to people in the scriptures, the angel says, "Be not afraid." This is strikingly similar to the first words (or similar words) articulated in many alleged alien being encounters today, be the message verbally or telepathically conveyed.

How long has this scenario been played out?

Rocky Incidents

The Minor Hill area of southcentral Tennessee was a site of a great deal of strange activity in the early 1970s. I became personally involved in 1975 thanks to a local newspaper columnist named Stanley Ingram who wrote for *The Pulaski Citizen*. I looked into stories of UFOs, MIBs, Bigfoot, and alien contact. I learned of one incident from a fellow investigator, Wyatt Cox. Some campers there one day heard footsteps coming down a dirt road nearby. They saw three tall black figures, which they initially thought were black people. They called out a friendly greeting to the tall dark strangers, but the figures remained silent. Then the figures detoured off the road and into a nearby creek, where they sank from sight. Then, much to the fright of the campers, rocks began flying out of the water, hitting them! One of the campers reportedly has never been the same since, suffering from a nervous condition with involuntary shaking.

Those tall silent figures failed to utter "be not afraid" to their unsuspecting viewers. The rock assault sounds like a poltergeist manifestation. I and many other investigators have confirmed through the years that, just as Keel had found, bizarre poltergeist occurrences frequently erupt in the homes of UFO experiencers soon after their close encounters.

In Minor Hill, I met UFO contactee David Swanner, who had described an unusual encounter as a young boy in 1946. He and other boys were walking to a church meeting one night when they observed a white robed figure with long blondish or red hair floating in the air and following them. Swanner said it "looked just like a man" and was about 25-30 feet off the ground. "We threw rocks at it," he recalled. "Never did hit it."

The Minor Hill episode with the campers reminds me of a personal episode described by Ivan T. Sanderson. He was in Sumatra in

1928, when suddenly dozens of shiny black pebbles from nowhere fell on a veranda near where he and some others were sitting. It was evening at the time. Curious, he and his friends marked some of the stones and threw them randomly into a nearby garden and shrubbery. "We must have thrown over a dozen such marked stones," he noted. "Within a minute they were all back! Nobody with a powerful flashlight or super-eyesight, could have found those little stones in that tangled mess...and thrown them back on to the veranda. Yet, they came back, all duly marked by us!"

Tim R. Swartz, an Indiana photojournalist and an Emmy-award winning television producer and videographer, investigated an odd poltergeist case in August 1984, when he was assigned to a TV station in Dayton, Ohio. The station received a call from a family in Springfield who was experiencing unwanted activity in their ranch-style farmhouse. They didn't want any publicity but needed help. Since Swartz had a personal interest in paranormal matters he talked with them several times on the phone, expressed a desire to meet, and reassured them that he would not produce anything to be broadcast. They agreed and soon he paid them a visit.

They were an elderly couple who were temporarily caring for two young grandchildren, a girl about 12 and a boy about nine. Swartz lugged one of his station's big cameras and a small 35mm camera. If there was any activity, he wanted to document it anyway, even if it wasn't going to be broadcast by his station. Though he had made sure his station's video camera was fully charged, after no more than five minutes every battery was dead, except for the 35mm camera's battery.

The activity had begun soon after the grandchildren had moved in and included raps on walls, furniture being moved about, and objects disappearing and reappearing in other locations. Swartz was seated on a couch talking to the couple, taking notes and sipping on lemonade when something quite unusual happened. All of a sudden, there was a huge bang like something large had struck the side of the house. The house shook. The grandparents indicated that more activity would follow.

The children were plainly visible down the hallway in a bedroom, playing a board game on a bed. "All of a sudden, from the center of the ceiling, small rocks started to fall down, maybe five or six in total," Swartz said. "But it looked to me like that they would just appear maybe a couple inches below the ceiling and then fall to the floor, and I have to admit I just sat there with these rocks falling down." He was so in shock he did not pick up his camera. "After they had collected them off the carpet I picked them up and they were slightly warm." The rocks were white and about the size of dimes and quarters, like the kind used on driveways.

"I got a bright idea, because I remembered something similar had happened to Ivan Sanderson," Swartz said. "I took out a magic marker and marked an X on these rocks. They had a relatively small backyard, past which was a cornfield – the corn was over your head. I went out the back door and chunked these rocks, one by one, in different directions into that cornfield, thinking, 'Ha! Find those!' I came back in, sat down, and almost as soon as I sat down here these rocks came back. They dropped down, one by one, and all of these rocks had an X on them. They were the exact same rocks that I had thrown out in the cornfield."

"This was the first time that the family had actually seen rocks actually being teleported, and that's what was happening. They were being teleported. I was seeing it. They were just as shocked as I was."

"I went up into the attic, which it wasn't much of an attic," Swartz continued. "It didn't even have a floor. You had to walk on the two-by-fours. I could see where the central light was because the rocks had come down from an area not too far away from where that central light was, but there were no holes on the ceiling, there was nobody hiding in the attic. So if it was a hoax it was a really good one. I don't know how they could have done it."

After that there were only a few minor incidents, and then the poltergeist activity ceased. Swartz was never able to explain what he had observed.

In the famous Bell Witch case of Adams, Tennessee, the John and Luce Bell family and their five children were besieged by a very powerful, vicious, but at times playful, mischievous series of poltergeist-type spirit disturbances. It began with their young 12-year-old daughter Elizabeth "Betsy" Bell in 1817. She became the main focus of these paranormal manifestations. She was witnessed receiving physical blows to her face, her hair painfully pulled, all by an unseen force. There were unexplained rappings on the windows and covers being pulled off of beds. Others also experienced the hair pulling, physical facial blows and covers being pulled. Although initially John Bell wanted to keep it all hushed, soon the word got out, and eventually neighbors even saw strange lights "like candles and lamps" moving about in the fields nearby. Farmers began to report inexplicable stone-throwing assaults too. One man witnessed several boys being pelted by sticks from a nearby thicket, though the sticks didn't have much force behind them, and instead of being scared the boys began laughing and threw the sticks back into the thicket. Soon the sticks came flying back out. The man watching this decided to take out his knife and cut notches into several of the sticks. Then he had the boys throw them back into the thicket, and again the sticks came flying back out, and this time the man was able to identify them as the same sticks as they had his notches on them. Included with the manifestations a voice from dark corners of the home eventually began communicating with the family and visitors. This activity went on until 1821. Skeptics and those who tried to rid the Bell home of this spirit suffered assaults as well. Some who spent the night found their bed covers being pulled off, and if they resisted they were slapped soundly on the face by this unseen presence. Two local preachers arrived to look into the disturbances and the Witch recited both of their Sunday sermons perfectly, word for word, and in perfect imitation of their very own voices. Even General Andrew Jackson left the Hermitage to pay a visit to the Bell's with a professional "witch layer" and several servants. John Bell was an old friend of the general. Jackson had intended to spend a week and deal with this spirit, but that very first night his witch layer was attacked by the Witch and fled in terror, with the servants right behind him. Jackson was forced to leave at that point, and reportedly his parting words to John Bell were that fighting this spirit was worse than having faced the British at the Battle of New Orleans.

A man in Palermo, Maine, who, along with many of his relatives was no stranger to paranormal and UFO phenomena and told me of an incident that happened to him one day in the spring of 1977. He had pulled out onto Route 3 from a Sunoco gas station in Palermo and was going about 45-50 miles per hour when he suddenly noticed a "tiny black ball" just three to four inches over the hood. "A few inches in front of the windshield it vanished," he told me. "Then I felt it hit my coat. It was as if someone tapped the coat very lightly. The object was about the size of a small marble."

What sort of world are we living in where rocks can just materialize out of the air, be thrown off to a fairly distant location and then almost instantly reappear? Who or what could be behind such manifestations?

Was Keel right? Is there this interactive intelligence that exists within what he called the "superspectrum" which usually co-exists unseen within our electromagnetic environment?

FIFTEEN
PARANORMAL BIGFOOTS?

While the majority of so-called cryptozoologists who document and try to track creatures like the elusive Bigfoot or Yeti believe that they're pursuing a physical apelike "missing link" yet to be identified by mainstream zoology, Keel felt that the truth was far stranger. "I've had reports where witnesses have seen a Bigfoot reach down to the ground and catch the hand of another Bigfoot, and pull it up out of the ground," he told author Andy Colvin. "The solid ground. [Then] the two of them would walk away. That's a pretty good indication that it's something other than an animal we're watching. We're watching the behavior of a paraphysical object."

Early on when I entered the UFO field back in the latter part of the 1960s, I investigated a family in rural Palermo, Maine. This family had a lot of UFO sightings, psychic experiences, and had also described seeing Bigfoot! The wife had said she had seen a man-like figure covered with long, shaggy whitish hair run from her car in huge leaps into the air. She said it was as though he had springs on his feet. Twice the husband had seen a grayish man-like figure himself that leapt across the road in front of his car. It was, he said, as though it was defying gravity as it seemed to effortlessly jump from one side of the two-lane country road to the other. This couple had also described some pretty wild encounters with ghost-like entities, details of which I had shared with Keel and which ended up in his book *Strange Creatures From Time and Space* (1970).

Back in May 1976, in rural Flintville, Tennessee, I came across citizens who were toting around rifles in fear of a Bigfoot-type creature that was seen by several in that area. There was one house where it reportedly grabbed at a 4-year-old boy. One witness though told me he was worried about people's safety from all of the rifle carrying Bigfoot hunters more than the so-called "monster" itself "I've lost a lot of sleep," he also complained. He had been getting a good number of crank phone calls at all hours of the night.

Reluctant initially to admit it, he eventually told me how he and others had frequently seen mysterious glowing balls of light, about the size of a streetlight, silently moving through the pine trees. He recalled how on one night a total of fifteen persons altogether had seen these lights. One night, later sometime in the summer of 1976, he and three others, he said, were startled to see a large "ball of fire" descend from the sky, over an estimated 1 ½ to 2 minute period of time, lighting the area up. It seemed to come down nearby, in a field, and made a swooshing type of noise. He thought that it had been a meteor, "as big as your car" he said, but soon afterwards when they searched the field there was no sign of any impact or debris.

I spoke with residents in three houses in a row. All described seeing the Bigfoot-type creature. Also on the scene I met a gentleman who had traveled all the way from New York to investigate these reports. His name was Lee Frank. He seemed like the right man for the job. A skin diver and photographer, I learned that he had spent six months at Scotland's famous Loch Ness. He later wrote an extensive article about his investigation in *High Times* magazine (January 1977). Though he never saw the creature himself, he had a number of very odd experiences. One night after he arrived, Frank was told how two of the locals hunting the creature had seen "great glowing spheres just above the trees several times." Frank joined them at the edge of the woods nearby waiting and watching, hearing something that sounded large stomping about. Eventually one of the men makes an unusual growl sound, that he says can attract the creature. Suddenly from the woods they hear heavy footsteps coming toward them. Within an estimated 25 feet, still under the cover of trees, there is suddenly a strange noise "like a loud mechanical clicking," Frank wrote. "Like baseball cards snapping against wheel spokes, only slow – about two clicks per second – and much louder, and very mechanical. The clicks come from a height of nine feet. In four seconds, the noise abruptly ends and there is nothing but dead silence."

A little later that night, Frank decides to try the Bigfoot call himself. "Then from a few feet into the woods comes the same grisly call, so loud it sounds like it's amplified over a PA system. It reverberates all around me and I get groggy with awe. It gets louder and louder and then dies out after 20 seconds."

On an earlier night, alone in the same area, walking a path that leads into the woods, he is about halfway across the field when he is startled by the odd silence that others had described. "Not a single sound. Not a bird, not a cricket. None of the sounds you always hear at night in woods. Nothing." He walks a little further when suddenly the silence is broken. "I hear a clear definite noise pierce the silence. A sort of ponging sound. Like a hammer striking sheet metal. Now there is no way anyone is bopping metal in those woods at this time of night, so at first I'm not quite sure how to react. Then I decide how to react. I scoop up my pack and gallop out of there." Author Jerome Clark mentioned Frank's experiences in Saga's *UFO Report* (May 1977) noting how the strange noise "like a hammer striking sheet metal" reported by Frank were similar to odd sounds described "during the famous Louisiana, Missouri, monster scare of July 1972."

In April 1977, I spent several days in and around Somerville, New Jersey, where a lot of Bigfoot encounters were being reported at the time. Just a couple of months prior to my visit a young man claimed he had had a face-to-face encounter with the creature one night! He said that at the same time, just a few feet behind the Bigfoot, there was a tiny pinpoint of light from which a "high pitched whistle" was originating. He found himself unable to move, and the creature seemed to be the same way until the light and whistle ceased to be, whereupon the creature turned and walked away and he went hastily in the other direction.

I wondered if the area was a "window," a kind of hotspot for anomalous activity, as quite a few people were reporting Bigfoot, UFOs, and I also visited a home with poltergeist activity.

In 1974 and 1975, I periodically joined Bigfoot hunters Duane and Ramona Hibner in the field, at Brooksville, Florida, which had become yet another hotspot for Bigfoot, UFOs and other spooky stuff. The town had become well-known in fact for its own world-famous UFO contactee John Reeves. Ramona showed me a stretch of country road, near where they had been investigating Bigfoot reports, where a "big ball of light" had come down out of the sky, touched down on the road it seemed in front of her car, and then shot back up into the night sky. A few months earlier, Duane had spotted a large UFO with lighted square windows low overhead at a ranch where he and Ramona had actually seen Bigfoot-type creatures themselves.

Noted author Nick Redfern (mysteriousuniverse.org) described what definitely sounds like a "window" located in the Piney Woods region of East Texas, in an 83,000-acre area of woodland known as the Big Thicket. It's a vast, heavily forested area with lots of wildlife, including alligators and bobcats. In addition, Redfern informs us that people have reported Bigfoot and large black leopards there as well. There's even an old road there known as Bragg Road, though locals call Ghost Light Road, because for many years now people have reported seeing mysterious lights there. "A small body of individuals have sworn that the large cats and the hairy humanoids – when spotted by the astonished and sometimes terrified onlooks – vanished before their eyes," Redfern wrote. "We're not talking about them making hasty getaways into the woods. Rather, we are talking about the 'animals' – in an instant – changing form from big cat and Bigfoot to a small, bright-lit globe of light."

Redfern wrote how three such reports had surfaced in 1977, from unconnected individuals. Two of the so-called "man-beast" and one of the "paranormal panther" in the Big Thicket. In all three instances the creatures became perfectly still. "Then, rather incredibly, they shrunk in size and transformed into small balls of light that vanished into the trees," Redfern added. "A near-identical incident occurred on Bragg Road itself in 1998, when a group of campers encountered an immense Bigfoot – in excess of eight-feet in height – which vanished in a flash of light and that left just one tell-tale card: a golf ball-sized globe of light that hovered around the immediate area for around twenty or so seconds and which then fizzled out of existence, and amid what was described as an electrical crackling noise." [I heard a witness to a Bigfoot encounter describe a similar sound years ago in Brooksville, Florida] Redfern later, in June 2005, met and spoke with one of the campers firsthand.

In 2007, Redfern made a trip to the Big Thicket and spoke to a wildlife officer who had seen one of these big cats herself. She admitted that prior to that she had been skeptical of such stories. She said it was drinking water from a small pool. She described how she stood transfixed to the spot and how the big cat's head casually turned in her direction. Then something very bizarre occurred as the creature was suddenly replaced by a glowing ball of light that seemed to melt into the pool of water, all of this amid a good deal of steam.

Remember Keel once speculated (refer back to Chapter 9) that some of the cryptids may "literally melt" away in the end. They may be short-lived tulpa-type projections or apparitions of some sort that Keel attributed possibly to the handiwork of an energy field of "intelligent energy (that) is intermingled with ours."

"That was the biggest outbreak in history anywhere, with UFO and Bigfoot sightings in Pennsylvania going back to 1973 until 1974," UFO and cryptid investigator Stan Gordon told me. He has been investigating UFOs and "monsters" going back to 1965. I first met Stan during a visit to his home in Greensburg, Pennsylvania, in August 1975. I got a little turned around in his town and stopped to ask the police for some directions. An officer at the counter kindly obliged, but before I left he joked with me saying if any Bigfoots were sighted please don't call them.

Some of Stan's cases had strong UFO elements associated with them. For example, there was one that was reported in Beaver, Pennsylvania, on the night of September 27, 1973, at about 9:30 p.m., when two shaken teenaged girls reported seeing a 7-8 foot tall Bigfoot-type creature, with brownish-red eyes, covered with white hair. In one of its hands, it was holding a glowing sphere! The father of one of the girls reportedly entered the woods the creature had disappeared into, to see what he could find. Around the time that he had entered the woods, the girls saw an object in the sky that shined a beam of light down into those same woods.

One case in particular, Stan will never forget. "It's so bizarre," he told me. "It's probably one of the strangest cases on record."

"There were about 15 people that night, October 25, 1973, in this rural area outside of Uniontown. They saw this object about as big as a barn, a bright red sphere. It was about a hundred feet off the ground coming down toward the pasture. The farmer's son was coming out to visit his father on his dad's property where this was happening and as they're going down the road he sees it and they go up to a neighbor's house to get a better vantage point. Then he and two young boys [fraternal twins, age 10] decide to go out to that field to investigate. Before he did he went to his dad's farm to grab a 30.06 rifle."

He grabs six rounds. Two are only tracers. "When they got up in the field they were shocked because about 250 feet away the object is on or close above the ground but now it's a bright white dome. Maybe a 100 feet or more in diameter. Bright white and like half a sphere, making this high-pitched whining sound and illuminating the whole area. They just cannot believe what they're seeing."

"Then their attention is drawn to a barbed wire fence about 75 feet away because along that fence are two huge creatures, one behind the other, moving in their direction. One is about 8 feet tall and the other is about 7 feet tall covered with long dark hair, arms almost to the ground, with glowing green eyes, a terrible stench, making baby crying type sounds. They're trying to figure out what they're seeing and realize these are not bear. What else could they be?"

"As they come closer one kid yells 'Fire! Shoot 'em! Shoot 'em!' The guy takes a shot – which is a tracer, and then he fires a second tracer, and its then the largest creature reaches out to grab that tracer round and the moment he does that he lets out this loud crying sound and the object in the field disappears. It doesn't take off. It just vanishes. The light and the sound go out. The creatures then turn around and start walking back to the woods."

"The guy starts firing live ammo into them with no effect. They run out of the field, get back to the truck, get back to the farmhouse, and get the family out of there, take them to a neighbor and call the police. Then a trooper arrives and they go up into the area to investigate. He [trooper] tells me later that that area where the object was on the ground had a soft luminescent glowing about 100-150 feet in diameter. He said if he'd had a newspaper he could have sat down in that glowing area and read the newspaper from the light off of the glowing area. Animals wouldn't go near it."

"And that was just the beginning of what turned into even stranger event as our team got up in the field that night to investigate. I never saw a UFO or Bigfoot in all the years I've been doing this, but what happened that night and what we documented highly suggested that there was a lot more to the UFO and Bigfoot phenomenon than any of us had any idea. And continuing years later, investigating case after case, more and more I'm convinced that this is a much stranger phenomena than a lot of people might accept."

So what happened? Stan and several of his investigative team members arrived on the scene around 1:30 a.m. They soon ventured out into the field where everything had happened, with the 22-year-old witness who had fired at the creatures, along with that young man's father. As one of the investigators named George Lutz was walking along with the witness asking him questions the witness suddenly became unresponsive. The man began to move back and forth in a jerky manner. Lutz, feeling that the man was about to faint, called for help. The man's father assisted and together they tried to support him. He began breathing deeply and then gave out a loud growl, sounding like an animal. He shook loose of Lutz and his father. They fell to the ground and the witness's dog ran at him, as if to attack. However, the young man began running after the dog, which ran away whimpering. He was swinging his arms and making growling sounds, at one point producing what was described as "an extremely loud, inhuman-like scream." Investigator Dennis Smeltzer, who majored in sociology, next reported that he felt light-headed, fearing that he was about to faint, and looking pale. Then another member of the team, who preferred not to be identified, reported that he felt as though he wasn't able to breathe well. Meanwhile the young man suddenly collapsed and fell face down in a very manured area. Then he began to come around and stated: "Get away from me. It's here. Get back."

Stan and others began smelling a very strong, sickening sulfur or rotten eggs type of odor. Meanwhile, the young male witness continued to act very strangely. He mumbled about how he'd protect them. Said he was seeing a man "in a black hat and cloak, carrying a sickle." He said that the cloaked figure said to him, "If Man doesn't straighten up, the end will come soon." He also stated, "There is a man here now who can save the world." He claimed that he could hear his name being called from the woods.

A well-attested UFO landing case with the presence of Bigfoot-type creatures had suddenly taken a very strange turn. The team wisely decided it was time to leave the field.

SIXTEEN
ALIEN EYES

In *The Eighth Tower* (1975) John Keel described a common archetype of the contact experience, something resembling a "floating eye." Alien abductee Barney Hill had "reported seeing a huge eye seemingly suspended in space in front of his windshield before he halted for the little men in black leather jackets..." Keel said.

Reviewing John Fuller's classic work *The Interrupted Journey* I failed to come across any reference of a single floating eye, although I found references that Barney had described "the eyes [two] don't have a body," even comparing them to the Cheshire cat in *Alice in Wonderland*. In the regression Barney first described seeing men standing in the road. "They won't talk to me," he said. "Only the eyes are talking to me. I-I-I-I don't understand that. Oh-the eyes don't have a body. They're just eyes." In a later regression, while describing his onboard encounter, Barney said, "When I was in the corridor, I was surprised that the leader didn't follow me into the room. But again-the eyes seemed to follow me. It was as if I knew the leader was elsewhere, but his effectiveness was there with me. Wherever he was, he was still able to convey messages to me, such as recognizing when I would become more fearful or needed calming down."

I found this interesting, because Albert Bender said that when the MIBs dematerialized "two glowing eyes lingered for a moment," and reminded him of the Cheshire cat. In quite a few UFO contact cases the "eyes" often seem telepathic and may exert control over the experiencer, which is what happened to Bender. "They beckoned me to approach them, and without hesitation I rose from the chair and walked to where they stood, for again I was helplessly controlled by their shining eyes," he said.

I contacted researcher Kathleen Marden, the niece of Betty Hill, about the "floating eye" detail and she confirmed that Keel had been wrong about the single eye aspect, that it was two eyes. But other contact experiencers have described similar eye related archetypes, whether one or two. On October 11, 1973, Charles Hickson, 45, a shipyard worker in Pascagoula, Mississippi, and a friend, Calvin Parker, 19, were night fishing in the Pascagoula River when both described how they were forcibly taken aboard a low hovering oval-shaped object with bright flashing blue lights. Hickson was taken into a room where he saw a thing that was "big and round that looked like a big eye that moved back and forth across my body." Paralyzed, he was moved around by two alien beings as the eye-like object checked him over. "I just kind of floated without touching anything," he said. "I didn't see any attachments for the eye. It was just kind of suspended in air."

When I met Hickson at his home in Gautier 10 days after the incident, he told me he now thought his abductors may have been robots. He drew a map of the location for me, and afterward New Orleans ufologist Milton Scott and I went to the location where the encounter had happened. We found the pier where they had been fishing. There was an old abandoned building nearby, and some junk cars and machinery. The ufonauts were floating gray beings with wrinkled looking skin, and about five feet two inches tall. They had lobster-like claws, three carrot-like protrusions where the nose and ears should have been, no visible eyes, and only a slit where the mouth would have been located.

We have long said that the eyes are the window or the gateway to the soul. Though it is considered a bit of a romantic notion, is it possible that the alien eyes may provide us something of a glimpse into theirs, if a soul is indeed what they have? They often seem quite different from our eyes and to exert hypnotic and telepathic affects upon their experiencers.

"A good many years ago, west of Calgary (Canada), a small boy, D.S., left his friend's house to run back home for supper," wrote long-time UFO researcher P. M. H. Edwards, Ph.D., F.T.C.L. "He crossed the field, heard a buzzing sound, was raised off the ground by an orange light-beam into a low-flying UFO which was inexplicably invisible to the neighbors. Extremely unusual-looking entities examined him through a large 'eye' suspended over him. Then they released him, programmed him to 'forget' the examination. However, he was so scared, that he rushed home and hid under his bed – one of his shoes was later found outside the house, on the roadway. His sister managed to persuade him to go downstairs for his meal; but he was speechless with terror. We arranged to have him put under hypnosis in Calgary, and his description of the beings was completely at variance with any others that we had heard. The case was therefore kept under wraps for ten years, until Hickson and Parker at Pascagoula were abducted while fishing off an old pier. Their account of the beings surprisingly fit that of D.S." (Alternate Perceptions, No. 37, Winter 1997)

In late 2016, I was talking on the phone with an experiencer in Tennessee who chased an orb that reminded him of an eye, through his house. He watched it disappear through the kitchen wall.

In the well-known report of a January 6, 1976 alien abduction of three women from Liberty, Kentucky, one of the experiencers named Mona Stafford later had an extraordinary apparition experience that began with a series of inner eye visions. Ohio ufologist Jim Miller, wrote an article about his investigation into this case for *The Ohio Sky Watcher* in the October-December 1976 issue. He said, "The story behind the face started January 9. Mona would close her eyes to go to sleep, and with her eyes closed the one eye appeared. It looked like an ordinary eye, but it would scare her so she would open her eyes quickly.

"July 7 was the first time that she saw two eyes. They also appeared as she closed her eyes, when she was about to go to sleep. Then, the night of July 19, Mona had been watching television and the last program went off the air. Mona sat starring at the snowy pattern when she felt as if someone was looking at her. She turned and saw a man's face with bright red hair and red beard, about five feet away looking at her. She turned away afraid to look again. She felt as if the man wanted her to look again. This time as she turned and saw it, she jumped up and the being vanished."

Keel took the "eye" motif of this phenomenon quite seriously and wrote about it more than once. In his *Anomaly* journal, #7, Fall 1971, he offered the following: "The case of Betty and Barney Hill began (with) the common (in psychic lore) impression of hypnotic eyes floating bodiless in front of the witnesses. ...When complete details of a contact experience are collected it is usually found that the witness either observed a flash of light or the bodiless eye at the outset. This is also extremely common in religious lore, in those cases in which angels and entities have appeared. The hypnotic eye is usually translated into the 'eye of God.'"

In *The Eighth Tower*, Keel wrote: "Some of our sea serpents, hairy humanoids, and silver-suited spacemen have huge self-luminous eyes. It may be that these 'eyes' are the only real things about some of these entities. The bodies to which they are seemingly attached are often shadowy and indistinct." He continued to write, however, that often the "floating eye" may be a tip-off that some of these experiences may have been "largely hallucinatory." He added, "Persons suffering from paranoia-schizophrenia see eyes everywhere. They turn on a water faucet and a huge eye oozes out."

In 2016, I had a phone conversation with a contactee in West Tennessee who had experiences with the greys. When he was 16 years old and living in the country, something odd happened to him one night when he was returning home. "When I was going inside the back door I felt an overwhelming presence staring at me and I knew exactly where it was without seeing it. When I looked in its direction all of a sudden I was looking through its eyes seeing me looking at it. It was like something in a movie. When I could see through my eyes again I heard it running at me. I ran inside and locked the door, collapsing on the floor. When I was looking through its eyes it lasted about 10 seconds."

Is the "eye" motif of some contact experiencers part of the telepathic process itself?

One experiencer had a similar episode when he was 10. He awakened around midnight and felt like he was floating above the bed, unable to move. A blinding light was coming in the bedroom window on the west side of the house. Suddenly, he became aware of seeing through someone else's eyes, approaching the house from the forest to the west. "I have come to understand it as a two-way channel that once open cannot work one way," this subject noted. "I am speaking about telepathy." Eventually this inner visual perception showed entry into the room. This person then saw what they looked like. They didn't realize till then that there was more than one. They had thin, large heads and black eyes. "They marched in perfect unison..."

The mesmerizing alien eyes are again and again a strong point of focus in many UFO contact reports. "She had those amazing, electrifying eyes...the huge, staring eyes of the old gods," Whitley Strieber wrote of his own encounter in *Communion* (1987). "Their eyes are often described as 'limitless,' 'haunting,' and 'baring the soul.'"

"Their eyes were very large," an experiencer in Virginia wrote me. "They were dark and glowed. These beings have a power through their eyes."

"They communicated with me telepathically, through the eyes," noted another experiencer who had described several encounters with grey beings.

"In Zechariah 5:1-5, the minor prophet described seeing a tube-shaped object flying in the air," Dr. Greg Little said in his book *Grand Illusions* (1994). "It was about 30 feet long and 15 feet wide. This flying 'curse,' as an angel called it, was used by God to identify thieves and liars. Earlier in his book Zechariah described seeing the 'eyes of God,' smaller lamp-shaped objects that travel across the earth collecting information on the doings and thoughts of earth's inhabitants."

Keel was interested in Zechariah's "flying roll" and other UFO phenomena to be found in the Bible, declaring that Enoch's legendary otherworldly excursions around 4,000 BC made him the first known contactee.

In the late 1970s, I met a gentleman in Huntsville, Alabama, who had a series of experiences with strange "circular patterns" in the sky that were, he said, "made of alternate concentric solid and dotted circles. There appeared to be electric surges from the dotted circles to the solid circles. The electrical activity pulsated at a low frequency and would give off a white and blue light."

Before each encounter, he would feel as though he was in a "highly charged field" that made his "skin tingle." The circular forms would swirl around and around. Over time he became aware of a telepathic communication that was going on between him and these objects. In the center of these circular displays was what resembled an eye. "During communication, the color of the pupil would vary in intensity and expand outward," he said. The pupil was white. He believed the "circular patterns" in the sky were mainly of a psychic nature.

On June 25, 1970, close to midnight, a housewife in Sharon, Massachusetts, observed an egg-shaped object with a number of smaller spherical objects, either attached or very close to it, flying slowly in a vertical descent into or close to a nearby field. The spheres flashed brilliant red and white lights. The object had a yellow corona around it.

A few years later, I dropped in to talk with her, but not just about her sighting. This housewife was deeply obsessed with the study of fairies and elemental beings and their possible connection to the UFO contact phenomenon, and naturally I was interested in learning all I could. We engaged in correspondence and in 1982 she wrote me: "I woke up one Saturday morning...I saw an eye floating in the sky, inside my head. I think this was after the 1970 experience. As I watched it black veils flew back and suddenly I was part of the entire universe. It's the greatest, Brent. You are the entire universe and at the same time have your individuality. Since then, especially this past year, I've had ecstatic feelings two to three times a week."

Visions? Jungian archetypes? Artifacts of alien intrusion? Or, alas, are the eyes of the old gods still watching us today, under the guise of UFO visitations?

SEVENTEEN
ENTRANCED MINDS

The use of hypnosis and its value as a tool for extracting hidden or forgotten memories connected with UFO encounters is a controversial and often heated subject of debate in ufology. Experiencers often report missing time, or amnesiac portions of repressed or forgotten memory concerning details of their close encounters, including involvement with non-human beings.

Wyoming psychologist Dr. R. Leo Sprinkle has devoted many years to regressing many experiencers with hypnosis and was able to recover a wide range of possible "memories" of onboard UFO medical examinations and assorted alien messages (many directed at how humankind threatens this world with nuclear destruction and how this needs to changed).

The memories of the beings acquired by Dr. Sprinkle and other researchers from the "experiencers" have been used to try and piece together and identify various extraterrestrial races, their alleged motives, and their places of origin.

How trustworthy are such memories?

Dr. Berthold Schwarz, psychiatrist
Many researchers are concerned that confabulatory aspects of hypnosis-induced recall may contaminate our data base. To minimize that, the qualifications of the hypnotist are important. A psychologist or psychiatrist is the ideal choice for regression.

The late Dr. Berthold Eric Schwarz, an eminent psychiatrist, commented, "The scalpel is no better than the surgeon who uses it. As in all things, there are potential dangers to the patient or subject and, at times, to the hypnotist unless he is aware of the vagaries of psychopathology, psychophysiology, etc. Hypnosis can be a great help in recovering many repressed areas connected with alleged UFO experiences and in some cases, this might be the ideal way to approach it. However, with time and careful questioning these matters might be more ideally integrated and handled in a therapeutic manner in a face-to-fact series of psychotherapeutic sessions."

Dr. Jacques Vallee (left) with John Keel (right)

Jacques Vallee told me in 2006, "I have studied over 70 abduction cases, in concert with psychiatrists trained in the use of the clinical hypnosis. These specialists were uniformly horrified when I showed them what some ufologists were doing and claiming on the basis of the regressions they were performing. In case after case, it becomes obvious that hypnosis is *not* a good way to bring back true memories. The psychiatric literature confirms this. In his famous book *The Fifty-Minute Hour,* Dr. Lindner explains why he considered, and then rejected, the use of hypnosis when asked by the FBI to treat a senior engineer who claimed to travel psychically to other planets. Hypnosis can turn a possible fantasy into an experience that becomes irreversible. I have received pathetic letters from famous UFO abductees asking me to help them find a new form of treatment, because they continue to experience traumatic experiences that do not fit into the rigid abduction model. Unfortunately, these people cannot be re-hypnotized in a professional manner after they have been subjected to the ludicrous process routinely followed in ufology today in the name of 'research.' Thousands of abductees have now been regressed hypnotically, and we know nothing more about the nature of the phenomenon, the alleged craft, or the entities associated with them. I still believe the abduction experience is part of the witnesses' reality, as Dr. Simon told me when we spent two days with Betty and Barney Hill at their place in New Hampshire, but hypnosis, in most cases, is neither the therapy of choice, nor the best way to explore what really happened to them."

I discussed the possibility of using hypnosis on a female subject in a phone conversation with John Keel. He exclaimed, "Don't do it. You'll only f—k her mind up." He said hypnotically retrieved memory could not guarantee accuracy and the end result could potentially mislead both the experiencer and the researcher.

Bob Rickard, founder and editor of *Fortean Times,* did an interview with Keel in 1992 and discussed with him the hypnotic work being done by Budd Hopkins and others with alien abductees. "They're dealing with the unconscious mind without reckoning on it being a trickster," Keel pointed out. Rickard asked why the researchers couldn't see that, to which Keel added, "They've been told this a thousand times. I've talked to Budd about this, and he refuses to read a book on hypnosis. This is the man who holds therapy groups for abductees. If they start talking about, say, poltergeist experiences, he stops them. He doesn't want to hear about that. He just wants to hear about the 'Greys.'"

Nonetheless, most will seemingly agree that hypnosis does have potential value within the right setting and context. Nandor Fodor, in his classic work, *An Encyclopaedia of Psychic Science*, wrote that hypnosis certainly possesses "therapeutical and psychological significance," and that conditions such as phobias, manias, inhibitions, pain, and a variety of other psychological and psychophysical based conditions could be greatly improved, if not in fact removed, with the use of hypnosis. He even commented on the appearances of "supernormal" capabilities. "The subject may see clairvoyantly, give psychometric descriptions, see into the future, read the past, make spiritual excursions to distant places, hear and see events occurring there and give correct medical diagnoses," he wrote.

Edgar Cayce, America's legendary "Sleeping Prophet," is perhaps a perfect example. Using self-induced hypnotic entrancement, Cayce gave 14,306 psychic readings, the majority of which dealt with holistic health and treatment of illnesses. Soviet parapsychologists have used hypnosis a lot in their work. Investigations into telepathy were conducted primarily at an institution known as the Leningrad University and Institute for Physiology. "The results obtained so far prove only that telepathy is possible when the volunteer acting as receiver is placed under hypnosis beforehand," Jacques Bergier and Louis Pauwels stated in *Impossible Possibilities* (1968; 1971).

In other chapters of this book we have already touched upon subjects such as altered states of consciousness, the role of the right brain hemisphere with paranormal manifestations and events, and the very curious surreal, subjective quality of many of these UFO contact experiences. Although seldom discussed in the mainstream ufological literature, hypnosis has played a strange interactive psychic role in a number of UFO-related cases.

In Massillon, Ohio, a hypnotist was regressing an alien abductee when unusual phenomena occurred. "Suddenly, a sort of half a helmet just floated into the room, right through the window [which had been closed], and settled down on his forehead," a witness told me. "Two pins appeared out of nowhere and slid through the helmet, into his temples, and at that precise moment he experienced a severe pain in his head. He hyperventilated, sweated profusely, and begged to come out. When he was aware he said the pain was so intense he knew that if he continued talking that pain would grow more so."

An abductee named Dan in northern Alabama was being regressed when presumed psychic interference erupted in that session as well. "To me, it appeared like a circulating column of water atop his head," an investigator who had been present explained to me. He told me that to the hypnotist "it appeared as a ball of flame." He continued, "I saw his light-sensitive sunglasses – you know, the type that change color automatically in harsh light – darken even though it was a darkened room.

"I channeled a being that called itself 'Xerra,'" Dan told me. "For me, it was very unnerving and I never want to feel that again!"

Robyn Andrews, a hypnotist in Atlanta, Georgia, worked with a male subject who had also been studied by the Mental and Psychiatric Research Center at the University of Virginia. He could be placed into very deep levels of hypnosis. Andrews worked with him a great deal because he was so unique and exceptional to anyone else she had ever worked with. Under hypnosis he would speak and write in other languages. "Some of the ancient Egyptian had been verified," she told me. "In the middle of these sessions he would start to channel a so-called alien," she said, "and that part I really was skeptical of." Then, at some point, this subject became ill, and she had been told that he was suffering from infectious hepatitis. However, he refused to go to the doctor for relief. Instead he insisted he be hypnotized. Reluctantly, Robyn agreed. Almost immediately the alien personality came through saying, "We're going to cure ____'s illness." The subject then stood up and made his way for the front door.

"There was ceramic tile on the front porch and concrete steps down to a concrete driveway, which is steep and curvy down to the street," Robyn said. "So we were very nervous because he was in deep trance walking down to the driveway, and then we saw it. There was a UFO over the house, huge and glowing. It was 8:30 at night. There was a poplar tree in the front yard that was about 100 feet tall, and it wasn't that far above that, just hovering, and with a glow around it. He stood out there and stretched his hands out, his palms up, looking up."

"He had been telling me about all of these encounters that he had had, which I didn't really believe at the time," Robyn confessed. "So then he turns around and heads back into the house. We, of course, have to follow him and get him settled and then rush back out there and it is gone then of course."

"Well, he was cured of whatever was the matter with him and after that night he never had any problems at all."

In April 1977, while investigating a wave of Bigfoot activity that had fallen below the media radar in the area of Somerville, New Jersey, I was introduced to a gentleman who had personally known the famed 1950s UFO contactee Howard Menger, then of High Bridge, there in New Jersey. He had become involved in investigations and had some odd experiences. In one instance, a bellhop at the Mount Airy Lodge at Mount Pocono, Pennsylvania, was allegedly burned when a UFO swooped down on him one night as he had stepped outside for some fresh air. During an investigation in the early 1960s, the bellhop was hypnotized and while entranced instructed the group to visit a nearby ravine where there was UFO activity. They went to the location, even though it was snowing at the time, and saw something quite inexplicable. This man told me that as he and others stood at the top of the ridge looking down in a gulley below that a vertical white beam of light shot up from the ground to a height of about 12 to 15 feet, near a tree. Suddenly the sides of the light bulged outward, forming an elliptical white light. Then it collapsed back into a single vertical light beam again and next went back into the ground. Down in the gulley a man named Rob and a hotel clerk had walked out into a clearing at that time. An unknown voice was heard by the two men saying, "Who's with you, Rob? Don't be afraid." The people on the ridge above, at a greater distance, heard no voice, but they did witness the strange manifestation of light. The next morning, they returned to the very site where the light had appeared and found that some of the branches on the tree nearby had bark on the undersides peeled off. They wondered if some force associated with the light beam had been responsible. "We checked the ground for footprints but there was nothing there but deer tracks and tracks of the two guys that went down there," he said. "It was marshy land." "If this was a hoax, it would have cost thousands of dollars," he told my psychiatrist friend Dr. Berthold Schwarz, in a separate interview.

EIGHTEEN
WHAT NEXT?

As Rosemary Ellen Guiley wrote in her foreword to this book, perhaps John Keel was somehow wired differently in some ways that made him more open to this vastly complex and perplexing multilayered mystery that he pursued with such diligence over the years. Perhaps it made him more capable at discerning the deeper meanings and implications behind the bewildering events and manifestations that he devoted so much of his time to studying and writing about. Keel chose to dig much, much deeper, below the proverbial surface of this mega-mystery, than the ufological mainstream with its biased singular focus on the "nuts and bolts" extraterrestrial theory alone. Instead he delved in-depth into comparative phenomena, from Marian apparitions to demonic manifestations, along with fairies, elementals, and cryptids, searching for possible causal relationships that might help to explain these widely varied phenomena. Even ghosts were on his radar. Remember Keel's remark I cited in chapter two, "Are ghosts really UFOs and UFO entities, or are UFOs really ghosts? Take your choice." As I have shared, there have certainly been some ghost-like apparitional UFOs and their "occupants."

Keel discovered distinctive, sobering, and for himself and many others, unusual and vexing parallels in the comparative and historical data of many anomalous reports. He urged researchers to take an alternative and multidisciplinary approach to the evidence. Keel believed that an earth-based intelligence capable of producing a wide-range of manifestations was most likely the true answer. The endless accounts of so-called ET visitors, who had such a huge and often contradictory variety of alleged identities, appearances, and origins from throughout the known and as yet uncharted universe, caused Keel to draw upon his former army training in psychological warfare and deception as possible explanations. He speculated that an intelligence operating behind the UFO phenomenon was deliberately concealing its true identity and purpose, for whatever reasons.

Obviously, there is much research and investigative work yet to be done. Pioneers such as Keel and Vallee have helped to map out this complex and enigmatic terrain. This is no time in ufological history to be myopic, focused singularly upon one favored theoretical explanation to the exclusion of all else. Confirmation bias, wherein you only accept or pursue evidence that fits with your personal perspective, has no place in this field. We must do much, much better. Dr. Hynek must be rolling over in his grave over the current sad state of mainstream ufology.

Keel long ago wrote that the UFO enigma "may eventually prove to be the most important story in history." Tragically, the full story has been largely dismissed, ignored and neglected by the mainstream's alleged "scientific" community. Many have cherry picked only that evidence that supports their biased version of an Extraterrestrial Hypothesis - "cult literature" as Keel called it – and have often turned to conspiracy theories in order to blame someone else like the Air Force or the CIA for their own lack of progress.

Keel was a genuine though often unrecognized pioneer in the field of ufology. He was often misunderstood and severely criticized for pursuing evidence and answers that seemed out of line with the pursuits and directions of the ufological mainstream. The average "nuts and bolts" ufologist typically found Keel's emphasis on components of psychic phenomena and the contactee syndrome as being especially misguided and saw such directions as unwanted distractions from what they perceived as an obvious and clear-cut truth. Keel, by the same token, had a difficult struggle with the mainstream's dogged resistance to his alternative ideas and the evidence that he had presented to support them. Much of his position arose from his own extensive field investigative work, adding to it that he was a seasoned journalist who had previously traveled to many corners of the globe, looking into many different mysteries. He had tried to track the legendary Yeti in Tibet, he'd encountered the revered lama Nyang-Pa who demonstrated mind reading skills to Keel, and in yet another instance he had observed the movements of a wooden stool that he was unable to explain. However, he was also a proficient magician who in his world travels exposed many fake miracle workers and psychics – a knowledge he tried to share with some parapsychologists so that they wouldn't be taken in by such trickery themselves.

You don't have to become a full-fledged Keelian, a person who fully adopts and embraces all of Keel's ideas and investigative approach, to recognize and appreciate his pioneering contributions and concepts. His influence has not only been to the field of ufology, but also to other potentially interrelated disciplines. When Keel first burst onto the UFO scene back in the 1960's and '70s with his many articles and books that challenged the status quo of mainstream ufology [a field Keel blasted as an "infant pseudoscience"] his alternative ideas and concepts drew heavily upon comparative religious and occult phenomena. His approach was perceived as a little too woo-woo for many at the time. However, over the years, the emphasis that Keel had made on the significance of the bewildering seeming contactee experience, the "missing time" episodes, and the unusual psychic events, all seem to be getting much more serious recognition these days. Such findings have become increasingly recognized as significant to growing numbers of serious researchers and scientists alike. It's no longer so woo-woo sounding today.

Today more and more people are finding themselves traversing those strange pathways that Keel had taken much criticism for delving into a few decades ago. On November 30, 2018, two distinguished medical scientists spoke at the Harvard Medical School about their findings from an extensive investigation that they have been conducting into experiencers of UAP (Unidentified

Aerial Phenomena) type occurrences. One of the doctors, Christopher "Kit" Green, had long been haunted by his memories going back to 1972 when he was assigned by CIA director Richard Helms to be an analyst and handler for such people as Israeli psychic Uri Geller and others. Psychic abilities were being seriously studied by scientists at California's then Stanford Research Institute. A skeptical Green found that in long-distance experiments with Geller at Stanford, with himself in Virginia, that Geller could somehow accurately see and know things that were too accurate to be explained as mere coincidence. Then in late 1974, while Geller was working with nuclear engineers at the Lawrence Livermore Nuclear Laboratory, where scientists were studying his psychokinesis abilities, these same scientists began to report disturbing, frightening phenomena. They suddenly began seeing mysterious balls of light and apparitional-type appearances, like large dark birds and an arm floating in the air, with a hook where a hand should have been. Two scientists were so scared they expressed intentions of quitting.

Today Green and his associate Dr. Garry Nolan of Stanford are conducting a comprehensive study of UAP experiencers, many of them from military backgrounds, some who have allegedly been injured by UAP beams of light. They're doing detailed medical studies, MRI scans, and believe they've detected an area of the brain that may act as a type of antenna for such manifestations – which with MRI scanning they've detected a higher density of neuronal connection between the head of the caudate and the putamen that appears absent with non-experiencers.

In his book *Real Magic* (2018), Dean Radin, Ph.D., chief scientist for the Institute of Noetic Sciences, previously assigned with Stanford's "remote viewing" Stargate program, speculated on how ETs perhaps advanced a few thousand years ahead of us might be capable of achieving very wonderous things. "If we can already see tiny space-time warps in our little laboratory psi experiments, then they'd be able to manipulate huge chunks of space-time like slabs of soft butter."

Over four decades ago when Dr. Radin was beginning to take his initial steps into this controversy with his studies into the implications of consciousness and non-local physics, Keel was already speculating on possible ET interactions that took similar factors into consideration. In a 1976 *Saga* magazine article he pondered "instantaneous astral travel," the parapsychological evidence for out-of-body projection, as well as the possibility of "time travel," and considered the possibility of astral ET intelligences. "If some humans have a capacity for this kind of time travel, then it is quite possible that intelligent beings in some distant star system may have the same ability to a very advanced degree," Keel wrote. He continued "if the cosmic time travelers are projecting only their consciousness to our planet they would arrive as shapeless energy forms. They could assume any form when perceived by the limited human senses."

"Some of the stories come from contact with subtle energies that have an intelligence and purpose," psychologist Greg Little has written. Dr. Little has previously described and outlined his thoughts on this matter in *Alternate Perceptions* magazine, as well as in his books *The Archetype Experience* (1984), *People of the Web* (1990), *Grand Illusions* (1994), and Andrew Collins' *LightQuest* (2012). Keel and Little had even chatted about this matter on the phone some and in a reprint of *Operation Trojan Horse* (IllumiNet Press, 1996) Keel acknowledged Little's own work on this matter. This is certainly an aspect that Keel directed a great deal of his attention to in his books *Operation Trojan Horse* (1970) and *The Eighth Tower* (1975).

The contactee stories are very puzzling and complex. Keel struggled to untangle the meaning behind such accounts. In his privately circulated newsletter *Anomaly* (#2) going back to September 1969, he described one of two major reactions that are frequently reported during the initial encounter event, being either extreme fear, bordering on hysteria, or complete euphoria. Following this, Keel noted, was a possible "expansion of awareness and perception", as well as a rapid deterioration of personality. He wrote how with the "expansion" phase the subject may gradually develop "higher IQ" as well as "heightened perceptions in all areas," including "ESP abilities." [These are traits that scientists like Green, Nolan, Radin, and others are currently very keenly interested in]

"Illumination often accompanies UFO sightings, particularly when the witnesses are caught in a beam of light from the objects," Keel wrote (*Our Haunted Planet*, 1971). "Their IQ later skyrockets, and their lives change appreciably."

"Psychic abilities appear to be hereditary, and this includes illumination," Keel added, which is another thing that Doctors Nolan and Green and other scientists are keen to unravel.

Keel noted a disturbing pattern with the expansion factor. He found how after a time the heightened perceptions could lead to "a slow deterioration of personality," and how the "contactee" could begin to suffer confabulation, develop obsessive-compulsive traits, becoming very preoccupied with the experience in a way similar to religious fanatics. He pointed out how they might become like "space age messiahs" striving to advance the proverbial "cause."

Other researchers have attempted to follow in Keel's footsteps and break the complex and confusing contactee syndrome down into meaningful components. Robert Anton Wilson, in *Second Look* magazine (September 1979), valiantly attempted to do so. He described how there were a wide variety of what he called "brain-change experiences in shamanic-religious history." He strove to break them down into various categories and show their similarities and possible "neurological" connections to the contactee experience.

"The UFO Encounter can trigger neurosomatic mutations from peace-bliss-serenity to anxiety-trauma-psychotic breakdown," Wilson noted. "Some contactees have actually become faith-healers, indicating a strong neurosomatic turn on in the positive direction, and others have required psychiatric care, indicating the other extreme."

The highest stage or level of experience, as far as Wilson was able to determine, was what he called the Contentless Vision which he felt was comparable to the White Light of the Void of Tibetan Buddhism, the Head in Cabala..."the 'ineffable,' beyond time, space, matter, and all concepts."

"As far as I can make out, this experience alone seems to be totally positive," he wrote. "Nobody seems to come out of it schizoid, paranoid fanatic, or even dogmatic. Olaf Stapledon described it as Agnostic Mysticism. It sees normal consciousness (the concensus-reality of the tribe), neurosomatic consciousness, metaprogramming consciousness, and even the Numinous Beings of archetypal consciousness as all relative – true in their own context, but not universally true. It even sees itself as relative, in the same way."

Did Keel encounter a Daemon?

In October 2007, I did a phone interview for *Alternate Perceptions* magazine with Anthony Peake, the British author of *Is There Life After Death – The Extraordinary Science of What Happens When You Die,* and in more recent years books such as *The Daemon, The Out-Of-Body Experience,* and *The Immortal Mind,* the latter of which he co-wrote with Ervin Laszlo. Peake weaves his conversations with a touch of delightful abandon, awe, and genuine high-strangeness, amid subjects like neurology, psychology, and hypnosis, that initially sound conventional enough, but suddenly delve deep into a wide-range of intriguing subject matter from quantum physics, Gnosticism, temporal lobe epilepsy, near-death experiences, deja vu, precognition, and what have you. The kicker is that all of these things, while interesting in and of themselves, take on a unique Theory of Everything that revolves around a central concept of Anthony's that he refers to as the Daemon-Eidolon Dyad.

I learned in our conversation that Peake had discovered Keel when he and some of his hippy friends in Liverpool read *Operation Trojan Horse* back in the early 1970s. They had found Keel's book very thought-provoking! Keel opened their minds to exciting new ideas and possibilities, and for Peake it helped to plant the seeds of To Keel the experiencer of presumed ET or spirit contact, and a variety of other forms of "psychic phenomena," might from time to time come under the influence, and in some cases even under the control (Keel even used the word "possession") of an interactive intelligence that ordinarily seems quite foreign and hidden from a person's everyday state of awareness. To Peake, that consciousness that Keel felt could be demonic-like, could instead be daemon-like. To the ancient Gnostics the daemon was one's higher self or "overself," perceived early on as a guardian spirit, adopted from the mystery religions of Greece and Rome, and referred to as the Neshamah of the Kabbalah. Similarly, to the ancient Egyptians there was the ka (guardian spirit form) and the ba (again the equivalent to the lower self). In modern language, it's the higher self and the lower self of consciousness. To Peake the everyday conscious self only has access to memories of this one conscious life, while the daemon, as he sees it, is largely a larger form of consciousness that we're usually unconscious of, except in certain unique and rare circumstances wherein altered states of consciousness occur, and where it is then capable, according to many documented accounts, of performing various remarkable mental feats, including what we call paranormal.

To Keel a psychic medium was quite often interacting with the same complex and enigmatic processes of the unconscious mind as the UFO contactee. Instead of calling them spirits or extraterrestrials, Keel preferred, as already explained, the term "ultraterrestrial" which he had acquired from his famed zoologist friend Ivan T. Sanderson, implying that we are dealing with interactive terrestrial-based intelligences rather than ETs. Sanderson even wrote a book entitled Invisible Residents (1970) speculating that an alien presence on this planet might reside in "underwater civilizations." There have been, after all, a good number of credible sounding reports of UFOs entering and exiting lakes, rivers and oceans around the earth. However, Keel leaned more toward psychic explanations, numerous examples of classic non-local reality and, he claimed, a simplified version of quantum physics that focused largely on apparent manipulations of the electromagnetic spectrum.

Peake found that people with temporal lobe epilepsy often seem prone to puzzling episodes of time dilation, déjà vu, precognition, and out-of-body experiences, as do near-death and UFO contact experiencers. Peake believes that hypnotherapist Ernest Hilgard's "hidden observer" and neuroscientist Dr. Michael Persinger's "sensed presence" all share characteristics in common with the ancient and archetypal daemon. Both Peake and Keel arrived at different perspectives but both covered similar data and recognized its overarching importance in trying to explain a mysterious "presence" that throughout humankind's recorded history has communicated messages through mediums, prophets, and, here of late, our UFO contact experiencers.

pointed out that the deeper one goes into a hypnotic trance state, the more likely one will encounter this "presence," the daemon, or what have you. Keel would have, of course, used "ultraterrestrial," or perhaps "elemental." At any rate, Peake recounted a case documented by the noted psychologist Charles Tart of a good hypnotic subject he called William. During one deep hypnosis session, there was an unexpected "intrusion" from a presence that was amused by the attempts of Tart and his colleagues to understand the human mind. Peake wrote that this amusement and "intrusion" is not a characteristic that one normally expects to encounter from a non-dominant brain hemisphere!
I found this story intriguing and so I shared with Peake details of Keel's 1967 hypnosis session with a UFO and MIB experiencer on Long Island, who also had a strange hypnotic intrusion. A woman he referred to as Jane (actually Jaye P. Paro, a radio personality at WBAB in Babylon, New York) who proved to be a good hypnotic subject, but soon after Keel performed tests to assure himself that she was in a deep trance state, he ran into difficulties. As he questioned her about her experiences, he found, to his amazement, he no longer had control of the session, for an apparent entity named Apol (pronounced Apple) began conversing with him instead. This personality explained that Robert Kennedy was in grave danger and made predictions about future plane crashes. Keel wrote: "The predicted plane crashes occurred right on schedule. I was slowly convincing myself that the entities were somehow tuned to the future." Keel also later found that he only had to ponder over a serious question and the phone would ring and Jane would be relaying a message from this Apol.

I couldn't help but notice a parallel between Keel's Apol and Peake's daemon. So I read that account directly out of The Mothman Prophecies to Peake to get his take on it.

"Apol, it's the daemon," Peake excitedly declared. "Again, it's the being inside that knows the future and he communicated directly with that higher self of Jane. The daemon is always in there and it's deeply rooted in the non-dominant hemisphere of the brain. In deep hypnotic trance situations people can encounter that being, which keeps all the memories of the past life, and has a knowledge of the future. It keeps itself dormant except when it's really needed, or when people are hypnotized."

"Mediums acted as oracles in ancient times, and people with this peculiar gift appeared in each new generation," Keel explained (Operation Trojan Horse, 1970). "Such persons seem to serve as instruments through which the ultraterrestrials can speak to us directly, and they often come up with amazingly accurate prophecies of the future and precise details of events that could seemingly be known only to the dead relatives of the people who consulted them."

Keel's approach to ufology was one deeply immersed in a wide range of sciences and belief systems in which he perceived interconnected relevance, whereas the vast majority of the UFO mainstreamers failed to understand why he took so many detours down avenues of thought that dealt heavily with the paranormal. His tree of knowledge had many, many branches! "I simply do not understand you," atmospheric physicist and UFO/ET advocate James E. McDonald complained in a letter to Keel. "You just spin one mystery inside another and never get anything across in any concrete terms."

Worldwide Keel's works have had quite a considerable impact and influence on other researchers and authors who have delved into the various aspects of psychic phenomena, consciousness, UFOs, quantum physics, and various other anomalous avenues and aspects that Keel opened their minds to. A few months ago, a medical doctor in California, who is a UFO experiencer himself, Skyped with me privately for two hours wanting to learn more about Keel from me as he had come upon things himself that were quite similar to what Keel had written. I've personally been in touch with many people all over the world who were very influenced by Keel, from such corners of the globe as Sweden, Germany, Australia, Brazil, and England. I found, as have many others, that Keel was absolutely dead on correct. I followed Keel's work closely and back around the mid-70s I traveled from Maine to Florida interviewing UFO researchers and witnesses myself. There were times I spent weeks on the go. I spent nearly the entire summer of 1975 doing this full time, and though I started out telling people I was a non-experiencer myself, eventually the phenomena seemed to turn "reflective," as Keel had expressed it, and I had apparent precognitive type dreams and impressions, EVP happenings (even a voice that identified itself as "John Keel" on multiple occasions, in the presence of others, and caught on recordings) and a variety of odd synchronistic incidents.

"Today many scientific disciplines are moving in the same direction, not realizing they are mapping a very old country," Keel further wrote (The Eighth Tower, 1975).

Today I notice more and more scientists are taking a serious look at what have previously been stigmatized as forbidden issues for academic pursuit. The tide seems to be shifting, there seems to be an increased openness to multidisciplinary exploration, and the whole Keelian landscape of the paranormal, UFO contact experiences, the connectivity of consciousness, the possibility of other dimensions, and the implications of quantum physics – all of it's being more openly and thoroughly discussed and explored by lay researchers and a good many scientists alike.

At this time, we're only barely able to scratch the proverbial surface of the UFO enigma and fathom its hidden components. We're like the parable of the blind men with each one touching a separate part of the elephant trying to figure out what it is in totality. In the UFO field we have lots of phenomena but an elusive gestalt whole phenomenon by which to fully discern and explain adequately the proverbial Theory of Everything that remains out of our reach at present.

Opinions and beliefs abound. There is an obvious caveat to the UFO conundrum wherein we have many talking heads loudly proclaiming answers, whereas no single theory yet has brought us, after over seven decades of trying, to a final, sweeping and singular conclusion that covers all the bases. For the time being perhaps it is as one of Ufology's Excluded Middle proponents Greg Bishop expressed "…it's not only stranger than we think, it's stranger than we can think."

At least for the present time. Let's not forget John Keel's memorable battle cry: Belief is the enemy!

Put that in your pipe and smoke it!

Credit: Hakan Blomqvist, Archives for UFO Research, Sweden

Bibliography

Collins, Andrew. Alien Energy: UFOs, Ritual Landscapes and the Human Mind. TN: Eagel Wing Books, April 2003

Collins, Andrew. LightQuest: Your Guide to Seeing and Interacting with UFOs, Mystery Lights & Plasma Intelligences, TN: Eagle Wings Books, 2012,

Devereux, Paul. Shamanism and the Mystery Lines. 1st ed. Minnesota: Llewellyn Publications, 1993.

Fernandes, Joaquim & D' Armada, Fina. Celestial Secret: The Hidden History of the Fatima Incident. TX: Anomalist Books, 20007.

Fodor, Nandor. An Encyclopaedia of Psychic Science. 1st Paperbound printing. New Jersey: Citadel Press. 1974.

Gaddis, Vincent H. Mysterious Fires and Lights. 1st ed. Dell Publishing Co., Inc. 1967.

Hynek, J. Allen, & Vallee, Jacques. The Edge of Reality:1st ed. Illinois: Henry Regnery Co. 1975.

Jung, Carl G. Flying Saucers: A Modern Myth of Things Seen in the Sky. New York: Signet. 1st ed. 1969.

Keel, John A. UFOs: Operation Trojan Horse. 1st ed. New York: G.P. Putnam. 1970.

Keel, John A. Creatures from Time and Space. 1st ed. Conn.: Fawcett Publications, Inc. 1970.

Keel, John A. Our Haunted Planet. 1st ed. Connecticut: Fawcett Gold Medal Book. 1970.

Keel, John A. The Eighth Tower. 1st ed. New York: Signet. 1975.

Keel, John A. The Mothman Prophecies. 1st ed. New York: Saturday Review Press. 1975.

Little, Gregory L. People of the Web. 1st ed. Tennessee: White Buffalo Books. 1990.

Little, Gregory L. Grand Illusions. 1st ed. Tennessee: White Buffalo Books. 1994.

Peake, Anthony. The Daemon. 1st ed. England: Arcturus. 2008.

Raynes, Brent. Visitors From Hidden Realms. 1st ed. Tennessee: Eagle Wing Books, Inc. 2004.

Raynes, Brent. On The Edge Of Reality. 1st ed. New Jersey: Global Communications. 2009.

Schwarz, Berthold E., M.D. UFO Dynamics: Psychiatric & Psychic Aspects of the UFO Syndrome. Book 1 & 2. 1st ed. Florida: Rainbow Books. 1983.

Smith, Susy. Voices of the Dead? 1st ed. New York: Signet. 1977.

Surprise, Kirby. Synchronicity. 1st ed. New Jersey: Career Press. 2012

Vallee, Jacques. Passport to Magonia. 1st ed. Illinois: Henry Regnery Co. 1969.

Vallee, Jacques. Dimensions. 1st ed. Ballantine Books, New York, 1989.

Vallee, Jacques. Confrontations. 1st ed. Ballantine Books, New York, 1990.

Vallee, Jacques. Revelations. 1st ed. Ballantine Books, New York, 1991.

ABOUT THE AUTHOR

Brent Raynes has been interested in UFO close encounters and the visitor experience since early 1967, when at age 14 he decided to become a "ufologist" after reading <u>Flying Saucers – Serious Business</u> by Frank Edwards. He is the editor of <u>Alternate Perceptions</u> online magazine (apmagazine.info), has given talks from Maine to Washington state, and authored three books; <u>Visitors from Hidden Realms</u> (2004), <u>On the Edge of Reality</u> (2009), and this book that you're reading now.

If you would like to contact Brent and share any personal thoughts, ideas, impressions, and/or experiences, he can be reached at: <u>brentraynes@yahoo.com</u>

Printed in Great Britain
by Amazon

56208361R00190